PHILLIPSBURG LIBRARY

6748 9100 102 639 7

DATE DUE

DATE DUE

DUE

5 26 99

D1417458

Reinventing Ourselves *after* Motherhood

Reinventing Ourselves *after* Motherhood

How Former Career Women

Refocus Their Personal and Professional Lives

after the Birth of a Child

WITHDRAWN

Phillipsburg Free Public Library

FREE PUBLIC LIBRARY
PHILLIPSBURG, N.J.

Susan Lewis

CB

CONTEMPORARY BOOKS

306.8743
LEW

rary of Congress Cataloging-in-Publication Data

/is, Susan.
   Reinventing ourselves after motherhood : how former career women refocus
their personal and professional lives after the birth of a child / Susan Lewis.
      p.   cm.
   Includes index.
   ISBN 0-8092-2906-4
   1. Mothers.   2. Motherhood.   1. Mothers—Employment.   I. Title.
HQ759.L4934   1999
306.874'3—dc21   98-30259
                                                                                  CIP

Excerpts on pages 16, 20, 87, 152, 181, 182, 234–35 from *The Feminine
Mystique* by Betty Friedan. Copyright © 1983, 1974, 1973, 1963 by Betty Friedan.
Reprinted by permission of W. W. Norton & Co., Inc.

Interior design by Robert S. Tinnon

Published by Contemporary Books
A division of NTC/Contemporary Publishing Group, Inc.
4255 West Touhy Avenue, Lincolnwood (Chicago), Illinois 60646-1975 U.S.A.
Copyright © 1999 by Susan Lewis
All rights reserved. No part of this book may be reproduced, stored in a retrieval
system, or transmitted in any form or by any means, electronic, mechanical,
photocopying, recording, or otherwise, without the prior permission of
NTC/Contemporary Publishing Group, Inc.
Printed in the United States of America
International Standard Book Number: 0-8092-2906-4
99 00 01 02 03 04 MV 19 18 17 16 15 14 13 12 11 10 9 8 7 6 5 4 3 2 1

For Joe,

and for Dan, Julia, Andrew, and Brian,

who make it all worthwhile

CONTENTS

Acknowledgments

Part of the joy of writing this book has been reaching beyond myself and exploring the lives of many interesting and engaging women, the richness of whose experiences and insights are often hidden behind the activities of their busy daily lives. The many women who participated in this book—those who filled out surveys, met with me, or spoke with me on the telephone—gave of their time and shared thoughts, feelings, and stories normally kept private. My deepest thanks and appreciation go to you, and I hope that this book honors the various choices you have made.

Thanks to Tracy Reigel of FEMALE (Formerly Employed Mothers on the Leading Edge) and to Elizabeth Nourian, Elizabeth Brooks, and Deborah Leavy of the Lawyers-at-Home subcommittee of the Philadelphia Bar Association for facilitating contacts with their members and introducing me to their efforts to support women's choices. Thanks also to the national nonprofit support organization Mothers at Home (MAH) for sharing research and statistics.

My agent, Barrie Van Dyck, believed in this project since its conception as a mere idea in the back of a New York taxicab. I thank her for her unflagging efforts, moral support, and friendship.

Thanks also to my editor, Kara Leverte, who trusted in this book, and to Kristen Eberhard and the other editors at NTC/Contemporary Publishing for shepherding it so carefully through the production process.

I appreciate the willingness of Ellie Kluger and Joyce Lewis, as well as writers group members John Bucholtz and Judy Trachtenburg, to read anything I wrote. Special thanks to Barrie Maguire and Larry Stains for their reading and rereading of chapters, for their honest critiques, and for their friendship throughout this process.

Thanks to my friends at Book Nook Press '97, whose initial eagerness for the idea helped me get this project going, and especially Cheryl Cheston, whose unrelenting enthusiasm, not to mention frequent help with research and ideas, was a constant source of inspiration. And without the members of my book group and their ambitious book selections, I would have had no "Dream After Reading Kafka."

I don't think my parents, Dan and Elaine Lewis, relatively private people, ever imagined that their elder daughter would turn from law to writing personal essays, and then write a book such as this one. Tremendously supportive while I wrestled with these issues about work and family, they watched grandchildren, read my manuscript, and arrived on my doorstep with emergency meals to feed six on nights when dinner preparation was the last thing on my mind.

Many an idea crystallized in my "short stress walks" with my sister Debbie Meloni, whose sometimes different point of view on these issues were always helpful, and whose love, support, and friendship I found essential for keeping this juggle going.

Finally, there is really no way to adequately thank my husband and children. Writing a book at home is probably hard on any family; writing a book that talks about the family is taking great license with the relationships I hold most dear. I thank you, Joe, Dan, Julia, Andrew, and Brian, for your patience and understanding when I growled, your picking up the slack around the house when I was working against deadlines, and your generosity and good humor in allowing me to share some moments of our life together.

Introduction

One evening in the spring, I was getting ready to meet my agent for dinner. My husband was working late.

To free myself for the evening out, I had to get some sort of dinner ready for the kids—preferably one that would not require the use of electricity or gas flames after I'd left. I also had to make sure the younger ones had their homework under control, give instructions to my eldest about the difference between being a big brother and being a good baby-sitter, and, finally, give instructions to the brothers and sister about being good baby-sittees.

Oh, and I had to get dressed in something better than my jeans.

As I sprinted from sink to stove to notepad to math worksheet, checking the clock and hoping there was gas in the car, my three boys, in succession, gave me grief about going out.

"But you were out two *nights* ago," complained the middle one, reaching for a piece of pizza.

"That was for Daddy's work," I replied.

"So why do you have to go out *tonight*?" the youngest wailed, tossing his head back in distress.

"Honey, this is *my* work. I'm meeting my agent about my book," I replied.

The eldest, nearly fourteen, straightened up from his slouch against the refrigerator door and eyed me dryly. "Well," he said, "we wouldn't want to get in the way of your career."

∾

Once upon a time, my career was law. Now my career, such as it is, is writing. But what I expend most of my emotional and physical energy on is raising my four kids.

This book is about the adjustments women today make when they leave or scale back their careers to be at home with their children. For the last ten years or so I've been writing personal essays about life at home with children, a recurring theme of which has been the contrast between the expectations of my teenage and young adult self and the realities of midlife as a mother at home with children.

I grew up thinking that intelligent, ambitious, well-educated women no longer stayed at home with children. I believed myself to be those things, and yet early in my thirties I stepped out of the practice of law and landed, not exactly feet first, in the world of diapers and playgrounds. I hadn't lost the desire for personal and professional fulfillment, yet children had added a dimension to my life that was much more significant, demanding, and compelling than I'd ever understood or imagined.

I felt as if there must be something wrong with me.

It took some time—because people didn't talk about these things—but I eventually discovered that I was not alone. There were many other women once driven by careers, now at home either full or part-time. They were women who'd had just as many "great expectations" as I'd had and who were struggling with similar issues, women who are still trying to reconcile their long-nurtured professional ambitions with their newfound great desires to be around for their children. (Such reconciliation is not always easy. I am not unaware of the irony of the last year or so, when I increasingly shut myself away from my children, so that I could write a book about how wonderful it is to be at home with children.)

And so began this book—not to whine, not to judge women whose choices are different, not to present a statistically significant study or announce a new social movement back to the home, but to reflect on the experience, to tell stories, to give voice to women who've changed their direction, and to laugh.

Despite social rhetoric about the importance of children, there has been and still is a common notion that women who choose to stay at home with their children are less ambitious, serious, and even reliable as professionals. I hope that by telling the stories of the women here—doctors, businesswomen, lawyers, accountants, teachers, scientists, artists—I will help debunk that myth and lessen the professional stigma many women feel when they introduce themselves with "I'm home with my kids."

Anchoring the narrative in my own experience, I've divided the book into three subjects. Part One examines our original expectations and the kinds of lives we led before having children. Part Two discusses the adjustments women make when faced with the reality of being at home—from dealing with domesticity to questions of identity to shifting relationships with husbands, children, and other women. Part Three looks at the new ways in which women at home are juggling their professional and personal desires.

Interwoven through the text are personal stories and anecdotes, as pictures illustrating the text.

Though every woman makes changes in her life when kids come along, this is not a book about every mother today. Nor is there any perfect way to balance our needs for work, family, and ourselves. There are mothers who want and need—by virtue of finances, personality, or other circumstances—to pursue full-time out-of-the-house careers, women who juggle work and family in ways that are best for them. And there are intelligent, interesting mothers who never intended to put career ahead of family, women who knew from the start that their lives needed to be family based.

The voices here are of well-educated women ranging in age from the late twenties to the midfifties who at some point decided to cut back, leave, or change their careers because of family. They come from different fields, different states, and different circumstances, both urban and suburban. I surveyed and talked to new mothers and women who were home with teenagers, women who'd resigned or scaled back as soon as their babies came, and women who, after twenty years in their professions, decided that they needed more time with their children. (For the most part, I've used first names only, fictitious names where requested.)

What these women have in common is that nearly all of them originally planned to make their careers their top priority, not because they didn't want children but because they grossly underestimated the emotional and physical commitment they'd want to give them. When expectations collided with reality, they adjusted, bucking social movements, professional training, and the expectations of their peers. They transformed not in intellect, ambition, or desire—none of these disappeared.

They had, instead, a change of heart. With that change of heart, they refocused their ambitions, reevaluated their priorities, and redefined the meaning of success.

They reinvented themselves.

Back in the kitchen, I raced around the table, pecking at cheeks and tops of heads, telling them I was really late now—I had to go—please do your homework—please don't fight—I'd be home by 9 or 9:30—or maybe 10. As guilt and a dash of resentment fought it out in my stomach, my nearly twelve-year-old daughter slid up to me, wrapped her arms around my neck, and cooed through a silken smile, "Don't worry, Mom, we'll be just fine."

I stopped and looked at my daughter, already maturing into a young woman in her ribbed T-shirt and wide-leg jeans, her high ponytail swept into a bun. I took a breath and relaxed. How fitting. My only daughter somehow sensed the conflict, the worry, the guilt, and the stress—all part of being a woman today—and she was eager to help. Don't worry, Mom, I'll take care of things, her deep brown eyes, shining with new maturity, seemed to say.

"Thanks, Julia," I said, relief soothing me like a warm summer breeze. I ran out the door into the driveway, around to the driver's side of my little car. Yanking open the door, I had one foot in when I heard the sound of bouncing, echoing rhythmically off the sidewalk across the street from the house. Looking up, I saw a boy nearly twelve—a classmate of Julia's—bouncing his basketball on the other side of the street. He was dribbling slowly, going nowhere, biding time, his eyes on our house.

I jumped into the car and turned the key.

"Hi," he shouted, his clear strong voice cutting through the engine's rumble. Bounce. Bounce. "Is Julia home?"

Reinventing Ourselves *after* Motherhood

PART ONE

GETTING OFF THE TRACK

CHAPTER ONE

"Well, I Just Can't Wait to Be King"

Great Expectations of a Generation Raised on Post-*Feminine Mystique* Feminism

I t is just after 11:00 on a Saturday night in June 1984, and things are not going according to plan—anyone's plan.

My plan was to spend the day shopping for baby furniture in New Jersey after a quick stop at the hospital for an examination, misleadingly referred to as a "nonstress test," in this forty-first week of my pregnancy.

My doctor's plan was to induce labor by injecting me, intravenously, with the drug pitocin, which I imagine races through one's blood vessels like a medicinal Paul Revere, rousing my sleeping uterus with the message "The baby is coming! The baby is coming!" to which the uterus responds with contractions spaced two minutes apart.

My husband's plan (at least plan B) was to try to remember his supporting player lines from Lamaze class, as well as what they told him about breathing (good) and panicking (bad).

None of us considered the baby's plan, which was, apparently, to stay put.

Fourteen hours after "stopping by the hospital," I am lying on my left side on a narrow bed in New York Hospital, my swelling skin covered by only a hospital gown, a sheet, and a monitor on a wide Velcro belt strapped around my giant belly. Yellowed plaster walls and overhead fluorescent lights surround us. A rapid, hoarse "Vwhomp-vwhomp, vwhomp-vwhomp, vwhomp-vwhomp" beats hypnotically from a speaker alongside the bed, reminding us—as if we could possibly forget—why we are here. Hallway noises—conversation bits and the squeaking of stretcher wheels—drift into the room. Someone is ordering pizza. Turning my head, I look across my shoulder at my husband, crumpled into his jeans and polo shirt in the pea-green vinyl chair next to the bed.

Every two minutes the lower part of me—or what I used to think of as me—ignites, twisting, squeezing, tightening. I puff, I pant, I breathe, and I plot my revenge. I think: they lied to me in Lamaze class. The instructors with their cheery smiles and earnest professional gazes said the puffing and panting and squeezing and tightening were for a purpose, the hurting had meaning, my cervix would open, labor would progress, my baby would be born.

My baby will never be born. He is a boat—a ship, an ocean liner—wedged and captive in the bottle of my belly. I scrunch my hips to shift my weight and stroke the curve of my abdomen with my palm.

My doctor, to whom I'd said good-bye hours ago, suddenly looms above me, wavering at the foot of my bed, like a silver-haired god in a lab coat. He is saying something about a heart rate dropping, about risks. About a cesarean section. Forms and a pen appear in my hands as the contractions sear and bind me like a fiery belt pulled tight.

I'm supposed to sign? I will sign anything. My husband stands, shifts, paces in the small space between the chair and the bed and the wall. New people crowd the room. Someone leads my husband from the room so they can insert a needle the size of a barbecue skewer up into my spine.

Then hands, arms surround me; I am lifted onto a stretcher. Watching the cracks in the corkboard ceiling slide by, I am being wheeled out the door, down the hall, turning into a room filled with large round lights and gleaming steel. Faces appear above me. Introductions are made. Dr. Sherlock. Dr. Holmes. Nurse Watson. Nice to meet you. Weird to meet you. My husband appears behind a pale green mask, wearing pale green scrubs, looking for all the world like an actor in a doctor show. As the late night shifts from stressful to surreal, it occurs to me that all of these people look like actors. Men in Green. And here I am, draped in white, the patient stretched out on the table. I am seized by a fervent wish that I had somehow been cast in another part.

The room is awash in pale green cotton. They raise a curtain, a drape, so that I can't see beyond my chest. Someone is pressing and pulling on my lower abdomen. Someone strong, someone heavy, too heavy. It is heavier than a person; it must be two people, or three; three men with a steamer trunk filled with iron weights, pushing down,

down, harder and harder. *What* are they doing? My husband—beginning to irritate me with his soft murmurs in my ear—is no help. He could stand up and report on what's happening, but he seems unduly fascinated with the side of my face. I don't remember this from class. I want to tell him to look, but I can't breathe; those men don't realize how hard they're pressing; they're going to crush me. Things are slipping around inside me.

Suddenly the pressure is gone. The startled cry of a baby fills the room.

A baby!

I'd been through the classes; I'd read the books. I'd thrown up enough times. I'd felt my abdomen expand, my bladder contract. I'd sat through meetings at work, my palm cradling the curvature of my belly behind my desk, waiting for the kicks. I'd lain in bed with the reading light on, my T-shirt pulled up, watching my stomach move. I knew I was going to have a baby.

But the reality—the reality of entering a room as six people, with arms and legs and thoughts and feelings and needs and plans and dreams, *six human beings*, and leaving as *seven* was beyond words or pictures or maternity policies or baby furniture.

I was unprepared for the ambush of birth—for the pain, for the stress, for the speechless joy.

Later, holding my baby, skin against skin, cupping his smooth firm foot in my palm, nudging my smallest finger into his tiny grasp, studying every crease and crevice of his wise little old man's face, I hadn't a clue as to how my life had changed.

I had come to think of myself as a lawyer—a lawyer who happened to be having a baby. That was another image they created in Lamaze class. The instructor was trying, I think, to reassure us in that hospital classroom, where we'd put our briefcases aside to sit on the floor, cradled in our partners' arms. There we'd imagine ourselves on the soft, pink sand of a lonely beach or some other far-off place of rest, learn soft cleansing breaths, try to prepare for the births of our children. At the end of each class we'd get up off the floor and pick up, with our briefcases, our old selves again. We were doctors, teachers, lawyers, bankers, managers, whatever—first. This baby was incidental, a passenger on the train on the fast track of my life—an important passenger, but not the engineer.

Ha.

I believed this for a while, for a great long while.

The concept of having a baby, like gross anatomy, hadn't changed much in the centuries since Eve first had the twins. Modern motherhood, I figured, like electricity, cellular telephones, and vcrs, had been figured out—with centuries to spare. I saw no conflict between simultaneously raising a child—or two or three—to adulthood and raising myself to the top of my profession.

I went back to work as a lawyer when my child was eight weeks old. Each morning I'd awaken him (though it was quite possibly the other way around) and change his diaper, chatting with him about the upcoming day. Then we'd settle into the bamboo rocker to nurse. For a while he would once again be physically part of me and I of him, our smells, our hearts, our stomach growls indistinguishable from one another, his velvet skin against my skin, his tiny fingers tapping my breast in time to the gentle creak of the rocking chair. When I could no longer feel the milk flowing miraculously through me (so incredibly, wonderfully, bizarre!), I'd gently pry him loose, change his diaper again, wriggle him out of his pajamas and into a clean soft stretchie for the day. I'd hand him off to a wonderful, loving woman, pick up my briefcase, lean over and kiss him again, turn my back, and leave.

Assumptions of the Culture

"I learned something from watching Power Rangers," my six-year-old announces to me one day in his never-ending war to persuade me that the antics of the superhero Power Rangers and Beetle Borgs qualify as educational television.

"Oh, yeah?" I say, slicing carrots.

He looks up at me, wide eyed and guileless. "I learned that girls can fix cars as well as boys can."

I stare. He has a smile with two loose teeth and wispy pale brown hair that defies gravity. A slight but sticky orange gleam above his upper lip suggests he's been sneaking Fruit Rollups again. I wonder sometimes if, in another life, he was the inspiration for Dennis the Menace. More and more often, I feel as if I am arguing with a clever con man who has stolen my son's little body. How does he know I care about girls fixing cars?

"Well, why *wouldn't* girls be able to fix cars?"

"No reason!" he says with a shrug of his narrow shoulders. A hole grows at the seams of the T-shirt he won't let me throw away. He climbs onto the kitchen stool and leans forward, bringing his round brown eyes level with mine. "Mom," he says, furrowing his pale eyebrows together, "some people don't believe in girls. In the show, this girl's father didn't believe she could, but she showed him he was wrong."

He straightens up, his lips twisted into a smirk, eyes steady on mine. "And that's what I learned watching Power Rangers. . . . It's educational, Mom. Really."

"Hmm." I am stymied in an argument with a person who hasn't existed as long as the run of a popular television show. But he is truly a product of his culture, and the way people behave on television influences the way he thinks about the world. Tv lessons—the good, the bad, and the ambiguous—may stay with him for years to come.

Popular culture's lessons in my childhood and adolescence were of a different sort, but no less pervasive. Never once did I contemplate being a housewife, a homemaker, or a stay-at-home mom. When, during my teenage years, my mother announced that she would begin using *homemaker* instead of *housewife* whenever anyone asked her occupation, I silently rolled my eyes. Homemaker, I decided, was a culturally invented psychic promotion, like the ubiquitous corporate vp, an effort to somehow revitalize the same old job. Whatever the title, I would not be the woman who sublimated her intellect and ambition to support her husband emotionally and domestically and raise his children.

I knew this without ever giving the subject much thought, without burning my bra or reading Betty Friedan's *The Feminine Mystique*. I knew it without taking women's studies courses in college or reading Simone de Beauvoir, Gloria Steinem, or Germaine Greer. By the early seventies the idea that women should be able to pursue the same academic and professional goals as men was no longer revolutionary—at least to an eighteen-year-old kid with her sights on the stars. The battles of the women's movement had been fought while I'd been climbing trees and putting on backyard shows, oblivious to national events that would shape my assumptions and expectations.

While I was a ten-year-old tomboy riding bikes and playing neighborhood baseball, *The Feminine Mystique* was published, exposing the unhappy trap in which a generation of married women found themselves. These women were the "happy housewife heroines": women whose identities, contributions, and aspirations were submerged into those of their husbands. The same year, the Equal Pay Act of 1963 had provided for "equal pay for men and women for jobs requiring equal skill, responsibility and effort."[1] The Civil Rights Act of 1964 prohibited sex discrimination in employment.[2]

When I was a fourteen-year-old girl coping with adolescent crushes and learning to play poker in my neighbor's garage, Executive Order 11375 of 1967 expanded affirmative action to include sex as a protected category (in addition to race, color, religion, and national origin) against which the federal government and employers with federal contracts could not discriminate.[3]

When I was a seventeen-year-old high school junior, a male classmate earnestly tried to persuade our English class that women should not be permitted to fly airplanes. I sat, incredulous, as he argued the folly of entrusting the safety of planeloads of people—let alone all those potential victims on the ground—to women, who were, he believed, through no fault of their own but by virtue of their biological destinies, too hormonally charged and prone to hysterics to handle any mid-air crisis. My friends and I laughed him off as a joke, an anachronism, a vestige of a time gone by.

The first of two daughters, I was both son and daughter to my physician father and housewife—er, homemaker—mother. If brothers had been around, maybe they would have taken out the trash and been the ones to rescue partially chewed squirrels from the jaws of our beagle, but as it was, as the older child, I did those things. It never occurred to me that I couldn't do whatever I wanted. If I ran up against someone who told me otherwise, I became only more determined.

By the time adulthood loomed as more than a distant fantasy of an endless childhood, the world had changed, and I left home to go to college with the assumption every generation makes anew: that I would be a modern person in the modern world.

In 1972 I entered an ivy-covered liberal arts school, which, until a few years before, had been all male and which still ran editorials in its school paper questioning the wisdom of admitting women. Such opinions I again discounted; I knew women had come to stay, and I didn't yet appreciate the fact that admittance to any male institution—from college to law firm, Little League team to business lunch club—was but half the battle.

In 1976, as the country celebrated its bicentennial, I graduated from college. It seemed obvious, at least to me, that our society had entered an age of gender enlightenment. My friends and I, simply by growing up with television, reading magazines, listening to records, and going to the movies, had subliminally absorbed the message of the modern day: that women were equally capable, equally talented, and equally able to succeed in whatever professional goals on which they set their sights.

Bright little girls no longer had to stifle curiosity, yield opinions in class, or choose coyness over competition. Young women need no longer set aside their own ambitions and dreams to service the dreams of others. Even TV's Laura Petrie, cute housewife and mother, had been replaced by Mary Richards, who had ambitions of her own.

As modern women, we would not be caught in the trap that had snared our mothers, so many of whom now seemed unfulfilled and unhappy once their children left the nest. Our generation of mothers would achieve a new level of personal success and fulfillment now that we could pursue the same professional opportunities as men. Nor was there any excuse not to succeed; the doors to the professions were apparently wide open.

We were a generation of women ready to believe in ourselves.

By the late seventies, when my friends and I were in law school, we felt we were on the brink of "becoming," the specifics of which we could not articulate. We felt though, that our careers would take off, ignited by graduation, fueled by the changing times.

Everything and anything was possible, and with youthful idealism we dreamed. We dreamed of becoming cabinet officers and world leaders, trailblazers in the arts, and foreign policy advisers. Maybe it was law school, maybe it was the time, maybe it was just our own extended adolescence. But parenthood was the furthest thought from our minds.

Occasionally when browsing through the ads in the *New York Times* magazine, we thought about children, but only in the context of a "break" from our true callings, whatever they should turn out to be.

If we had composed a to-do list for our lives, it would have read:

1. Graduate from law school and pass the bar exam.
2. Get a prestigious entry-level job that will shine on résumé.
3. Reach thirty, at which point identity will become clear.
4. Move on to cabinet officer, policy guru, etc.
5. Take a year off, have a baby, buy a Snugli, and sail around the world.

P.S.: Fall in love anytime along the way.

It is 1978, and I am interviewing for a state supreme court clerkship after law school. The search has been narrowed down to two of us—a male student from another law school and me. I spend the day with the justice. We talk case law, we talk theory, we have lunch. I find him intelligent, funny, and nice to be around. I hope he finds me the same. I want this job.

In a few days, my faculty reference calls me. He says he's talked to the justice. The other guy got the job. I ask if he said why? My professor hesitates. "I'm not sure. He liked you very, very much, and he said something very strange. He said, 'She's just the kind of girl I'd want my son to marry.'"

I dug my heels in and went to Wall Street.

Assumptions Unraveled

Back in my first few weeks of law school, living in Greenwich Village in 1976 was a quick lesson in growing up and growing tough. But aside from accustoming myself to the many lives that make up the city, there was law school itself. In law school I was surrounded—in every class, every meal, every room, every walk through the park—by law students. *These people are going to be my friends, neighbors, classmates, colleagues for the next three years, and my God, what am I doing here?*

I had my image of law students: mental sponges, absorbing contracts and torts, regulations and legislative orders. Of course they were all very intelligent, but my God, probably none of them knew how to play the guitar.

(I, of course, could just about make it through the easy chords of "Fire and Rain.")

Because this was now my life, my sentence for the next three years, I persevered. One day at lunch in the dorm dining room, I joined a table of these dry types I thought I knew so well. We talked about torts class and proximate cause and all the work. Suddenly the conversation moved on, from work to play and where we were from, where we had been, and where we might go from here. That day at lunch I met four incredible friends, each with his or her own distinctive personality and character. The guy with the blue suede sneakers turned out to be the Bronx-raised son of a labor union leader, a history major from Columbia with a razor-sharp mind for history and politics. The bookish-looking mild-mannered man from Princeton was of Greek ancestry, sang a great barbershop tenor, and had a sense of mischief about him that always made me laugh. The woman with the L. L. Bean vest and corduroys was someone with whom I was destined to spend many hours deliberating and debating everything from questions of constitutional law and federal jurisdictional authority to the relative merits of James Tayor versus the Rolling Stones to which annual date book would most effectively organize our lives. She lived in a loft with her medical student husband and, having already worked a few years in Manhattan, also knew where to find the best souvlaki in the Village. I even met a student who, when he'd closed the law books for the day, picked a mean James Taylor on his guitar.

Fast forward through three years of law school, five years amid the suits of Wall Street, a year or two in a midtown corporation, and a blur of years having one-two-three-four kids. I am sitting at a lunch table in the Philadelphia suburbs in a meticulously landscaped backyard with five other women—all, like me, mothers of children at our elementary school. Billed as a planning meeting, it is a luncheon for volunteers at the Book Nook Press, a parent-run school publishing center that each year helps every child in the school produce an original, bound, illustrated storybook.

I have long resisted this sort of thing—school committee meetings, luncheons, gardening workshops. My excuse has been time, which is in large part valid. But there has also been that image—like a ghostly apparition of June Cleaver rising up with a tray of slice-and-bake cookies—keeping me at bay.

I am not one of them.

"They" are stay-at-home moms. They do this all the time—meet, have lunch, talk about the kids. They play tennis, do car pools, get their nails done, exchange recipes, plan parties.

And like it.

I am not one of them, I tell myself, feeling like Meg from *A Wrinkle in Time*, resisting absorption into IT, the terrible pulsing being, that destroys the power of independent thought.[4] Beneath my sweater and jeans lurks a woman of substance: my dreams and aspirations go well beyond a successful bake sale, a perfectly sewn Halloween costume. If I've taken a wrong turn, I will, in time, find my way out.

We don't really know one another. We introduce ourselves by identifying our children: the mother of Andrew in first grade, Julia in third, Dan in fifth, and so on. Those of us with children in the same grade or, better yet, the same class, bond by discussing teachers, homework, and other school experiences. Then, as with the shifting of the late spring breeze, the conversation pivots, with a question thrown out, seemingly spoken by no one and yet by everyone at once: What did you do before kids?

I discover that I am sitting with an investment analyst, a Russian teacher with an MBA, an employee benefits consultant, and a nurse who headed up a surgical trauma unit.

We are all women with pasts, pasts put temporarily aside or in some cases discarded; women once known by their degrees, their titles, the call letters after their names, who now find themselves most frequently called Mom.

This was not a gathering of unhappy housewives out of *The Feminine Mystique*. Nor were these women contented homemakers. All, like me, were living with conflict, some juggling kids and scaled-back careers, some trying to tread water professionally while being there for the kids, some searching for new personal direction, having decided that the path they'd originally trod led too far away from home.

All had discovered that life plans mapped out at eighteen or twenty or even twenty-five hadn't meshed with the reality of either work or family life. And all of these professional, well-educated, capable women had chosen somewhere along the way to be around for their children.

They had done what some early feminists (as well as some today) thought (and think) unforgivable. "No woman should be authorized to stay at home to raise her children," said Simone de Beauvoir in a dialogue with Betty Friedan in 1975.[5] To those whom philosophy professor and author Christina Hoff Sommers calls *gender feminists*, women who choose to stay at home with children were at worst traitors and at best pitiful dupes of a patriarchical society:

> Although they may disagree politically about what measures to take with women who make the wrong choices, de Beauvoir and her latter day descendants share a common posture: They condescend to, patronize, and pity the benighted females who, because they have been "socialized" in the sex/gender system, cannot help wanting the wrong things in life.[6]

"Who Are Those Guys?"
The Stereotypes Persist

I never intended to quit my career. I used to imagine what it might be like, to have the courage, the resolve, the determination to take charge of my life that way. It must be incredibly difficult to leave the security of a workplace, a routine, a place where—to borrow from television— "everybody knows your name" and where you've established an adult identity for yourself. I always thought it would be like skydiving for the first time—hoping that the parachute would work but not really knowing for sure, hoping that it would be a pleasant ride, but fearing that you might just hurtle through space, crashing into nothingness.

One deterrent was that I didn't know anyone at home. Except my mother—and women from her generation. I assumed most of them lived in the suburbs.

More than not knowing at-home mothers, I didn't know anyone who had quit—or tried to change—her career. Nor was much written about women who had done so. The Department of Labor statistics count people who earn paychecks. There is no mechanism for counting those who give them up. The *New York Times* ran an article in November 1997 about what women tell their children when they go off to work each morning. Mention of the women who decide to stay home is almost an aside:

> For some working women, the early morning tears are soon forgotten in the press of the day's events—just as most of the children quickly dry their eyes and go about their business. For others—*and no one knows how many*—the emotional baggage becomes too heavy to haul to the office, leading some to give up their jobs or cut back their hours, often relegating themselves to the so-called mommy track.[7]

"No one knows how many" women leave the fast track to accommodate family in part because so many women today try to disguise any such motivation. In a world where it's easier to get the afternoon off to pick up your car from the shop than to acknowledge that you have a first-grade play to attend, women are still advised to minimize family demands on their work time.

Giving up a career or scaling back or in any way readjusting one's professional expectations because of the kids was not and is still not—in many circles—a respected choice. When corporate women leave the work force, many are loath to give family or children as the reason, in part because they believe that to do so would confirm the stereotypes. Brenda Barnes's resignation of her high-ranking job at Pepsi, along with her explanation that she wanted to spend more time with her family, became a lead story in the *Wall Street Journal*.[8] Outraged "working" women called in and wrote to Sue Shellenbarger's "Work and Family" column. "'This has set the rest of us back a long time,' [a New York marketing consultant] lamented. 'It verifies all the worst stereotypes about women in the workplace.'"[9]

The problem with this kind of reaction is that it also confirms the negative stereotype—not of a working mother but of a mother at home with children. How does this woman think Ms. Barnes will be spending her days?

The *Wall Street Journal*'s column "Managing Your Career" on November 11, 1997, proclaimed, "Colleagues Often Have the Wrong Ideas About Why Women Quit." In it columnist Carol Hymowitz admonishes that when women are not "candid" enough about their professional motives for leaving jobs, they leave the impression that they are going home to family. Yet when they are "candid," the men they leave still may not believe them. "I was adamant that I not be perceived as leaving to spend more time with my children, because that wasn't what was driving me," said a woman leaving a financial services company to start her own business.[10]

Again, why so adamant? Why such effort to distance oneself from family? Women so outraged by stereotypes, so insistent on disassociating themselves from home life must have another stereotype in mind. The illustration running with the article shows a man waving to a departing female colleague. The bubble showing his thoughts pictures an aproned woman embracing two kids—while the woman is picturing herself conductor of a symphony orchestra.

I question whether the aproned woman in the *Wall Street Journal* article exists anymore or whether she ever existed as we now imagine her. Whether or not she does, this book is not about that woman.

This book is about an evolving breed of at-home mothers, women who left their office jobs, scaled back, reorganized their professional activities, or otherwise redirected their talents *because of conflicts between pursuing careers and raising children*. They are working through the seeming contradictions: acknowledging the validity of traditional motivations (i.e., wanting to be at home with their children) without succumbing to traditional stereotypes (i.e., the 1950s vision of what a wife and mother should be). In the process they are discovering and creating new ways of balancing all of the meaningful parts of their lives.

Some of at-home motherhood is much the same as it was when Betty Friedan wrote of the "enormous demands" of the role of "modern housewife":

> . . . wife, mistress, mother, nurse, consumer, cook, chauffeur; expert on interior decoration, child care, appliance repair, furniture refinishing, nutrition, and education. . . . Her day is fragmented as she rushes from dishwasher to washing machine to telephone to dryer to station wagon to supermarket, and delivers Johnny to the Little League field, takes Janey to dancing class, gets the lawnmower fixed and meets the 6:45. She can never spend more than 15 minutes on any one thing; she has no time to read books, only magazines; even if she had time, she has

lost the power to concentrate. At the end of the day, she is so terribly tired that sometimes her husband has to take over and put the children to bed."[11]

But much of it is different. Women who chose to change their careers to spend more time with their families have brought to at-home motherhood their expectations, education, creativity, skills, business savvy, and often a sense of guilt that they are not somehow "doing it all."

It is not easy to leave a career, scale back, or start anew. Many women describe it as taking a huge risk. This book examines what some women did, why and how they changed their careers, the adjustments they've had to make, the growth they've experienced, and the balance they seek.

CHAPTER TWO

Courtrooms, Boardrooms, Operating Rooms

Work and the Jobs We Held

Thirty-five years after Betty Friedan wrote *The Feminine Mystique,* the debate about women, home, and work still rages, despite a generation of women who have reaped the benefits of the revolution. Women have joined the ranks of doctors, lawyers, politicians, scientists, investment bankers, conductors, movie producers, executives, entrepreneurs, construction workers, and pilots while continuing to fill traditional roles as teachers, nurses, models, actresses, and bookkeepers. Even Barbie has begun thinking about more than what to wear in her pink convertible or how to furnish her dream house. A generation of girls have grown into women with the expectation that we would work in the world in whichever way our skills and talents led us, contribute to society in some visible way, and slip a family in along the way. "It wasn't as if you had a choice," says Jill, a thirty-six-year-old Princeton-educated civil engineer. "Before you were expected to stay home. Now you're expected to work—and be able to do it all."

Our expectations blossomed at different levels of our education. Allison, a thirty-four-year-old lawyer and mother of two small boys, remembers it being an "anathema to think about staying home as a mom," and that as early as sixth grade she knew she wanted to achieve in a high-status way: "The teacher was going around the room talking about careers and aspirations for people in the class. When my sixth-grade teacher said to me, 'I think you will be a teacher,' I was insulted, because that was traditionally a women's role. . . . It was a male teacher—that's the irony, that I would be offended—because I thought, you think that's the highest I can achieve?"

By the time many women were in college, childhood fantasies had flowered into extraordinarily ambitious career dreams. Where once little girls grew up wanting to be princesses, now we were thinking in terms of becoming kings. Sherry, thirty-six, a mother of two and a part-time editor, remembers thinking during her years at Princeton that she and her friends "were all going to do something important." "I didn't know what," she says, "but it would be significant. I thought about becoming a lawyer, not because I wanted to be a lawyer, but so I could be attorney general."

Professional schools only heightened such feelings for women like Jessica, a physician who went to Yale Medical School in the seventies, where "there was a real expectation there that people would not just graduate from med school and work part-time. It was not subtle. . . . They trained people to take leadership roles."

Such expectations were sprouting beyond the classroom doors in other fields as well. Cathy, forty-three, a former urban planner, whose mother was a social worker and whose father was a doctor, says: "My original goal was to be head of the Department of Public Welfare for the state of Pennsylvania. . . . My goals were assumptions more than real goals. It was always assumed that I'd grow up to do something socially productive. I'm a Quaker, and it's kind of expected that your work will be good for society."

In an atmosphere of such single-minded ambition, the idea of family life, says Cynthia, a former editor of *Business Week*, "didn't even occur to you. You're not being trained to live that kind of life. You're being trained to live in a professional world where everybody goes to work every day."

Thoughts of children were often little more than vague expectations and fuzzy fantasies—family planning Scarlett O'Hara style: "I'll think about it tomorrow." Says Christine, thirty-eight, a legislative analyst, "I always assumed I would work. I didn't get married until I was twenty-nine, and I would joke with friends about going to a sperm bank if I didn't meet 'Mr. Close-to-Perfect.' I envisioned myself as a single corporate mom."

When Is Work Considered Work?

Asking why women work is a little like asking why we breathe, why kids slide on their knees down a freshly waxed hallway, why dogs sleep in the sun. Freud said that a man's work "at least gives him a secure place in a portion of reality, in the human community."[1] Everybody—or nearly everybody—works! What is work, other than productive activity?

The debate about working mothers is not so much about whether they work but about the kind of work women do and why they do it—whether for love of the work, for money, or simply to get the job done. Flipping burgers at McDonald's and negotiating terms of international peace as secretary of state are both work. So are cleaning house, teaching a child to read, and raking leaves.

The circumstances under which work is done change its character as well. You can rake leaves for exercise or because you have small children poised at the end of the yard readying themselves for takeoff. You can rake them because someone is paying you to do so, or you can do it because they're your leaves and they'll kill your grass if you don't.

But when money is paid, work achieves a different status. Juliet Schor points out in her book *The Overworked American* that most economists "[identify] work with income-generating activity,"[2] consequently

> ... if a man marries his housekeeper, the gross national product will fall. ... The paid labor of the housekeeper is replaced by the unmarketed services of the wife, and the country looks to be poorer as a result. The reality is that the actual work being performed may well be identical ...[3]

Implicit in the public debate about whether women should "work," is the notion that work is paid work. But the concept of work was not always defined by a paycheck. Schor cites economist Nancy Folbre's observation:

> In 1800, women whose work consisted of caring for their families without pay were widely considered productive workers. By 1900, however, they had been formally relegated to the census category of "depen-

dents" that included infants, young children, the sick and the elderly. The dominant discourse characterized women as "supported" by their husbands.[4]

When Does Paid Work Become a Career?

(When it follows you home at night,
competing with Little League games,
school fairs, and raking those leaves.)

When today we talk about women and work, even within the category of paid work outside the household, there are distinctions, often unstated. Although Betty Friedan, in *The Feminine Mystique*, went so far as to characterize the home as a "comfortable concentration camp," she did not advocate taking just any job, nor did she advocate work for the sake of working. In condemning volunteer work as lacking sufficient responsibility and commitment, she also criticized women who "apply for jobs as receptionists or saleswomen, jobs well below their actual abilities. These are also ways of evading growth."[5]

People have been working—for money, for love, for necessities, and for all combinations of such for thousands of years. That women work is not new. The feminist revolution opened the doors not to work itself but to high-status work.

Studs Terkel wrote in 1972 about the importance of status to men and women alike:

> Is it any wonder that . . . status rather than the work itself becomes important? Thus the prevalence of euphemisms in work as well as in war. The janitor is a building engineer; the garbage man, a sanitary engineer; the man at the rendering plant, a factory mechanic; the gravedigger, a caretaker. They are not themselves ashamed of their work, but society, they feel, looks down upon them as a lesser species.[6]

But public debate about mothers and "work" often ignores these distinctions. In its story about what working women tell their children about why they "work," the *New York Times* quoted statistics that show 63 percent of women with children under six, and 70 percent of married women with children under eighteen "work" at least part-time. Although many feel a financial need to work, the author points out, others work because they like it.

> Although a second income helps pay the bills, working really is not about the money for some of these women, especially after higher tax rates and the cost of child care kick in. Instead, going to work becomes similar to an illicit pleasure, almost akin to sneaking off to have an affair.[7]

Even if you lump together all women who work for money (the only ones picked up by the Department of Labor Statistics)—the ninety-hour-a-week lawyers with the nursery school teachers with the nurses-on-shift with the part-time physicians and home-based marketing consultants—the real question demanded by the children is not so much "Why do you work?" but "Why do you leave me?" or "Why do you do work that takes you from me?"

There are many women mixed up in all these statistics who have dramatically changed the ways in which they work. Because they have left the fast track of their often corporate lives, they are to some the women who "couldn't cut it," who "sold out," who sacrificed their careers for their families.

When you're on a speeding train, hurtling toward the next station in your career, it's difficult to focus clearly on things off the track. Perception is distorted; reality blurs. People without children or with a "wife" at home, i.e., those who have never let themselves slow down, carry a picture of what they imagine life outside to be, but they may not have a clue as to what life at home today is really like.

At least I hadn't.

It takes a lot of nerve to jump from that train into the uncharted brush of family life, uncertain of whether you'll ever be able to run fast enough to get back on. And if you do return, certainly, you'll have a lot of explaining to do.

To understand why we left and why it was so difficult, it helps to understand what it was like to be there.

In Deep Career

I was on the bottom rung of a ladder at the top of the world.

I am curled around a pile of books at my desk in my fiftieth-floor office during my first year of work. One wall is entirely windows, framing a panoramic view of blue sky and cloud patterns stretched out over the island of Manhattan, an irregular mass of concrete and glass shapes edged by rivers creeping up its sides, disappearing into the blue-gray horizon.

The carpeted office is still, the quiet clicks from the secretarial stations barely audible down the hallway. Books open, papers spread around me, I am deep in the pages of an SEC case, lost in thought. Suddenly a shadow falls across the page, the warmth of a body looms behind me, an arm plunges across in the space in front of me. I startle in my seat and stifle a scream.

It is the pencil man: a little elderly man in a blue messenger uniform who is hired solely—as far as any of us know—to sharpen pencils.

Work life was incredibly seductive.

Between 1979 and 1984, I lived in an apartment in Manhattan and worked as an associate at a large New York law firm. The people with whom and for whom I worked were from the highest echelons of the legal profession. The firm represented major banks and corporations, prominent politicians and celebrities. The partners came from Harvard and Yale, presidents' cabinets, and federal administrative agencies. Firm parties were thrown at Tavern on the Green, at the Top of the World Trade Center, and on ships chartered to sail around Manhattan.

As the years slid by, I worked more and more, took the subway less and less, coming home late at night in client-charged limousines, fleets of which roam lower Manhattan after dark. The pencil man disappeared as the firm soared into the computer age. But the work remained and grew to fill my days and often my nights. Colleagues became my friends. Work became my life. Though I was married to my college boyfriend, we lived an eighties yuppie lifestyle, going our separate ways, meeting for an occasional late night burrito and refried beans at the tiny Mexican restaurant up the street from our apartment. We were, like many of our friends, married people living single lives. In fact, it was better than being single, for our time and energy could be devoted exclusively to our careers, without the distraction of dating or working on a relationship. Neither of us had a problem with this. My husband was, after all, on a career climb of his own. And ours were just two of the ladders all over the town.

I may have attributed this workaholism to law or New York or my own particular personality. But it was happening everywhere and in many different fields: Women were stepping into boardrooms, scrubbing up for operating rooms, making their cases in courtrooms all over the country. We weren't punching clocks, biding time, or keeping busy. We were creating identities for ourselves, securing places in our own visions of reality.

The roles we've since taken on—as wives, mothers, scout leaders, school and community volunteers—often cover up but do not erase those early footholds we'd seized, those identities we'd fashioned. They are still part of our individual histories, contributing significantly to the women we are today. What follows are seven early snapshots: These women will surface later in the book, with reflections from later in their lives. They are presented here only as different examples of how deeply involved in our various careers we became.

Cathy: Nonprofit Fast-Tracker

Before children entered her life, Cathy raced along a nonprofit fast track. Financially independent at age twenty, she was used to working for money but wanted her work to be of real value to society. Originally headed for social work as a therapist, her experience in inner-city hospitals made her think that she should refocus her efforts: "I realized that treatment in the hospital was great, but the city was pathological. . . . It didn't matter how healthy you could help people become; if they had to go back to an environment like that, they would crumble again."

After working as a community liaison at a community health center, Cathy took a job at a community development think tank, where she worked on energy conservation and utility advocacy. She threw herself into her work, helping low-income people weatherize their homes and reduce their utility bills, as well as networking with state and local politicans.

"I always had two jobs at once. I think what's really significant about this time was that I had no responsibility except to myself and no family to take care of. . . . I could devote myself entirely—blood, guts, and soul—to work. . . . I had the energy, the inclination, the time. . . .

"I developed a training school—we called it a school for citizens, and it was for people who wanted to improve their communities in any area, and it helped them learn the skills they needed to be able to turn their ideas into programs or to turn programs into actual institutions.

"It was very exciting. I was in the right place at the right time, and I was the right age. . . . I went to town meetings every night, civic association meetings on weekends. I did a lot of writing. I got very involved in fund-raising. . . . In the course of it I developed a lot of leadership skills myself."

By the age of thirty-five, Cathy had been offered a top job in her field—as executive director of a nonprofit association providing management advice, services, and advocacy for arts organizations.

Lisa: Neurobiologist

Lisa spent her early professional days "slicing brains." A scientist with an undergraduate degree in psychology, a master's in science, and a PhD in neurobiology, she did postdoctoral work that involved studying sexually mediated neuro-endocrine reflexes, such as brain activity during milk letdown in lactation.

"I would inject the animals with a radioactive form of glucose that would be taken in by the cell but not metabolized. . . . The radioactive tracer would sit there . . . two weeks later we'd get a picture of the neural activity during that particular twenty-second period during injection and take-up of that deoxyglucose . . . it was fascinating."

Lisa never read *The Feminine Mystique*; nor did she think much in terms of feminism. She simply wanted a career in science, a field that she expected would be incompatible with having children. She loved her work and published in *Brain Research, Science, Animal Physiology, Animal Behavior,* and a host of other publications; she was listed in *Who's Who in Science and Technology*. Lab research, writing, lecturing, and traveling filled her days.

"One thing I liked about science was the intellectual camaraderie. Going to conferences and talking to somebody who is working on a different species, working toward solving the same questions that you are, is wonderful. It's like good sex. . . . That intellectual give and take was just fabulous—it was the high point of my years in science."

Jill: Civil Engineer

Jill knew when she went into engineering at Princeton in the eighties, that it was still considered "a man's field." That, in fact, was part of the reason her mother urged her to consider it: "I went into engineering basically because my mom said, 'You're good at science and math, you're a woman, it's not a woman's field, so it'll be easy to get a job.' And it seemed like a good field, so I said, 'Fine,' not really thinking about [whether] it would be boring [or] interesting. . . . My mother wanted to make sure that if I ended up in a bad marriage I would have the means to support myself . . . I would have a marketable degree."

So Jill armed herself with a degree in civil engineering, with a concentration in structures. After college she headed for New York, where, as one of two women engineers in a firm of 150, she did "the typical Manhattan thing: subway in the morning, subway in the evening." "I dealt with roads and bridges and buildings—designing them, the geometry of laying everything out in terms of roadway; in terms of bridges and buildings, figuring out how big different members have to be to support the weight."

After a year she moved out of New York to a forensic engineering company with more women but a "weird" attitude about them. "Our department was called the harem," she says. Gathering experience while searching for her niche, she made two more moves over the next several years until she found a company close to home, which was very family oriented, though it still had few women engineers.

Sally: Investment Banker and Financial Reporter

Like Jill, Sally considered it an advantage to become skilled in a field populated by men. In 1991, armed with her Yale BA in Chinese, she headed straight into an investment banking program, an experience she says "was the best thing I could have done after college as a woman."

A "high-pressure job," she says, particularly in finance, "can always get you immediate respect in a conversation with a man. . . . It put me in an entirely different category [from other women].

"It was the equivalent of playing on the Little League team with boys. It's OK, you were cool, you were accepted. . . . They knew how to have a conversation with you. It wasn't awkward. That was huge for me."

Working eighty to ninety hours a week in such an environment was excellent experience and taught Sally not only finance but how to deal with corporate executives. After the two-year program ended, she was twenty-six and landed a job as general reporter at the *Wall Street Journal.* A short time later she moved to one of the regular sections and was assigned to write a daily column on the stock market, an area of the *Journal* that felt "more like a men's bastion." That column, she remembers thinking, "was 'supposed' to be written by gray-haired men." Nevertheless, she worked hard and with few exceptions had positive experiences working with people inside as well as outside the paper.

Cheryl: Director of Research

Cheryl graduated from college with a degree in English in 1969, the year before Sally was born—the same year a man first walked on the moon and thousands gathered at Woodstock, but still a time when a woman's BA in English was little more than a ticket to a darn good secretarial job. She never sought a particular career, but after a couple of secretarial jobs, the acquisition of a real estate license, registration with the SEC, and some months working on the renovation of a friend's house (learning everything "from constructing walls and laying floors to plumbing and shingling"), she found herself on the way to a career with an investment house. In 1974 she began as an editor for investment research, adding analytical writing and increasing levels of responsibility. By 1979 she was a chartered financial analyst and a vice president. ("There were thousands of them," she says. "Not a big deal.") In 1983 she was promoted to senior VP and director of research and asked to join the board of directors. Her position now required early mornings (out of the house by 7:00) and late nights, along with dinner meetings and receptions. With it came significant responsibility, money, and visibility within her profession.

"I traveled all over the country, could call anybody anywhere, and usually got through. The firm and the department were growing, and I spent a good deal of time recruiting analysts and developing the research product. The people I worked with were exceptionally bright and highly motivated. They were what I liked best about the job."

Lorraine: Manager of Employee Benefits

Like Cheryl, Lorraine didn't actively plan for a career. Growing up in Hartford, Connecticut, she was the first in her family to go to college, and the last place she imagined herself was in business. Yet by the time she was twenty-seven, she was so thoroughly immersed in her work that she couldn't imagine life without it. Working at a small insurance brokerage firm, she began to discover talents she never knew she had. As a consultant for employee benefits, she gave speeches to roomfuls of male executives—and found she loved it. Her employer began to handle investments as well.

"I *was* the employee benefits department. I had four people working for me. Their clients were my clients, small closely held companies. . . . Having an employer with a thousand employees was a very big thing. I had a lot of clients, a lot of volume. The clients needed a lot of hand holding, a lot of creative ways to solve their problems. I was doing things like public speaking, running meetings. . . . I got very wrapped up in my job. . . . And I was very good at what I did."

Alice: Model, Makeup Artist, Businesswoman

At nineteen, Alice couldn't have anticipated the life she'd be leading in twenty years—as the thirty-nine-year-old at-home suburban American mother of two children. Born in England, Alice has a quiet manner, a pleasant smile, and a life before children that carried her all over the world. By the time she was twenty-four, Alice had lived in four countries, with as many different jobs, any one of which could have been considered a career. Brought up in a proper English family, the daughter of an industrialist, seventeen-year-old Alice went from finishing school in

Switzerland to Spain with her older sister. There they found modeling jobs. With her classic bone structure and blond good looks, Alice soon found herself working in the Far East, doing runway and print work.

"[Modeling] is extremely good work for doing absolutely nothing, but if somebody's willing to pay you money to take a photograph, you'd be stupid to say no. I never thought of it as a feminist issue. I thought I had the upper hand. I never felt exploited. It was a pretty gutsy thing."

Their father's death took the sisters home to London, where her sister married and Alice began learning other aspects of the fashion business, working as a makeup artist and teaching girls how to model. By the time she was twenty-one she and a partner had opened up their own modeling school and agency in London. The agency did well and had a steady stream of clients.

"Running the agency was very hard work, very stressful. You were sandwiched between the models and the photographers, and everyone would scream at everyone else, and I was starting to get burned out."

Along with burnout, problems in the partnership were beginning to appear. Then one of the girls in the agency became sick with cancer. When the girl's family asked Alice if she'd accompany their daughter on a visit to her father in South Africa, Alice said yes. It was a good time, she reasoned, to make a change.

Closing the business, Alice left for South Africa, figuring she'd stay a month or two. Once there, however, she met a man who was working as a guide in the tourist business coming to Africa from South America. Learning that Alice was proficient in Spanish, he offered her a job. She accepted.

Little did she realize that sheperding busloads of tourists around Africa would in some ways prepare her for her future role as an American mom.

"I'd have to get up at 6:00 every day . . . because I'd have to get everyone checked out, pay the hotel bills, make sure everyone had everything. . . . There would be forty-five people who in South America were doctors and lawyers and very respectable people, and they get on the bus, and suddenly . . . they're on vacation, on holiday, and they become totally irresponsible. . . . Everyone's telling me they're carsick and have to sit in the front . . . and the same people are always late, the same people are always losing their keys. . . ."

Alice discovered that her Spanish wasn't as good as she'd thought, and worse, the Castilian Spanish she'd learned in Spain and the Spanish spoken in South America uses different expressions.

"I was always putting my foot in it. . . . Once I was explaining an ostrich farm, and it was explained to me . . . after they had managed to scrape themselves off the floor . . . that I had said that the farmer went out and gathered up his balls and put them in the incubator and left them there for seventy days until they hatched . . . oh, God."

After a year of this, Alice decided she'd had enough of the tourist trade in South Africa. She'd been a model, a makeup artist, a teacher, a business executive, and a tour guide. She was all of twenty-three years old.

Although her mother introduced her to friends as "my daughter, my career girl," Alice didn't feel driven by career as much as by the desire to do something interesting at any given moment in her life. Boyfriends came and went, but Alice didn't want to be tied down to a life of domesticity: "Actually, I regarded the whole notion of marriage as a drag. I'd never had to answer to anybody . . . I didn't want to be controlled."

Careers "R" Us

The more immersed in work we became, the more we identified with our co-workers, and the more foreign the concept of a life at home with kids became.

It is 1980. The followers of the Ayatollah Khomeini are holding fifty-three American hostages in the American Embassy in Iran. I am hostage to the life of a lawyer: for an average of sixty hours a week I inhabit the concrete canyons of Wall Street, a place that looks like the old black and white photos of Eastern Bloc countries, its citizens in uniforms hustling with grim determination through a gray urban landscape.

Over the course of the first year or so I chuck my unstructured dresses for tailored suits, my funky pink suits for worsted gray wool, my open cotton shirts for high-necked blouses. I even try, for a day or two, those dumb little ribbon ties. I don't recognize myself in the reflection of the firm's glass door. I look like a feminized man—a masculinized woman. I think I look ridiculous.

There are only seven women in our entering class of twenty-five new associates. I, who have always been friends with men, now seek out the company of other women. Only one of us has children, about whom she rarely speaks. We, like all good associates, model ourselves after the partners, all but one of whom are men. There are issues here, buried under the stacks of case files that line my office floor. Work seems an invincible master, but time marches on, and the unacknowledged conflict quietly and steadily builds.

"Women aren't serious about the law," grumbles one balding partner in his rumpled Brooks Brothers suit. "It's only a question of when the babies come." Astonished that he would say this to my face, I react reflexively; I am horrified that anyone would think I would be distracted by something as outdated and traditional as a baby. The women associates begin to bond, and at the same time we watch one another. The actions of any of us, we feel, reflect on us all. We can work as hard as anyone, we say. And it is true.

Other women lawyers report similar dynamics among the women in their professional lives. Sheryl was an associate at a big firm and knew that one of the other women had adopted a child. Although Sheryl was curious about how the woman was working it all out, her efforts to learn about the experience went nowhere. "She acted as if nothing had changed. She was working more and more. There was no discussion. She didn't want to share information. It was almost as if she didn't want to be seen as having a child."

Allison was also a lawyer with a big city firm and remembers a woman who took her work with her when she went into labor:

"She was editing a summary judgment motion when she went into labor. She was so determined not to be distracted by having a child that she was calling in corrections between contractions."

Nor was this effort to model ourselves after men limited to those of us in the legal profession. In *Women and the Work/Family Dilemma*, authors Deborah J. Swiss and Judith P. Walker surveyed women who had graduated from Harvard's professional schools in medicine, law, and business over a ten-year period. They found that

[w]hen women first entered the male-dominated professions of business, law and medicine, they visibly demonstrated their buy-in to the male work ethic by looking and acting as much like the men as they could.

Conservative gray flannel suits and silk ties were their camouflage, symbols of their desire to fit in easily and without fanfare. They recognized that "image" is a powerful component to succeeding in the workplace.[8]

The stronger our career identities became, the weaker our sense of home and family and its place in our lives became.

Pat was immersed in her work as a city planner and was not particularly concerned about a family in the future: "If I fell in love with and married a guy who didn't want children, I would not have children. I also perceived at-home moms as underachievers. Women who sold out."

Before her first son was born in 1994, Bobbie was a New York banker, heading up departments involved in corporate lending, corporate buyouts, and entrepreneurial private banking. She had started out in banking in the midseventies, when there were few senior women to act as role models: "When I was in banking, I knew what my handicaps were. I was a woman in a white shoe firm, I was ethnic, I looked very young. They tried to hit on me; it happened quite a bit with clients and even with senior management at the bank. I made it a point to work harder than every single one of them. I worked longer hours, and I'd still go out and have a beer with the guys because I knew that was important. And that's how my life was for years. I didn't turn down an assignment. . . .

"This was who I was—'Bobbie the banker who works with X, Y, and Z,' and I got a lot of fulfillment out of that. I never viewed myself as a mommy person."

The absence of real in-the-flesh role models for any other family life than the man-with-a-wife-at-home was significant. When I thought about combining a fast-track career and a home life, my ideas were gleaned from the media more than from any real-life woman I knew who was doing it. And the more prestige I associated with my work, the less I thought of women who were at home with children.

I wasn't alone. Lucy, now an artist and at-home mother of three, was, in 1983, a marketing consultant working fifty hours a week. She remembers thinking, "There's no way I can have children and have a job like this. It's too stressful. . . . Secretaries had kids. . . . The men had kids. And the wives were at home with the kids. . . . The men treated me differently. They treated me like one of them. I felt like I was an equal, and I felt like the wives were inferior. That's the truth. That's the way the business world operated then, and it probably does to some extent now, though probably to a lesser extent because so many women are working with kids."

This absence of role models went beyond the business world. Lisa remembers that as a college student headed for a career in science she concluded that to succeed she would have to forgo having children: "I had no women role models who were professors with children. . . . They had no children at all. Many of them weren't even married. I concluded that science and children don't go together. . . . My mother was a very smart lady . . . but she stayed home, cleaned house, drove the children from one place to another, and she was bored most of the time. And I didn't want to live my life that way."

Even in recent years professional life seemed disproportionately populated by single people or men with wives at home to take care of their children. Tracy, thirty-four, now at home with three small girls, was a communications specialist at a large investment house until 1994. She recalls that "There weren't women who had children. Either they were just married or they weren't married. Most of them were single and didn't have any kids. Unless they were men. . . . My sister-in-law, my husband's sister, has four children, and she never really worked, except for odd jobs. . . . She had her third when my husband and I got married. . . . Back when I was working, here I am, like twenty-five, and I'm thinking, 'Man, she is out of touch.' You'd talk to her about a movie, she's like, 'Huh?' I knew she had four kids, but I thought . . . 'what do you do all day?' And that was my perception of her. Here I was, with this important job (ha-ha). I knew what I wanted, and I did this, and here she was . . . big deal. I mean, anybody could take care of kids."

Anne, now thirty-eight with a one-year-old, put off having children for fear of what it would do to her career momentum as a college teacher. Her perceptions of women at home, though not precisely "negative," were not consistent with her image of herself: "I guess I had certain perceptions of women who stayed at home as . . . doing laundry and, you know, those things you see on TV commercials. And I guess that's partly why I thought they were not like me."

Indeed, what one woman had gleaned from a college English lit class in 1968 remained the dominant theme nearly thirty years later: "The overwhelming message was not that there were choices to be made but that being home was bad and career was good. . . . The result for me was that everything having to do with home and children and families and housekeeping was a real negative.... And I had this impression that women at home were ... dumb.... [She smiles.] The women who play tennis are the dumb ones, the ones who do lunch and get their nails done."

From Career Women to Working Mothers

It is 1982, and unemployment in America is the highest in forty-two years, a fact of which I am barely aware, so many hours do I spend at the office in my work-is-life-is-work period. I am having a conversation with my lawyer friend Steve, whose advertising executive wife has told him she wants to move to the suburbs and have kids. I am surprised and feel a little sorry for him, thinking how mismatched they must be: he, ambitious, intelligent, a real achiever, and she, a successful advertising executive, who wants to throw it all away for a life of station wagons and kids in the burbs.

By now it's not the idea of children that disturbs me; I just see no reason to equate kids with suburbs, station wagons, and being at home, associations I make with my sixties childhood. I want to be a contemporary mom, raising kids whose playgrounds are museums and who are fluent in Japanese menus.

One day in the fall of 1983, a home pregnancy test tube turns blue; suddenly it is my turn.

My best friend at work is beside herself. We have a bigger secret than the identity of a new takeover target, a client's strategy for litigation, or who's on the inside partnership track. And I have a problem.

I discover that I am not one of those people who have easy pregnancies, who never felt better, who don't miss a day of work. I do not get a spring in my step, good color in my cheeks. I most definitely do not glow.

I throw up. A lot. At unpredictable times, not limited to early morning. Chills rack my body; my head feels like cotton. I hunch over my work and nibble crackers all day.

It does occur to me that perhaps a sixty-plus-hour-a-week job is pushing it for my new state of being. It does not yet occur to me to stay at home. Now, more than ever, I believe myself to be different from those stay-at-home moms.

CHAPTER THREE

"No, No, We Won't Go!"

Motherhood and the Choice—
How Did We End Up Home Again?

I t is the fall of 1984, and all is right with my world. Take-charge woman of the eighties that I am, I have planned my life well. I have an exciting job as in-house counsel at a company in the broadcasting/entertainment field, a move I made five months into my pregnancy, partly because I like the field and partly so that I could get home by 6:30—practically a part-time job by my old law firm's standards. My apartment is a five-minute cab ride, twenty-minute bus ride, or thirty-minute walk from work. The guy I've loved since college—now my husband and the father of my child—is making his way up the orchestra management ladder at Lincoln Center—even closer to home than my job. And every night I go home to the only real-life miracle to which I've been witness: a child with pink satin skin, slate blue eyes, and a white knuckle grip on my heart.

I have this working mother thing down cold. My soft leather briefcase, its zipper teeth clenched tight, bulges with the shape of a breast pump I use to express milk when I can't make it home for lunch. The thirty-six-year-old woman I've hired to watch my baby has a soft, melodious voice, a sunlike smile, and her own kids to go home to every night.

Sure, there are moments. Moments when my briefcase leaks milky drops that bleed into my papers and follow me in a trail of drips down the office corridor. Times when, as the daylight at my office window fades into blackness, a crisis erupts at work, triggering the domino effect I dread: I can't get home on time, my husband can't get home on time, and my babysitter must get home (to relieve her babysitter, etc.); the upshot of which is, hours later, I retrieve my infant son creeping around in his pajamas backstage at the orchestra. And there are those moments when I overhear my boss—herself a working mother—telling someone with a sigh that it would have been more expedient to have hired a childless person without a life.

But so it goes. The delicate balance, the skillful juggle. Then, like a New York snowstorm in April, life showers a few surprises on me, reminding, me, perhaps, just who is—or at least who is not—in control of things here.

First, my company, a start-up venture in the direct broadcasting satellite business, files for reorganization under Chapter 11 of the Bankruptcy Code, in the process laying off me and nearly all its other employees. At about the same time, my husband receives a very good offer from the Philadelphia Orchestra. We decide he should take it, which means moving from New York. Soon thereafter, I discover I'm pregnant with our second child.

Well. OK. Fine. We'll switch to Plan B, in which we move to Philadelphia midpregnancy. I unpack, get settled, and, during the last half of my pregnancy, scope out the market for great jobs. Network a little, give birth to my second child (a girl would even things out), start work, and resume my professional life in the perfect, exciting, challenging, flexible job close to home.

> Four days before the move, I am lying on my back on the examining table of my obstetrician's office while the cold end of a microphone slides around clear jelly smeared all over my lower abdomen. With gentle but firm pressure it glides, exploring, pausing, and meandering in a seemingly random path like the arc of a child's index finger in his first finger painting. It moves to the right to my hipbone, back to the left, down a little, up. The nurse holding the microphone and I listen, barely breathing ourselves, straining to hear through the heavy stillness in the small white room what should be a faint and rapid heartbeat.
>
> The silence settles like a shroud.
>
> "It may be too early," says the nurse, straightening up, her lips curving upward in not quite a smile.
>
> The doctor comes in and repeats the drill, the microphone less cold this time, moving back and forth, around and down.
>
> "Tell you what," he says, helping me sit up. "It's probably just a little too early, but you'll feel better if you get this checked out. You can call and schedule an ultrasound for tomorrow morning. That way you'll have some peace of mind for the move."

I'm not worried; I am, in fact, excited at the chance to see an early ultrasound. Let's bring our son, I suggest to his father, so he can see the baby, too.

Three days before the move I am on my back on another examining table, in another room in another office, in another part of the city, again with the jelly, again with the microphone. This time the room is dark, and the microphone is hooked up to a TV monitor. I turn my head to study the fuzzy black and white shapes sliding in and out of focus on the screen.

"Can you see the baby?" I ask the technician.

"Not yet," she mumbles, frowning at the monitor. "I'll be right back." She leaves and a few minutes later, returns with a doctor to study the screen.

"Is there a problem?" I ask, feeling cold.

I am sitting in a dark office on a raw day in September and a man I've never met is telling me that the baby growing inside me has died, disintegrated, disappeared within me. My abdomen is still swollen, my stomach still queasy, my dreams of a sister or brother for my child still vivid in my mind.

The man I don't know hands me a black telephone receiver. "I was afraid of this," says my doctor on the phone.

Two days before the move, I am lying on a stretcher in the hospital, having difficulty believing this is happening. Tears slip down the side of my face into my hair. My husband is holding my hand; they are wheeling me down the hall. Last night I had nightmares that they cut me open, took my child from me, and they'd been wrong. My baby wasn't dead or disintegrated. How absurd. How can I let them do this? A harrowing feeling creeps over me—my arms, my shoulders, the skin on my scalp—a terrible crawling dread that something horrible is about to happen, not, as they've told me, that it has already occurred. "What if they're wrong?" I plead, groggily, grabbing for my husband's hand. "What if they're wrong? I keep thinking that they're wrong."

The day before our lease runs out, I am going through the motions of a woman packing to move. I feel so very empty, as if they took out much of the rest of me when they removed the remains of my baby. I sit on the floor wrapping jelly glasses in newspaper, and when my fifteen-month-old toddles over to me, I pull him onto my lap and rock.

We move to Philadelphia and for me it suddenly has the feel of a clean break. For the moment I am a woman without a past, with only the present, and a future no longer clear.

I am a woman without a plan.

Of course I had a plan. I always had another plan. It's just that life kept intervening.

Here I was, in a new place—worse than a new place, actually—the place that knew me as a child. In New York, I had left behind my job, my friends, my professional colleagues and connections—virtually everyone and everything connected with my adult identity. I needed to get my grown-up self established, to meet people who didn't call me Susie or remember how short my bangs were in seventh grade.

When I left New York, I did not intend to leave my work. But now that I had made a break, I knew enough about the working mother juggle to know that it would grow only more complicated as time went on, and I wanted to find the ideal situation—with good child care, transportation, a job with some flexibility if things went awry—rather than jump into a position that would turn out to be impossible.

Plus, I wanted more kids.

Pregnancies, even normal pregnancies, take time (and however wonderful and miraculous, can seem interminable as the anticipation grows along with your waistline). When I'd switched jobs during my first pregnancy, I'd gone through the whole interviewing-while-pregnant thing—with my suit jacket buttoned and pulled down over an unfastened skirt waist, kind of like squeezing a pumpkin into a small paper lunch bag. I'd gone to interview lunches where I'd talked on automatic pilot about SEC rules and federal cases while concentrating all of my effort on smiling and not throwing up.

Leaping into another law firm, or even a corporate job—which no longer seemed so part-time—didn't seem wise, until I'd at least had another child.

So I stalled. I paged through the classifieds, I went on a few interviews. I took acting lessons and worked as an intern two days a week at a television production company. Never during this time did I consider myself a stay-at-home mom. And in February, four months after we'd moved, I was pregnant with our second child.

As a new life was forming within me, another life was forming around me, affixing itself like toy plastic balls to a Velcro dartboard—bit by bit, grin by giggle, hug by precious hug—to my expectations, my plans, my concept of life and what kind of work was worthwhile.

At the time, I felt as if I was doing this alone and that the possibility of connecting with like-minded women was remote, in part because I was in such a state of conflict and confusion. What I've discovered is that there were, and are, many women at home for whom staying home was not the plan, not by any stretch of their professional imaginations.

Plans unravel, baby-sitters quit, kids get sick, and careers sometimes lose their luster. Try explaining the plan to a sobbing child whose fingers must be peeled one by one off your coat or even to a teenager whose once wide eyes now seem permanently narrowed in a suspicious stare. Faced with a living, breathing, drooling, crying, giggling, clutching, exploring little person that miraculously has your eyes and his chin, sleeps with his rump in the air, and claps his hands in delight at any stupid thing you say—the most well-thought-out strategies just don't carry a lot of weight.

But why I left my career was not as simple as all that, because as enchanting as my baby was, to leave a career, particularly in 1985, involved giving up—or altering—so much of what my life had been to that point. More than the way I filled my days, my career was a source of identity and security. To leave that for a life that was unknown or, worse, filled with negative associations of dependency and loss of self was agonizingly difficult. I wasn't quite sure why I had done it.

But I began, slowly, to realize that I wasn't alone.

All the women with whom I spoke had stories; stories filled with conflict, anger, doubt, love, guilt, denial, ambition, confusion, pride. Some left their jobs early in their professional lives, others retired well into their careers, others settled for scaled back versions of their original goals. Some women wanted to be there for their infants; others left work to be more available to teenagers. Some went from full-time office job employment to at-home status cold turkey. Others made more gradual transitions. Still others evolved from original careers to other, more flexible, child-friendly careers.

Nearly all the women with whom I spoke considered themselves capable and talented in their original careers. Yet they also found themselves in conflict of a magnitude they had never anticipated—a conflict of time, of energy, and of passions—because neither work nor family life, each with its own rewards and frustrations, was what they'd once imagined them to be.

In this chapter, then, are individual stories organized loosely by the different circumstances and reasons that careers didn't progress quite the way they were planned:

- Some women were blindsided by the powerful emotional pull a baby can exert merely by being there. They simply had no idea how hard they'd fall in love and how consuming it would be.
- Some of the best-laid plans, grounded as they were in preparent knowledge of the world, didn't begin to adequately cover the everyday contingencies of having kids— and having more kids.
- It would have been easier to juggle careers and family if we'd all had wives. When a baby joined two high pressure careers in a marriage, something had to give: from his and her careers to one career (his) and a baby (hers).
- When the father's career changed cities, the mother (who has two jobs now anyway) sometimes left her career behind.
- In the jigsaw puzzle craziness of life with a newborn, work sometimes seemed the only place that was still "normal," that is, until one or more of the pieces to the puzzle became lost between the sofa cushions: when the kids were sick . . . when child care fell apart . . . when it seemed as if everything that could possibly go wrong did . . . when scheduling became a nightmare . . . when work no longer worked or filled a need.
- Some women, after years of juggling, decided to "retire" while they still had some years with the children at home.
- Other women left work unexpectedly and then decided it was fate.

Underestimating the Power and the Pull

In the early stages, when our careers were revving up with energy and enthusiasm, no one talked about babies. No one—not our peers, not our superiors, not school counselors. The subject was considered sexist, inconsistent with ambition, and simply inappropriate. What's more, I, at least, vastly underestimated the complexity involved in merging a professional life with motherhood. Many women thought as I did, that a baby could easily slip into our professionally dictated routines.

(I once thought the first year of a baby's life would be an ideal time to buy a boat and learn to sail around the world.) Women years later admit that they hadn't a clue as to how someone so small could present such enormous disruption in their lives.

Alice, who had run her own business and traveled and worked in countries all over the world, didn't expect as little a thing as a baby to slow her down. She had, at the time, settled down to study communications at the University of Houston, with plans to integrate her business experience and education to work in public relations. But when, at age twenty-seven, she was seven months pregnant, her husband was transferred to Spain. When the baby was six weeks old, the family moved there.

"You know, I assumed the baby would be no big deal. . . . I'd strap the baby on my back, enroll in the university wherever I was. . . . You think everybody else makes a big deal about this, but my baby's going to be different. But I couldn't get my act together to go back to school. I was nursing . . . the classes were at odd times. . . ." She shakes her head. "I just couldn't see my way through it. At the time it seemed an insurmountable problem."

A baby—an insurmountable problem and an extraordinary pull. Many women I interviewed recounted feelings of wonder they experienced with their babies, feelings that often were at odds with what they'd known about themselves. For some women, such emotions were strong enough to keep them home.

Pat at thirty-five had all intentions of resuming work as a city planner after the birth of her child. Always self-sufficient, she found the idea of any kind of dependency a tough one to swallow.

"It was very hard," she remembers. "First of all, I had put myself through college. I put myself through graduate school. I had developed a career on my own. I had never depended on anyone else; there was no one to depend on. . . . You go with your gut, and intuition, but it was a tremendous decision for me."

Now fifty-two, with a seventeen-year-old and her own consulting business, she sits at my dining room table, oblivious to its fork marks or the crack between the leaves that is caulked with crumbs. She remembers the pride she had in her work: "I had developed, by that point in my career, a very good reputation as a project manager. When the Greater Philadelphia Chamber of Commerce wanted to develop the regional retail council, they wanted to interview me. I had very strong ties in economic development and the real estate community. . . . I had worked with national developers as part of a team to consider redeveloping the central core of Philadelphia."

Unlike the stereotypical stay-at-home mom, Pat lived in the city in a neighborhood of two-income couples. There was great incentive to go back to work, not only because there were opportunities waiting or because she expected to do so, but because everyone else was doing it. "Everyone on my block was more or less my age—two doctors, two lawyers, two Indian chiefs." Pat grins with the memory. "Everybody was having babies at the same time. Everybody went back to work." She pauses. "Except me." Voice breaking, she looks away. I study a sticky spot near the edge of my tape recorder. My dining room grows larger and more quiet. After a moment, Pat looks back across the table, her eyes moist, her face flushed. Her lips part without sound, ready and yet not ready to give voice to something she perhaps doesn't usually put into words. "I fell in love."

I smile, and my eyes moisten with the memory of another child so sweet.

Pat grabs at a tissue and shakes her head, composing herself. "It really gets to me sometimes." She grins and leans across the table. "I used to get *euphoric* at the sound of a lullabye—and I had never even baby-sat in my whole life! I had never been around children. And then there's this thing—this . . . reason for being."

∾

Like Pat, Cynthia had never considered herself a "baby person."

"I'd never oohed and aahhed over people's kids. Kids were like, ugh, I couldn't be bothered."

In the midst of a fast-track career in journalism, first at Associated Press ("I worked in the middle of the night, every weekend—the most godawful hours you could imagine—and didn't think anything about it"), then as an editor and writer at *Business Week*, the idea of having a baby took Cynthia somewhat by surprise:

"We'd been married for five years. I was twenty-nine, and it was as if somebody had switched on a light—I wanted to have a baby. . . .

No one I knew was pregnant, no one I knew wanted to be pregnant, no one I knew *thought* about being pregnant. But all of a sudden I had this overriding desire to have a baby. I didn't know what I was going to do with it once I had it."

Like many women immersed in their careers, Cynthia worked during her entire pregnancy and left with full intentions of returning after a minimal maternity leave. "I had no plans to stay at home. I worked until Friday. Sam was born on Monday. My baby shower consisted of my group of journalism friends from *Business Week* giving me a drinking luncheon at a Korean restaurant. I said, 'Good-bye, I'll see you in a few weeks,' and didn't think anything of it."

Three days later, Cynthia had her baby; with him came a heavy dose of reality. "It was a rough delivery. Sam was a difficult baby, requiring a lot of attention from the very start. He wouldn't eat if he was distracted. He wouldn't sleep if he was in the wrong direction. He needed a lot of attention. I found it really difficult. . . . All of a sudden, I was trapped with this baby in this town where I didn't know anybody.

"But by the same token, I felt a real need to care-give. I didn't want to bring in somebody else to take over and abdicate my responsibilities. If somebody else came and did it, why did I bother to do this— if I was going to have somebody else raise my kid?"

Cynthia had three months' maternity leave. Toward the end of the three months she called work and made it six.

Still she anguished.

"It was me and my conscience struggling with what to do. . . . As the weeks went by, I got more and more attached to this kid. By the end of the six months, I could not imagine being away from him all day. I couldn't imagine it! Who knows him the way I do? Who's going to be able to take care of his needs the way I can? Nobody. And I'm going to miss so much. Every day. When babies are that little, every minute is a development. . . . You can see their whole personalities unfolding before your eyes. I couldn't imagine missing that.

"I had endlessly boring, long conversations with Eliot about what to do. . . . It wasn't as if he was pushing me one way or the other. . . . Finally, one night, I just was crying all the time, because I didn't want to go back.

"So I didn't. I just couldn't see giving this experience over to someone else."

∾

With other women, the pull intensified after they were back at work.

Laurie, at thirty, was thoroughly engaged in her career as a sportswear buyer in the corporate buying department at a clothing company. When she became pregnant, she was purchasing in New York City and Los Angeles and designing and manufacturing sportswear lines overseas for eleven hundred stores, making frequent trips to the Far East.

She had no thoughts that pregnancy or a baby would slow her down.

"I never intended—from the moment of conception—to ever cut back or alter my work plan. After I had my first OB-GYN appointment at ten weeks, I was contacting au pair agencies for applications. I had my child care arranged before I even contemplated a name for our baby!"

After the birth of her daughter, Laurie experienced a pull she'd never anticipated: "The last four weeks of maternity leave I cried a lot. It seemed so unnatural to leave the most precious thing in our lives. I bonded so quickly and beautifully with Katherine—she was a great baby!"

But her career awaited like a carriage to the ball, and Laurie admits that she was also "excited to get back with my close-knit gang and catch up. I was still in my honeymoon period. It was great to wear my Ann Taylor clothes and talk shop. But then it took me exactly three weeks— that's only fifteen working days—to realize that society had sold me the biggest load of goods. I was pissed! Not at my husband, not at the au pair, not at the company—at something far larger. I couldn't even put a face on what I was angry at! I thought I could have it all . . . wrong! There's a cost for doing it all, and it's never the job or career that gets the shaft!"

After six months of designing lines, meeting deadlines in the Orient, or commuting to New York City three times a week, she realized that "my dream career had turned into a nightmare."

As to defining moments, Laurie, now forty and working several part-time jobs around the lives of her seven-year-old boy and ten-year-old girl, remembers: "I'd be sitting in the lunchroom having other new moms tell me that missing the first real laugh, the first real step, was really not so bad, that it will be the first when the mother sees it for the first time. These were women I respected, and such bullshit was coming out of their mouths! It was almost like they had resigned themselves to a certain fate . . . a certain mold. I swore I'd never become like them. . . .

"Then one evening, coming home after a long day, the au pair greeted me at the back door with Katherine in her arms. She gave Katherine to me, and Katherine put her arms out, clearly wanting to go back to the au pair. I felt like crap and questioned why I was working so hard to make this whole thing work, making all the pieces fit together. Why did society tell me that I could do it all? That's a bunch of crap! Money was definitely a concern, since I was making most of it! I took a real leap of faith, because moneywise, I should have continued working. . . ."

The Best-Laid Plans

Lucy, at twenty-nine, was someone who had thought she'd mapped out a workable strategy for combining her work as a marketing consultant with motherhood. Like me, she left one job to take another she perceived as more compatible with a life with kids. "What I was thinking was that if I could work out of my home, then I could have children." She gestures toward the doorway and laughs. "I thought having children meant, you know, keeping them in the next room. . . . So I went and got a job with a smaller firm, 'cause I thought then I could either work for them or have my own little consulting business. That's why I made the move, because I knew I couldn't have children and stay [at the large firm]."

But pregnancy itself began to change Lucy's life in ways she'd not expected: "When I got pregnant, I felt something halfway between impending doom and a calm excitement. You know your life is going to change, but you have no idea really how much. You're being treated without the same kind of professional respect at work. Before they knew I was pregnant, I was really being groomed . . . they were looking for somebody to eventually be a partner. As soon as I was pregnant, it became clear that this was not going to be the result. Somehow or other I just felt that if I had been there for two years and then gotten pregnant it would have been totally different."

Her transition to stay-at-home mother, says Lucy, just evolved: ". . . I became immersed in babies—with every little thing. About two months after the baby was born, I remember Bill calling me and saying, 'How about doing some stuff at home, like maybe media buying?'—something that didn't require my coming into the office. It also didn't require a brain. But it wasn't interesting to me. I'd sit at the computer, and I'd start to write up these plans. I couldn't do it during her nap time, plus with nursing—I was nursing every hour and a half, so I finally hired a baby-sitter. I'd be trying to work, and I'd hear the baby crying and think, 'I don't want to be in here doing this. I want to be playing with my baby.'"

From His and Her Careers to One Career (His) and a Baby (Hers)

Just as my career plans didn't factor in much family time, neither did those of my husband. The shock of combining work and motherhood hit particularly hard in situations where fast-track husbands offered little in the way of child-care trade-offs.

"I just thought I'd be the contemporary mom," says Pam, mother of two boys, nine and twelve, speaking of her plans to continue as RN coordinator of a neurosurgical trauma team after her son was born. When she was twenty-four years old, she had nabbed the job she'd wanted since switching her major from music to biology—as an epilepsy research center nurse in Baylor College of Medicine, in Texas. Working for six pediatric neurologists, she ran two research studies and functioned as the nurse for the Epilepsy Center. The combination of academic research and family contact was exhilarating, and fourteen years later she recalls it with a gentle but animated Texas drawl:

"It was my job to teach the families how to keep kids with epilepsy normal, not to protect them too much. They were just kids with seizures. . . . We were doing a drug trial, to determine what was more effective. I had a lot of contact with families. I'd see them in family clinic, draw their blood, change their dosages, do the exams, so I had the clinical side of it, too.

"Then the other study was for the FDA about a severe and rare seizure disorder, where kids who are normal at birth sometime before the age of one go into status [epilepticus] and never come out. The brain is constantly in seizure activity; whether you stop the physical seizures or not, the brain is still just haywire, and the kids never develop past that.

"We were testing drugs that might stop the seizures, so while I ran the study in the research unit in the children's hospital, I did a lot of teaching. I developed a booklet to teach the parents about what the kids had. The prognosis was terrible, but you'd explain to them what the study was, what we hoped to do, what the limits were, what the realities were, and . . . be there for them."

When her husband was transferred to Seattle, Pam went with him. She got a job as nurse coordinator for the neurosurgery team at the University of Washington. There she helped with research studies and was responsible for all the team's patients who went through the OR. She'd triage patients, see them in clinic, arrange for staffing of the operating rooms, and follow the patients in ICU through rehab.

When she became pregnant, she went to see the head of the department, not intending to ask for much time off. "He said, 'Write whatever leave you want. I'll sign it. Just come back.' So I wrote four months and thought, 'Plenty of time!'"

After the baby was born, Pam began having doubts. The picture of her continuing a job that—before her baby—had taken nearly all her time and energy was troublesome, especially set against the backdrop of her husband's overly long hours. The hours home together in the evening had been too few when it had been just the two of them.

She remembers that by the time her son was three months old, "I looked at him and thought, 'There is no way.' I looked at my hours and Ted's hours—nobody worked less than a ten-hour day. I thought, 'What is the point?' I talked with Ted, and we said, 'If we're home for two hours a day to wave at the kid, we're not the ones raising him.'"

Following (His) Dreams

"When we moved, I was sure I was going to get another job . . . and I'm not sure when I dropped those expectations. . . . I was in crisis a lot of the time."

As in my case, it was not having a baby, but relocating from one city to another that tripped up Sherry's career climb. Now an at-home mother of two boys, ages eight and twelve, and a freelance editor, she never imagined herself carving out her working life at home. A Princeton graduate, she had always planned to pursue her career first, integrating a family life along the way. In fact, when her boyfriend, a banker, had proposed marriage a month after her college graduation, she said no.

"He had this great job in New York. But I said, 'No, I can't, because *I* don't have a job. I need to come into this marriage with my own job and money and without the feeling that I'm being rescued.'"

Once her job at a publishing company was in place, she agreed to get married. They moved back down to Princeton, which was an equally long commute for both of them. After about a year, though, Sherry was confronted with two life-changing events: She was offered what she describes as her "ideal, dream job" as a manuscript editor at Princeton University Press. Three days before—at the tender age of twenty-three, she had discovered she was pregnant.

"There was no question I was going to take the job. It was a surprise that I was pregnant—it wasn't part of the master plan or anything. I didn't mind, but it wasn't what we'd intended for just then.... So I spent the first two and a half months on the job knowing I was pregnant, not quite showing, not knowing what I was going to do, always intending to go back to work after. I was still in that mode, where my career, such as it was, was not firm or established. I really had to put some time in and get experience, and I couldn't, even if I wanted to, take some time off. I worked up till my due date and came back three and a half months later."

As with many other new mothers balancing one baby and a career, working with one child seemed very doable to Sherry. Good day care was close and convenient, and work was only a few minutes away from home. But her husband, John, was miserable commuting over three hours a day to a job with Wall Street banking hours. When a job opportunity came up for him in Detroit near both of their families, they decided to move.

Remembers Sherry, "I was going to take a little time to set up the house, get things unpacked, and then, I, *of course*, was going to go out and find a job. But that never happened."

Getting another job never happened in part because her days filled without it. Princeton University Press had given her some freelance work, which, along with the house, the baby, and a new baby on the way, didn't leave her time to brood. Yet she harbored anxiety.

"Not that many presses were freelancing, so I didn't feel as if there would be a steady stream of manuscripts. But I knew that there would be enough so that—and this was important—I could go to a party and say, 'Well, I'm freelancing.' In those early years, that was important."

Sherry pauses, searching for an explanation: "You get past a certain point, and you realize, 'Hey, wait a second. Why do I need to get a job?' ... You get out of that stressful got-to-pick-up-the-laundry, got-to-get-the-grocery-shopping-done-in-those-few-hours, got-to-use-lunch-to-pick-up-the-mail. You get out of that, and it takes such pressure off. You realize that this is the way you're supposed to feel and the way you were feeling before is not the way you're supposed to feel. . . . "

"Working Mother" Stress: The Search for Normalcy

Several days after giving birth to my first child, I am lying in the hospital, exhausted. When I look down at the eight-inch slash across my abdomen, the scene where the woodsman frees grandmother from the wolf in *Little Red Riding Hood* comes to mind. Through the open door, babies cry, stretchers squeak, and telephones ring, all through the day. At night, people come in to dab at my wound, check my pulse, press my abdomen. Every few hours my baby appears, and huddled together on the sheets, we together try to figure out this nursing thing. He seems to be getting it, but with each of his determined sucks, pain rockets through my breast, while cramps ripple through my abdomen. This was good, they'd said, because it helps to shrink the uterus back to normal size. But my muscles pull, the stitches tug, and I silently worry that I myself will wrench apart. Day turns into night turns into day and another night.

I think to myself that I can't wait to go home and get some rest.

It is only on the morning that I hobble home in baby steps, gingerly holding my so featherweight, so alive, so terrifyingly real little human being, that it hits me: There is no rest—at least not the deep, long, dreamless, sleep-until-ten kind of rest of the preparent person I was, oh, a week or so ago.

Maybe, I think, things will be normal at work.

Returning to work seemed like the obvious, natural, logical thing to do. Many women recall the same feelings. Lorraine, whose job it was to manage employee benefit plans for her company, remembers that, as a thirty-one-year-old new mother, being at work felt much more normal than being at home:

"[When the baby was an infant], I was bored silly at home. My social life revolved around the people I worked with. People in my neighborhood I never really connected with. It was very enticing to go back. I loved what I did, and Peter was very happy to have extra money, because he was concerned about living on one paycheck."

When child care fell easily into place, life could seem to be the best of all possible worlds. Cheryl, director of research at a regional brokerage firm, had her first child at thirty-seven and was back at work after six weeks:

"I hired someone who was incredibly wonderful. She was intelligent, she'd worked as a nurse, she was incredibly caring, and she was a little older than I. She was at an age where she didn't have to prove anything to anybody. She took care of him, and then [after my second was born] the two of them probably a lot better than I could have, because that was something I had not been brought up to even think of . . . and so she was there, and I was at work, and everything was just fine. And she even liked my dog."

Other women were juggling as well. Barbara went into banking right out of college as a credit analyst. In those first few years of working, she met and married her husband, worked toward an MBA at night, moved into the commercial lending side of banking and, at twenty-seven, had a son, hardly skipping a beat.

"I must have interviewed forty-two [nannies], finally found a really nice girl, very quiet, from the islands, and went back to work at the bank. I'd have spilled milk down my back. And I wouldn't see it, but I'd be wearing a navy blue blazer, and the men would be saying, "Uh, Barbara, you have spit-up all down your back." And I'd have to take the train to New York. . . . It was hectic, we'd be going in all different directions. Mark was traveling for his job; I was traveling. The baby-sitter'd get there at 5:30, so I'd catch the train, do a full day, and come home at 7:00. . . . But a lot of my friends downtown had kids and worked, and you just didn't think about it. Of course, you were going back to work. I had a very good job, loved the people. It was also at a time when we were with a very stimulating international crowd from both of our jobs. We'd entertain them, stay up late. Everyone was working, there was no question about it. You had kids, they stayed home with nannies, and you went back to work. I didn't even hesitate. . . . I wasn't very good with infants. And Jake was a real screamer until about four months."

Many of us who returned to work recognized ourselves in Arlie Russel Hochschild's book *The Time Bind*, where she posits a "new model of family and work life" in which "a tired parent flees a world of unresolved quarrels and unwashed laundry for the reliable, orderliness, harmony, and the managed cheer of work."[1]

But the flip side of harmony is the dissonance that can result when any of the parts play out of tune: when kids—or husbands or aging parents—are sick or have significant problems in their lives, when jobs relocate or change in quality or intensity, when child care is bad or good child care leaves, then work sometimes doesn't work anymore.

Sick Kids

With her demanding career in neurobiology, Lisa had not originally planned on having children. Her husband, though, was crazy about kids, and as time went on Lisa softened to the idea. "I finally said, 'Oh, what the heck. Other people do this all the time.'" After the birth of her daughter, Lisa, by now thirty-three, decided that "it was kinda fun." She now very much wanted a second child, although parenting was turning out to be as inconsistent with her career as she'd feared, particularly when her baby was sick, which was often: "The babysitter'd call me at work and say, 'The baby's throwing up.' So I'd go home and drive the baby to the doctor. Or I'd wake up in the morning, and the baby'd have a high fever. I'd cancel my meetings, I'd cancel my classes, take the baby to the doctor."

When Lisa had her second child at thirty-five, life became "complete chaos": "We moved. I lost my child-care person because she did not drive. . . . I had grant proposals due, and I was just too tired. I just couldn't do it anymore. My blood pressure was 160 over 100, I was losing the competition for jobs with the guys I'd gone to graduate school with, because they were free to go to Baltimore, to take a job at Johns Hopkins. They were free to go to Maine, to take a job at

Bates College. . . . All the people I'd gone through the trenches with were going on and I was stuck. . . . I was so tired, I just couldn't do it anymore. I said, 'I have to choose. I can abandon these kids and go get a job in some other state, or I can focus on what my responsibilities are here,' and that's what I did."

Child-Care Crises

As Lisa and many other women can attest, sick children and child-care problems often go together, for the baby-sitter who seems perfectly capable of playing with your healthy child sometimes falls apart in an emergency. With a sick child, the child care giver's judgment becomes more critical.

But finding care for even a healthy child can seem overwhelming. "I don't think I've ever been faced with a more difficult or constant challenge—choosing and lining up child care, living on edge with that every day," says twenty-eight-year-old freelance writer Sally, who in her preparent days tackled the world of corporate finance as both an investment banker and a reporter for the *Wall Street Journal*. When she moved out of New York in connection with her husband's job change, she left the *Journal* to work freelance and broaden her writing experience. When her first child was born, she was working part-time at an investment house, writing quarterly and monthly investment letters.

"I hired someone, and she was to start on a Monday. Sunday night she called and said she wasn't able to work for us. So then the nanny agency had to find somebody else. But in the meantime I had to call work and say, 'I can't come in for this month.' . . . I had to go through the whole process again. Fortunately work was very flexible. Then they lined someone else up. I went through the whole process again. This was in August, so it was the middle of September before I got someone. She started and was good and reliable, and I was pleased with her. The one problem was that I didn't feel as if she was as engaging with the baby as I wanted someone to be—or as I would be. So I felt like when I was done working, I had to come home and be 'on' rather than relaxing.

"She was here from September to December, went home for the Christmas vacation. We went out of town. We called back the night before to check our messages, and she'd left a message that she wasn't coming back to our state. So I had to call work and say I couldn't come in in January.

"Because I've done it part-time, I might have had an easier time if I was looking for someone full-time, but that would just increase the pressure and the worry that if it didn't work out, I'd be letting a full-time job down."

What's more, as the number of children increases, so do the complications in finding good child care.

Tracy, now thirty-four and the mother of three girls ages five, three, and one, got married right out of college but always knew that she'd work. After majoring in finance and health care administration in college, she thought perhaps she'd combine her finance background with health care. Finding a job at a mutual fund/investment company, she moved up through different positions to communications representative, in the course of which she'd travel all over the country, giving presentations about investments, talking about various funds.

"By this time I knew I enjoyed working. I'd been there for six years. I liked it. I knew I'd continue. I had plans to come back part-time. After two months [back at work after her baby was born] another job came up, and it was a promotion. My boss said, 'Do you want this?' and I said, 'Yeah!'"

Tracy worked full-time for the next two years until her second child was born, when she took ten weeks of paid leave and six months of unpaid leave under the Family Leave Act. She returned to work part-time (three full days a week) but found day care to be a problem.

"I had a baby-sitter who was leaving after two months. . . . I had my older daughter in a day-care situation that didn't take infants. So I figured I could put her back, but I had to find day care for my other child.

"I did find someone, this woman at her house, but I would have had to drop Lauren off at one place and then drive to the other sitter and drop Megan off. My husband didn't do that—drop them off or pick them up—mainly because he had to be in earlier. Often he'd get home late, and I just didn't want them in day care for twelve hours a day. . . . He would do it once in a while, but mainly it was my responsibility."

When It Seems As If
Everything That Can Go Wrong Does

Christine, like many women who love their careers, made continual adaptations to try to work things out over the births of her three children.

She had worked her way to what she still considers a great job: communications analyst for one of the nation's largest communications companies. Most of her colleagues had law degrees, but Christine, armed with a bachelor's degree in biology and economics, had started with the company right out of college and worked her way up. Starting as a management trainee with assignments such as construction foreman, she ascended the company structure, assuming positions of more responsibility and money, carving out a place for herself in the growing industry. Her marriage at twenty-nine and decision to have children didn't change her career plans. "I was sure I wanted to work when we had kids. I was one of six kids, and my mom worked as a nurse. I mean, I thought, how hard could it be?"

Christine had her first child at age thirty-two, shortly after she and her husband had moved from the city to a house in a nearby suburb. She couldn't wait to get back to work, where, now, as a senior communications analyst, she was studying proposed legislation, writing speeches for company officials, and attending legistative and regulatory hearings, thoroughly immersed in her career. "It was a great job where I could read how we did in the headlines of the newspaper. It was very exciting."

What's more, work was where her friends were.

Child care was simple, with her mother, who lived nearby, babysitting. "It couldn't have been easier," she says.

But over the next six years life became increasingly more difficult. Shortly after Christine returned to work after her second child was born, the baby began experiencing breathing problems: "At seven months he started a weird thing where he would stop breathing when he got a 'big' hurt, like if he got a shot at the doctor's or fell or something. He'd suck in all this air, the way babies do, but instead of then giving a great big sob, he'd just stop breathing. His eyes would roll up in his head and he'd pass out. When he was unconscious, he'd start breathing again. But you have no idea what it's like to see your child stop breathing."

Once it began, it continued to happen, at different times, different places: a hotel room on vacation when he fell off the bed, in the back-yard, at friends' houses. Alex could stop breathing anytime, anywhere.

"It happened one night when I was in Macy's trying on swimsuits at dinnertime. I'd taken the kids [then one-and-a-half and three-and-a-half] with me, and they were playing in the empty dressing rooms, giggling and running around. I was lifting my leg to step into a bathing suit when Alex came racing into the room and got my knee in his face. He started to cry and then suddenly stopped breathing again. There I am, standing there half naked in an empty dressing room (wondering if the security cameras are watching) with my child not breathing."

It was terrifying. Christine learned that she could prevent her son from passing out if she hugged him very close as soon as he was startled or hurt, before he began crying. But it wasn't a technique she felt comfortable trusting to any baby-sitter, and even when she did leave him, it became impossible to relax enough to concentrate on work. "My mother couldn't watch him as much as I needed, and I couldn't deal with the idea of anyone else."

Sufficiently frightened by the problem, which was diagnosed as pallid breath holding, Christine took a two-year leave of absence. Pleasantly surprised by the calm that came to her household when she was at home, she nevertheless felt cut off from the outside world. At the end of her leave she returned to work, pregnant with her third child.

After her daughter was born, Christine took a year's maternity leave. She returned to work part-time, with the understanding that in three months she would become full-time. Finally, she thought, she was getting back on track. But within a month of part-time work, which included business trips and working through holidays, anything that could have gone wrong at home did:

First the baby-sitter announced she was quitting to go back to school—and agreed to stay only as long as it took for Christine to find someone else.

Then, on the evening of Christine's second day at work, Jessi, her six-year-old daughter, caught her finger in the rest room door of a neighborhood restaurant. The family bundled up the sobbing little girl, along with her three-year-old brother and one-year-old sister, and went home. Christine and her husband, who is a doctor, both examined their daughter's finger. She could bend it, and they concluded that it was probably just bruised. Christine recalls, "I said to her, 'Well, it'll be sore for a few days until it gets better.' I gave her Tylenol 'round the clock and then forgot about it."

About three weeks later, her daughter was roughhousing with her brother, rolling all over the family room. Suddenly Jessi broke away screaming, "*That's my sore finger! He hurt my sore finger!*"

Christine stopped rushing dinner to the table. "What do you mean, it's your sore finger?" she asked, a slow sense of horror overtaking her.

Her daughter blinked eyelashes matted with tears. "You said it would be sore for a little while."

Recalls Christine, "It was awful. I felt terrible. I took her to the doctor, and he said it had been broken [for a month], but it was now mending itself. The thing that got to me was, my husband didn't notice it either. And he's a doctor. But I realized that even though I was back at work, doing business trips and everything, the kids' stuff was still my realm."

To complicate matters, Christine's youngest child, now fourteen months, began experiencing pallid breath holding, the condition that had so frightened her with her second.

When her normally cheerful middle child began acting out temper tantrums—in one episode, throwing the baby's high chair across the room—Christine made her decision. "There was just less of me to go around," she says. "And it was clear to me that this wasn't helping my marriage . . . I knew I had to leave. It was a very hard decision to step out, because . . . my job was very unique and exciting. Although it was impossible to excel at work, even more important, I really needed to do this mothering well, and I wasn't.

"The vice president didn't want me to leave—we'd worked together so well for ten years. He was worried that he couldn't find someone to do what I did, and he offered to let me work part-time. I offered to do projects from home. . . . Nine months later they haven't called. It was such a hard decision to make. Now that I look back, it was the only decision."

Scheduling Nightmares

Kate didn't plan to quit either her broadcasting or teaching jobs when she had children. At thirty-four, she'd been in radio for twelve years and was not about to let it all slide away. Her mother had left a career in theater, something Kate never understood. By the time she was in college, there was no question in Kate's mind that she would make a career in broadcasting. In contrast to theater, radio lured her with immediate opportunities to be on the air and working. With the melodious speaking voice of a singer and a love of organizing, by her junior year she was running the campus radio station.

When she married her college boyfriend in the fall of 1974, she was aiming her career sights on New York: "I thought I would spend about ten years paying dues, work my way into New York City, work my way up the hierarchy, and eventually do something like work at WNEW-AM, which is an all-news station."

By the time she became pregnant with her first child, Kate, at thirty-four, was on her way. Working at Station WMCA in New York and teaching at Hofstra, she juggled responsibilities and learned to appear to be awake at odd hours of the day: "To do a morning show, you get up at 4:00. You're in at 5:00, on the air at 6:00, sometimes 5:30. I was living on Long Island; the studio was in Queens. I left that job at 10:00 in the morning. I had to be at Hofstra by 11:00 because I taught a class. Sometimes I taught at St. John's. I was what they call 'variously employed,' but I was making a living."

But in the middle of her pregnancy, her doctors told Kate to cut down her stress. She dropped the radio job but continued to teach. Her baby girl was born in July—in the parking lot of the local hospital. Kate planned to take the fall off, teach again in the spring, and resume her career climb.

But her plans began to unravel. First, child care was complicated—and each situation had its own unsettling aspects. Kate tried placing Claire with at-home mothers who took additional children into their homes. One home was troubling, says Kate, because when she picked her up, "the mommy would say, 'She was very good. We sat and watched television the whole day. . . .'"

They found another woman who was, in Kate's words, "a really wonderful, cheerful mom who let them watch television for only a little while.

She had this great big sunny playroom and only three children there. The only catch was that this woman has this incredible Canarsi accent!" Kate bellows. She mimics, "Oh my gawd, yau nevah hoyd anyting like tis waw-man in yaw hole life. It was like someting from a mooovie!!!

"Then Claire started picking it up. She was two years old, and she'd come home and say, "*Hey, Maw,* wat's fa dinna?"

Kate laughs. "Claire loved it there. She was throwing up at night, but she loved child care."

Claire's throwing up was, of course, another issue. In 1987 Kate's husband, Ed, took a job in Philadelphia. It was just after the stock market crash, and the sale of their house fell through. So Ed went to Philadelphia, and Kate stayed on Long Island with Claire, teaching, and trying to sell the house.

"Claire threw up every weeknight during the fall and spring. I was teaching at Hofstra, and it was very stressful. I would lie awake at night waiting for her to throw up. I was getting no sleep. Her weight was going down and down. She'd be fine on the weekends when Frank was here."

The house eventually sold, the family finally moved, and Claire stopped throwing up. In their new home, Kate calculated that between her daughter's adjustment to a new place and the nature of the radio business, it would take about a year to get work. She began to scout out child care for her daughter, now nearly three.

That fall Claire started at a nursery/day-care facility at a local private school that boasted an enrollment of a number of children with two-career families. Kate had still not found work and started Claire there at only three days a week. Meanwhile, the search for child care (Claire, at three, had now been through four day-care situations in New York) and the months of sleepless nights began to take their toll: clouds of doubt were gathering over Kate's resolve to pursue her career.

"I'd go in to pick up Claire from school, and there were a lot of kids whose mothers are anesthesiologists, lawyers, cardiologists. I would walk in the door and be swamped with kids yelling, '*Mommy! Mommy!*' Not that I was *their* mommy, but that I was *a* mommy. There were two kids there who were really close, nearly inseparable. They used to put photographs of the kids on the wall, and there were pictures of these two kids from the time they were infants. These kids saw more of each other than of their own families . . . they always had their thumbs in their mouths—practically in the other's mouth, they were so attached."

And so between the sickness and the day care and the nature of broadcasting—a career that was receding further into Kate's past, Kate began to question what she really believed.

"My mother . . . said to me [about leaving her career in the theater], 'Well, acting didn't seem important anymore, and you children seemed important.' That made no sense to me until I found myself saying to myself, 'Who the hell cares about toxic oil spill or whether they hear it from me or somebody else? Claire is sick this morning. That's important.' . . . I finally said to Ed, 'I'm not going back to radio where you have no control over your schedule. You have a schedule and someone changes it.' We'd need a full-time housekeeper," which, Kate says, they couldn't afford.

She never went back.

When Work No Longer Works

Lorraine resigned her position as consultant for employee benefits six weeks before her first baby was born, not sure what she was going to do. She found herself "bored silly" at home, drawn to people from work who would call her for advice or ask her to attend meetings. Soon she found herself falling back into work, arranging day care as she went.

Every parent's worst nightmare became a reality when for Lorraine her child was nearly four. Just before his birthday, her son came home from camp complaining of severe stomachache; soon afterward he was diagnosed with Wilms' tumor, a form of childhood cancer. After nearly a year of treatments and extended hospital visits, her son, just shy of his fifth birthday, died.

Work's role in this tragedy was to keep Lorraine going, to serve as the glue holding life together in a year ripped and ravaged by unspeakable sadness. Her friends at work banded together. Lorraine remembers, "We had a Jewish funeral at our Catholic church. All my friends were Jewish, and they took over. They came and sat shiva at my house. I don't know what I would have done without them."

Mingled with the grief over her son's death were the raging hormones and conflicting passions that accompany a new baby; a month earlier, Lorraine's second son had been born within blocks of the same hospital where her first son lay dying. At sea in a storm of emotions, Lorraine, at thirty-five, plunged back into the only constant in her life: work.

"Michael was one month old when Christopher died. Two weeks later, I brought him to the office. I just did not know what to do at home. I had been so involved—even while Christopher was sick. My career and what I was doing were just blossoming incredibly. It wasn't as if I was anxious to get back. I didn't know what else to do. So I went back."

Two years later Lorraine had another boy and was back to work two weeks later. Now with two boys and an ever-increasing workload, she began to feel some strain. In addition, her situation at work became less than ideal.

"The wonderful situation I had with the company changed the year before. When I was pregnant with Joshua, they decided that they didn't want to be in the employee benefits business. They wanted to set me up in my own business, and I didn't want to do that. The company ended up selling my business to another company. I went into partnership with them."

When she became pregnant with what would be her last child, Lorraine began to think about slowing down the pace of her life, which now had the normal stresses of two-career families: "Two little babies, getting them up, packing their lunch, getting their diapers, the whole thing. Getting dressed in a suit, Peter and I arguing about who had the more important meeting that day, who could afford to have blanket-sleeper lint and spit up on his or her suit. We had two car seats in each car, because we never knew who was going to pick them up. So I decided I was going to take a longer period of time after the new baby was born. And within a week or two, they decided that I needed to take a pay cut and work more. I had negotiated a four-day week after Joshua was born, but I probably worked more than I ever did. They told me I'd have to take a dramatic cut. I went home to Peter and constructed a letter. I never went back to work."

Been There (at Work); Done That

Rachel worked for twenty years—sixteen of them as a "working mother" before she decided to call it quits for a while. Over the course of those sixteen years she'd had five children and four big jobs. Unlike many other professional women at the time, Rachel married early, at twenty-one, after which she soared through law school and landed in an old white shoe Philadelphia law firm, doing litigation and corporate work. At twenty-seven she had her first child and was back at work six weeks later.

"I was very involved in my career, and I didn't want to give up anything. But about eight or nine months into it, I realized that I was walking into work crying." Long hours combined with a pull from home and a feeling that the quality of her assignments had decreased. "They had started treating me as a nonentity pretty soon after I'd had the baby. I was working ten, eleven hours a day, weekends, and I wasn't seeing him at all. . . . I realized that this wasn't what I wanted to do."

Still very much career driven, Rachel decided to take charge of her life: she went to work part-time for a smaller law firm and simultaneously opened her own business—a video dating service. "Corporate documents had driven me totally crazy," she says. She also became pregnant with her second child.

After two years of running the business, her husband was transferred to Israel. There, now with two children, she worked as a lawyer in an electronics company and became pregnant with their third child.

Two months after her third child was born, they moved back to the United States. For the first time she got what she describes as "a mommy track cushy job"—as a securities lawyer for an insurance company. "It was a full-time job, but it was out in the suburbs and had regular hours."

Rachel enjoyed her securities work, but she'd become increasingly frustrated with the law and believed that business could offer more opportunities for creative work. About the time she became pregnant with her fourth child, she began an executive MBA program at Wharton.

With her MBA—and now four children—Rachel obtained a four-day-a-week job as head of licensing for a publishing company, licensing electronic rights all over the world.

At this point Rachel appeared to be one of those women we all now hate, living proof that Superwoman is alive and well. Her drive was seemingly endless—she says she never seriously thought about taking time off and reflects, "I never had that option financially, and I was always career focused—outwardly focused. I was always an overachiever—probably the result of insecurities; I think overachievers always feel they have to prove themselves to somebody else."

But after about four years and an increasingly stressful job situation, Rachel and her husband decided that they could manage financially without her salary, and she quit. For the first time in nearly twenty years of juggling kids and career, she was home "more or less" full-time.

When Fate Holds a Mirror

Jill didn't enjoy engineering as much as she'd hoped and expected to love her career. Since she'd been good at science and math, the male-dominated field of engineering seemed a good place to carve a niche for herself as a woman. She entered the profession in 1984 with a degree from Princeton in civil engineering with a concentration in structures. Experience in different firms layered on education, and by the time she was twenty-eight, she had become skilled in civil engineering design of roads, bridges, and buildings as well as forensic engineering.

That year, when their first child was born, she and her husband assumed without question that she'd continue her engineering work.

"Michael is very nurturing and all that but kind of figured with this whole women's movement that women want to work. He just assumed that I'd go back to work. . . . Nothing was ever discussed."

Jill returned to work part-time, which she continued through the birth of her second child in 1993. In January of 1997 she was laid off in a company downsizing move. While collecting unemployment, she thought about her options and realized that this "break" might be an opportunity to rethink the direction her life was taking.

"I'd been unhappy with engineering. It's boring. When unemployment ran out, I thought, 'Do I really want to go back to this? If I go back, it would probably have to be full-time, because no one's going to hire a part-time person.' And I realized that one of the last big projects I worked on involved knocking down a large wooded area and putting up a strip mall. To go back to a field that I wasn't happy with in the first place to do projects like that really rubbed me the wrong way. I decided at that point that it was time to stay home with my kids. . . . Without kids, I'd still be an engineer, just because I wouldn't have any reason to take a step back and look."

The Role of Fear

Similarly, had I stayed in New York, I suspect that however stressful my life, I might still be in an office somewhere, practicing law, motivated in equal parts by ambition, peer pressure, and fear. No one I knew quit work. Before I'd left New York, a fellow lawyer and a good friend expressed concerns about my move. "If you move to the suburbs of Philadelphia, you might never be heard of again."

A number of the women expressed anxiety and guilt about leaving their work, particularly with respect to the reactions of their colleagues. Remembers Barbara, now a newspaper associate publisher, that when she left her job as a banker, "A lot of men and women did feel that you were bailing out and hurting the cause for women. I had men coming over to my house when I was sitting there feeding Ben, my second son, and they were saying, 'Why are you doing this? Why are you leaving? You're abandoning women. You're a role model.' . . . They would give you all kinds of grief."

Tara, at thirty-five, was an environmental scientist and project manager for an environmental consulting firm. After managing a $5 million project and supervising a staff of twenty-five, she hoped to work out a part-time arrangement after the birth of her child. Although her due date coincided with significant downsizing by her company, one opportunity with a former employer looked promising. The obstacles? The company wanted her to work four days a week. After researching child-care options and evaluating her family finances, Tara wanted a two-day-a-week deal.

"After a day of crying, I finally decided that I couldn't accept the job. When I called my potential future employer to tell her, she was shocked, sounded angry, and was cold. Since she was a mom, I thought she might understand. And since I had enjoyed meeting her, I felt I had lost a friend."

Even women who were simply scaling back—not leaving their careers—felt pressure not to do so. Adelaide was a thirty-one-year-old associate at a large city law firm when she decided to go part-time to be able to spend more time with her two-and-a-half-year-old daughter. "I was 'warned' by the women [at the firm] that my leaving to go part-time was playing into the stereotype that women aren't serious about their careers and that I would never get a decent job after working part-time."

Jessica, a graduate of Yale medical school, suffered similar anxieties, felt similar pressure, when she went into part-time practice after her first child was born. "I'd always felt the expectations of other people that I would do everything and that I'd work full-time. It was really very hard [to do otherwise]. I didn't want to fall into that category of women—the 'Oh, we sent you through med school, and here's just another woman running off to raise her kids. . . .'

"I think a lot of the pressures were internalized. No one outwardly expressed the view that I was taking an easier route or that I wasn't doing what I was supposed to do. [But] there was always the question of whether people were taking you seriously enough."

Jessica had planned that when she had children she'd continue to work full-time. "I assumed you could do it all. I never really looked at the time frame—how much time I would devote to each one."

After her second and third children were born, she continued to limit her medical hours, finding that family life became only more complicated.

"You think the issues are big when you have one kid. . . . With each kid, it became more difficult time-wise. I'll never forget. We had a carpool for preschool with two other moms who were both working. One was full-time; one was part-time. We carpooled to preschool. And one of them forgot the kids one time. It wasn't a big issue, because we knew the principal would stay until every single child was picked up, but still. . . . When the first mom did this, I said, 'How could she do this? How could she forget the children?' And then the second mom did it, and I said, 'How could *she* do this?'

"And then once when it was my turn, I forgot. And I got the call from the principal. I totally forgot the carpool. I was still at the office catching up on paperwork. That's when I began to realize that things weren't quite so easy as they'd been with one."

Women in other professions found the juggling more complicated than they'd ever anticipated—and felt similar pressures, internalized or otherwise—not to leave. Patricia, now an at-home mother of three, was one of twelve female musicians in the Philadelphia Orchestra, which plays a full-season concert schedule as well as making annual three- to four-week domestic and foreign tours. She deliberated long and hard about leaving what she considered "a great job" but after fifteen years—eight of which were spent juggling the competing demands of work and family, administering baby-sitters on two shifts, and coping with increasingly competitive schedules of her husband and three children, by then ages eight, five, and three—she decided to resign her position in the orchestra.

"It took me a while to decide, because I remember my teacher used to treat the women as if they weren't real musicians. He'd push the men real hard, and women he'd just assumed were going to leave the school and become mothers. He even told me that once.

"It was a difficult decision, because if you quit, you can never go back. . . . You don't audition again at age fifty."

In her book *When Work Doesn't Work Anymore*, Elizabeth Perle McKenna talks about the role of fear in women's reluctance to leave unsatisfactory work situations:

Behind all forces of resistance is fear. . . . Having some fear of the unknown is sure proof of sanity. But then there is the overwhelming fear that keeps us in bad marriages, unhealthy relationships, and limiting work situations. That kind of fear tells us we will lose our identities, our place in society, and the food on our tables, it tells us we will never be able to take another vacation, our children will not go to college, and we will never have meaningful work again. That manner of fear concludes that we should hold on to what we've got with all we've got—no matter what.[2]

When we walked away from our jobs, many of us took the fear along.

PART TWO

STRANGERS IN AN EVEN STRANGER LAND

Metamorphin Time:
A Dream After Reading Kafka

As Gini Samuels awoke from unsettling dreams one morning, she found herself transformed in her bed into a large apricot poodle. She lay curled in a ball nestled against the pillow, one floppy ear warm against her face and partially covering one eye, which is no doubt why she had slept so long. Raising her head, she saw out of the other eye that the clock read 7:40. The side of the bed where her husband slept was empty, the covers thrown back carelessly across the floral sheets.

This startled her because she had always been a light sleeper and was always the first one up, hopping out of bed at the first signs of morning. She had to make sure her oldest son was up and out to catch the 7:15 bus to school. She then would empty the dishwasher, make lunches for the younger three, prepare breakfasts, sign any permission slips, write necessary checks, and make sure the children cleaned up their rooms and practiced their instruments before leaving for school at 8:45.

Yet the bedroom was silent, with the door closed, the way it was on those weekend mornings when her husband got up first to meet his basketball buddies at the gym.

And, of course, there was her situation. At first she assumed that this was an extension of her dream, which had, in fact, been about a dog. Her children had been begging her for months to get a dog, and in her dream they had gotten one, which had then escaped. She'd been very upset (in the dream) because their house was bordered by busy streets, and she'd been running through the streets chasing the children, who were chasing the dog, who was chasing a squirrel. Just as she'd heard the loud blaring of horns and crushing sounds of metal, the dream had ended or perhaps switched scenarios to her current situation. But as her head cleared, it seemed not to be a dream at all.

The bedroom was the same as it always had been: four walls, a queen-sized bed, a chair in the corner on which lay a pile of unmatched socks. Yesterday she'd dumped a pile of laundry on her husband's side of the bed as a not so subtle hint that he needed to help out a little more at home, and he'd pushed it to her side when he lay down to watch the game. She'd stood there, in front of the TV, folding the shirts and pants and underwear. She'd left the socks as a compromise. He'd then moved the entire pile to the chair before turning out the lights for the night.

She stretched her long arms—or what she had thought of as arms, though both of them were now covered, along with the rest of her body, with soft curly hair—and opened her mouth in a wide yawn. Pushing with her haunches, she rose unsteadily on all fours, trying to find her way out of the covers. She stepped gingerly to the edge of the bed, wondering if there was a way to ease off or if she should just jump.

A loud banging on the bedroom door startled her, and she leapt, with surprising agility, onto the soft carpet.

"*MOOOMMMM!* I have to be at band practice early today!" came her daughter's plaintive cry. "Brian won't put on his socks and shoes, and Andrew hit him with the package of Golden Grahams!"

Gini's ears perked up, and she stared at the door.

"*MOOOMMMM!*" She recognized the anguished sob of her youngest child, who was no doubt in the throes of another battle with his brother. Gini padded over to the door and sniffed at the crack, smelling graham cracker and toothpaste, and suddenly feeling very hungry. "*Momm! I can't find my socks and Andrew took all of the Golden Grahams and I didn't have any, and now there are no more!*"

"Where is Andrew?" Gini started to ask but recoiled at the sharp barking sound that filled the room. The voices from the other side of the door stopped abruptly, and there was a long moment of silence. Gini wondered if they could hear her heart pounding.

"Mom, do you have a dog in there?" came her daughter's excited voice. "They got us a dog! They got us a dog! That's why the door is closed!" she said excitedly.

Gini closed her mouth and trotted back to the other side of the bedroom, suddenly panicked. Things were certainly getting out of hand, and she was in no position to explain what was going on, let alone settle fights, drive her daughter to band practice, or find Brian's socks—though the last job would probably be the one thing that in her current condition she could do better than ever before.

"Mom!! The door is locked. Let us in!"

"Mom! I have to go!"

"Mom!"

The sounds of voices receded into Gini's consciousness. The bed with its rumpled covers looked soft and inviting. She leapt up and circled twice before settling down in a cool spot right smack in the middle of the bed. With her hind legs tucked easily under her, she burrowed her head between her folded front paws and closed her eyes.

CHAPTER FOUR

Fear of Frying
(and Baking and Broiling)

Altered Activities and Practical Problems

It is evening on a school night, 1968. Leaving my homework spread out over my desk in the pink bedroom with white eyelet curtains that I share with my little sister, I head toward dinner. My mother bustles in our brightly lit kitchen amid the aromas of baked chicken and potatoes in the oven and string beans simmering on the stove. Yellow flowered curtains frame the window, which overlooks the driveway and our quiet suburban cul-de-sac. The flash of headlights across the pane means that my father is home.

Hugs are first, then a kiss for my mom. He pours himself a martini and stirs it with his finger. I slice a tomato and set the table with placemats and stainless. My sister, with coaxing, puts out the napkins.

A candle glows from the center of the octagonal oak table. My father lowers the lights on the dimmer, while my sister, mother, and I bring out the plates, with portions already arranged on each. We gather 'round, taking our seats, mine as always between my mother and sister, across from my father. We bow our heads, listen to my father say the grace, and then begin.

Cut to an evening on a school night, 1998. I bustle in our brightly lit kitchen amid the sounds of piano keys banging from the living room and a quarrel erupting between two children fighting for space to lay out their homework papers at the breakfast room table. Pulling out of the refrigerator, in succession, three shriveled green peppers, two plastic containers of leftover pasta shells, a half a jar of marinara sauce, a plastic bag of chicken pieces with bread crumbs and a bag of ready-to-eat baby carrots, I contemplate whether we have enough or whether I can find something in the freezer to microwave. Looking up, I suddenly notice that my six-year-old sits hunched intently over a bowl of Fruit Loops.

"Brian, who said you could have cereal?" I say, sidestepping the dog who is doing figure eights around my legs.

"I was hungry," he says through a colored mouthful.

"But it's almost dinnertime."

"This can be my dinner," he smiles, grabbing another handful as the phone rings. Two adolescents make a grab for it.

I glance at the clock. "That better not be your father saying he's late."

My son listens into the phone and smiles. "Mom, it's Dad. He's going to be late."

"Fine, tell him we may start without him. Brian, Fruit Loops aren't dinner."

My six-year-old's pale eyebrows descend and settle in a studied frown. He looks at his bowl of Fruit Loops, then over at my dinner buffet of ice frosted plastic and Tupperware. "Mah-um," he says, stretching me into a two-syllable word, "I don't like that."

I whip lids off some containers, ball up plastic wrap stretched over others. "Look! Chicken, pasta, carrots. You have to have something besides Fruit Loops."

"Fine." Scratching a stool across the wood floor to the refrigerator, he climbs up and pulls open the top door of the freezer. "I'll have frozen pepperoni to go with it."

I look back at the assortment of leftovers, my mind racing. "Five carrots with it."

"CarrotsIhatecarrots!"

"Green pepper."

"Fine, I'll have carrots and frozen pepperoni."

"Deal."

I have discovered five distinct attitudes about domesticity and housework, which I have held in successive phases of my life since I've no longer been able to bolt out of the house at 8:00 each morning, leaving the dishes and the dirty laundry to someone else:

1. Domestic work is not a job, implied by all those "Do you work?" questions.
2. Domestic work is not *my* job. Hey, I'm a lawyer.
3. Domestic work is an impossible, overwhelming, endless job.
4. I am Superwoman. Watch me clean.
5. A little dirt never hurt anyone.

1. Not a Job

"Holding down a job is a lot more difficult
than lying around the house all day."
RICKI RICARDO to his wife, Lucy, on a 1952
episode of the *I Love Lucy* television series

The stereotypes are numerous, from as many sources: women at home lie around the house all day, watching the soaps, eating bonbons, or, as Fred tells Ricky in the job-switching episode, "sometimes they get up to play canasta."

Even experience—our own memories of growing up with dinners prepared and clean clothes in the dresser drawers didn't leave us with an appreciation for what our mothers did. They made it all look so easy.

Christine, the former legislative analyst now at home with her three children, comments, "It still amazes me that parenting was such a shock, because I was one of six kids and I thought I knew what was involved. I knew how to take care of kids, all the functional things. What I didn't calculate into it was all those nights I was sleeping and my mother was still awake, doing laundry, writing notes, sewing the prom dress."

Juliet Schor writes in her book *The Overworked American* of the prevalence of the "housewife" phenomenon in the first half of the twentieth century, due to both discrimination and social mores:

> The lady of leisure may have been a powerful ideological symbol, but it was a reality for only the tiniest fraction of the populace. Middle class women "faced a paradoxical set of expectations. They were to work but . . . not seem to work. . . . They were to run a household, yet return themselves in the census as unemployed."[1]

It is the fall of 1985. My husband, one-year-old son, and I have packed up our little Toyota Tercel and moved. We have moved out of the security of the city with its sidewalks and subways, concrete and glass towers, off the edge of the page of my poster of New York, beyond the real world of working professionals. We have headed for a parallel universe rumored to be populated by housewives with small children pulling at their apron strings.

We have moved to the suburbs.

In our case, the suburbs of Philadelphia.

My second pregnancy, the timing of which was so perfect in my master plan, is gone and with it my sense of order and control over my life. I have no job, no professional contacts, no friends, no plan, and I am afraid.

I am afraid of the gray station wagon with the extra child seat in the back; I am afraid of the four bedroom house, the quiet, too quiet, neighborhood street. I am afraid of the leafy green suburbs with winding roads that stretch from city life to professional oblivion.

I believed that, in New York, I had learned to deal with car salesmen who would focus their man-to-man eyes on my husband while ringing up a bill on my credit card; slap-on-the-back real estate agents who would talk property values with my husband and flirt with me about closet space. But then I was armed. Now, without my job, my fancy business card, my reason to be somewhere else, I feel vulnerable.

I am vulnerable to play groups and coffee klatches; I am suspicious of nursery schools that schedule "mothers' meetings" at 10:00 A.M. and special "Daddy days" once a year. I am afraid of my own mother, who now lives five minutes away and in *Twilight Zone* fashion seems to telephone every morning at 9:00 to ask what I am cooking for dinner that night. I fear that everything intellectual or dignified I've become, my whole adult self, may be sucked away, swallowed up, erased. I will become a bad imitation of my mother, bad because, unlike my mother, I don't even like to cook.

It is 1989 and my assignment is simple: A batch of cupcakes for my son's birthday celebration for kindergarten the next day. I have written briefs for federal court; worked on multimillion dollar deals. How difficult can a batch of cupcakes be?

Under watchful blue eyes from across the table, I set out the mix, the egg, and the milk. I turn on the radio to the baby boomer station and begin crooning, "You make me feel like a natural woman." I pour the oil and smile through the markings of the Pyrex measuring cup at my captivated child.

Opening the mix, I startle at how brilliant a color the cake mix is, so iridescent that it would, I am sure, glow in the dark. I crack the egg. I pour the milk. I dump them all together. I plug in the mixer. And then I see the spot.

It is a small, bright red spot, no bigger than a deer tick, that swims toward the center and in a fraction of a second is swallowed by the rotating blades, leaving an orange streak of color. Yanking the plug, I stare at the bowl of goop, then over at my curious son.

"Is it time to cook it?" he asks.

"Uh, maybe, almost," I say, picking up the box and searching for an ingredient in vanilla cake mix that could conceivably be red. . . . Who can tell?

Pouring the cupcakes into the tin, I debate. I can either assume that nothing is wrong—just a weird red spot, not poison. Probably not—or I can be totally irrational and panic; let my imagination run wild with fears about tamperers and bacteria and people who die from bad tuna.

Maybe there are red spots in all cupcake mixes.

I sigh. A real mother would be using flour and baking powder and organically grown chocolate chips.

I'm sure they're fine. I'll just send them in. I can laugh about the whole thing and even tell the teacher. "Excuse me, there was a red spot in the mix, which I'm sure was nothing (chuckle chuckle), but I just want you to know in case. . . ."

Maybe not.

Thirty minutes later, when they emerge from the oven, there is no sign of the red spot, but the cupcakes are very . . . short, as if too tired to make it all the way to the top of the paper liners.

"Mom," my son says seriously, staring at me from under thick brown lashes.

"Yes? . . . Sweetie?"

He frowns at the cupcakes, then looks pleadingly at me. "Can we just buy some?"

2. Not My Job

Housewife—n. 1. the woman in charge of a household, esp. a wife who does all or most of the cleaning and cooking in her own household and who holds no other job[2]

I did not leave my lawyer job to become a housewife. At times over the years, the house has indeed seemed to swell with its own domineering and demanding personality, times when I feel as if a giant scoreboard somewhere reads: HOME 98, VISITOR (ME) 0. But as anyone who has dropped by my house unannounced can attest, floors that shine, uncluttered rooms, and midday baking have never been at the top of my priorities. Nor do the women with whom I've spoken—even those who are good at it—attribute housework as a motivating factor for leaving or scaling back their jobs. This is another important difference between housewives of the fifties and stay-at-home moms at the millennium. Women who leave careers are in most cases staying at home because of the conflicts created by having children, not because of the house or because of any inclination toward domesticity. From that difference flows considerable angst, because, in most cases, the house responsibilities are part of the arrangement. Activities we had largely ignored, shared with spouses, or hired someone else to do were now smack in the middle of our job descriptions. Suddenly the house looked a lot dirtier than we remembered it, and we couldn't blame the help.

Rachel, a practicing lawyer and businesswoman for nearly twenty years before scaling back to spend more time with her family, says that being responsible for chores around the house was a jolt:

"It was almost the first issue. My husband would walk in the door and I'd say, "There's no dinner. . . . Was I supposed to get dinner? . . . Suddenly, dinner became my responsibility. Well, I have to tell you, that's an adjustment I have barely made after almost two years. Even if it was just pasta, my husband didn't care what I had, but I had to have a plan. . . . He was right, but I couldn't admit that it was my job."

And I didn't consider it my job, either, at least not at first. Domesticity, for those of us who didn't gravitate toward cookbooks and homemade Halloween costumes, had a terrifying ring to it. After being a lawyer, billing out at over $100 an hour, I had become rather compulsive about productivity and fell prey to some rather self important ideas about what kind of work was worth my time. This was not a good frame of mind in which to begin a life with small children at home.

It is snack time at my house, which means it is about ten minutes after the time the kids last ate. Our fourth and final child is sleeping peacefully, hunched up in his baby car seat, and I'm feeling rather proud of the fact that I remembered to buy grapes—real fruit—as an alternative to the sticky stuff that claims to be fruit something or other but was called candy when I was a kid. Grapes are one of the few digestible substances on which my kids and I can actually agree.

"I want some. I want some."

"Hold on, guys, they're coming," I say, running the water over the bunch, wondering why they look so . . . so purple. A thought crosses my mind, and I promptly dismiss it. No, I couldn't have.

"Here they are," I say nervously, handing small clumps to outstretched hands.

They grab and devour and suddenly scream, "Eewwww! Nuts! They have nuts in them!"

My heart sinks, and I know the awful truth. I bought the wrong kind. At home, as in the law, you pay for your mistakes. Before a riot erupts, I grab them all back and begin slicing and digging and extolling the virtues of half-grapes with holes: "Isn't this neat? Don't they look like little boats, guys?" It takes about thirty minutes of slicing and digging to fix the things. Billed at my hourly rate, these grapes would be worth roughly $47 per pound.[3]

I was still thinking like a lawyer, in the way I valued my time and energy. I didn't think I was leaving my career at all. Like a lover after a bad breakup, I went through phases of grief and denial. I wasn't actually *staying* at home, I reasoned. This wasn't my job. How could I have traded a job for which I had years of education and training for a job in which I had no education or training? Left a position that carried with it a certain measure of deference to my knowledge ("So you're on Wall Street? What do you think about the arms embargo/ trade deficit/independent counsel/etc.?") for a job which everyone from my mother-in-law to the lady on the street corner thinks she knows better than I do and tells me so ("Isn't that child too hot/too cold/too loud/too tired?"). For what possible reason could I have left a career with a very good salary for a job that pays nothing; worse, that you sometimes pay other people to help you? How could I have abandoned a career where support staff do things like remember my birthday and keep track of my vacation days for a job with no cake unless I make it and no vacation?

Ever present and oblivious to my deliberations was my child— transformed one day as if by magic from a helpless baby to a tool-obsessed toddler—a weird kid, if you want to know the truth. There he'd be, pushing aside his teddy bears to cuddle a plastic hammer in bed at night. There he'd stand, crying in bewilderment as the moving men paraded back and forth, in and out of the only home he'd ever known, carrying away his boxes of toys, the rug, the mirror, the crib from his room. My son's cheek, when he was sad, felt like wet velvet against my face. My son's eyes, when he was happy, danced with delight. Or perhaps they were reflecting the delight in mine.

I was confused. I knew I wanted a job, a good job, one that was interesting, paid well, and was close to home. And I knew one other thing even more.

I wanted more kids.

Wanting more children complicated things, for, as a lawyer friend advised me, every baby has a way of setting you back a bit.

Other women remember feeling similarly stuck. Says Lucy, the former marketing consultant, "My original plan was to have kids one-two-three, two years apart. When that didn't happen . . . I was so upset. Part of it was that I felt I had to have my kids and then get back to whatever I wanted to do."

Career, aspirations, and adult identity seemed to be in a holding pattern, forcing me and my self-important ideas to move on.

3. An Impossible, Overwhelming, Endless Job: The Work in "Not Working"

"The backbreaking, physical drudgery of taking care of a house is exhausting. The cleaning, the laundry. . . . If you don't do it, you just take it for granted."
CYNTHIA, former editor at *Business Week*

Many of us who for years believed that women at home with children "didn't work" experienced one of life's little ironies when we cut back to spend time at home. Not only did it seem like work, but it seemed like endless work, with little feedback or external gratification. Says Paula, formerly in teaching and sales advertising for cable TV, "I missed the feelings of 'a job well done' and had to retool such markers, finding gratification in 'a house well cleaned'! When can one ever say that her parenting is a 'job well done'?"

Marie, a former controller and chief financial officer, now working freelance and staying home with her four sons, would no doubt agree.

"The laundry never ends, the house remains clean for only a short period after cleaning, and it seems as though I just finish clearing one meal and another is due!"

Having achieved a measure of professional success, it can be startling to discover that home life could present such a challenge.

"The sheer logistics of it are amazing," says Julia, who was a succesful stockbroker and then president of her own retail business before she decided to sell it to be at home with her son.

It is overwhelming, due both to the nature of the work and to our unrealistic expectations. Some of us feel inexplicably guilty about not being able to meet those expectations. Says Suzanne, a former controller, "I feel guilty now about my housewife skills. I'm not a good cleaner, and I hate to plan meals, food shop, etc. I used to get away with that because I worked, but now I feel as if I have no excuse not to be doing these things. My husband is disappointed that the quality of our meals hasn't improved...."

Despite our memories of watching Donna Reed or June Cleaver, we knew real women didn't clean house in high heels or pearls. Still, we'd had mothers who'd gotten the job done without complaining. Compared to either our colleagues back at the office or fuzzy memories of our mothers or even the expectations of our husbands, many women wound up feeling both insecure and inadequate.

Lucy remembers comparing her life to her mother's: "My mother had seven children and went back and got her doctorate after she had us . . . I was the second oldest . . . Whenever I would complain to her about a problem I was having with the baby, saying, [sighing] oh my gosh . . . she'd say, 'Can you imagine having three under three?' It made me feel like I wasn't measuring up."

Tracy, the communications specialist who'd once found it difficult to understand what women at home did all day, was worried that she wouldn't have the patience to be home with children:

"My mother was always a patient person. My father was not like that, and I was more like him. I thought, 'If I ever have kids, I'm going to be a mess.'

"There are days when I get really stressed out. I could always do what I wanted to do when I wanted to do it. And with kids, you can't. I tried. Somebody gets upset, and it's usually me. I've learned to live my life around them, but it's taken a while. . . . When I worked, if I wanted to go to the mall, I'd do it at my lunch hour. If I wanted to eat a hot lunch, I could do it—all in one sitting. Or I would take breakfast to work and eat it there. There are days now when I don't eat breakfast until 11:30!"

4. I Am Superwoman. Watch Me Clean

Acknowledging the work in being at home only fueled my determination to fully master it. Although images of house cleaners in heels had lost their potency, Superwoman was still out there—her curves poured into a business suit—in magazines, TV, even perfume ads. So if we weren't bringing home the bacon, at least we could learn to cook it. Complicating the fact that we were home was the guilt that went with giving up an income. Juliet Schor writes:

> [Women] felt (and feel) that the "luxury" of staying home entails a moral obligation to hard work. Of course, this is a difficult point to prove. But it is suggestive that until just recently, as "housewifery" is dying out, the twentieth-century housewife's work week has not been exceeded by her husband.[4]

Meghan, thirty-two, an elementary schoool teacher with a graduate degree in education, feels now that she's home (working part-time) the domestic work is unending: "It seems that the more you're home, the more there is to do, and the more you think you have to do yourself. Being at home means I should clean my own house, do the cooking, the family entertaining at holidays, the homemade crafts for the seasons, decorating, painting, planning, etc. . . . I usually try to do it all."

Pat, the former city planner, remembers how difficult it was to shoulder such a load with an infant by her side: "I felt because I was not earning an income that it was my job to do everything. . . . I just assumed that because I had been Superwoman in my career I could be Superwoman at home. . . . If I had studied and gotten my As, how could this be any harder? But I was frantic. . . . The kid didn't sleep through the night for two years. The kid never woke up when he wasn't screaming. The kid *never* slept. There were hostages in Iran at the time. I remember days when I was nursing him where I would watch the TV in my nightgown, and Walter Cronkite would say, 'This is the 178th day of captivity,' and I used to say, 'No shit.'"

5. A Little Dirt Never Hurt Anyone

It is 1985, and I decide to face reality: Given that I don't want to jump back into an all-encompassing legal career, and I am rotten at cleaning the house, I decide to become a television producer. Or at least I can learn to be one while my children are small. I show up at the studio owned by the father of an old high school boyfriend of mine, who hires me as a two-day-a-week unpaid intern so that I can start to "learn the business."

We're shooting a commercial for freezers. Cool. All the excitement of television is around me: lights, camera, action. My action—or job—it turns out, is to make all the plastic food that will be in the freezer compartment look really, really frosted. I spend what seems like hours in a windowless studio spraying a white substance—what I can only describe as "guk"—all over the "food," while trying to ignore the large red warning letters on the can (extremely toxic: use only in well-ventilated areas). After the commercial is shot, I spend even more hours at an old utility sink in a back room under a flickering fluorescent light, scrubbing and scouring, trying to remove that which I only hours ago so effectively put on. As I stand there at the sink, my back aching, my hands and arms awash in bubbles and flecks of spray paint, I think, "I gave up housework for this?"

It began to sink in—as the last specks of paint submerged into the murky sludge of suds—that every job, whether in a glass and chrome high-rise office, a suburban kitchen, or a basement sound studio, has its tedious aspects. The trick to adjusting to domesticity—for me, anyway—was putting it into perspective.

As for the tedium, if I never delighted in it, at least I began to mind it less. Cheryl, another woman who was dead set against domestic chores, recalls a similar transformation. "At first, I was loath to do housework because it was what housewives did," she says. "Eventually I realized that a lot of things I thought I hated doing I hated the notion of. I got to the point where I was doing something 'productive' all the time, and I realized I had taken away all my downtime—my creative, mind-wandering time. And then I thought, 'If I do laundry, that's good downtime. When you fold laundry, you can watch TV, or listen to a book or music, or think. I started putting back in these things, like weeding the garden. The further you allow yourself to drift afield and consider the way other people live, other people in this country, other people in other countries, other people in other times, then you can really question the way people are living their lives today and decide whether there's something wrong here, and that is the other part of the equation that made it work for me."

Similarly, I began to realize that not everything can be reduced to economics. While I still calculated the money saved by wallpapering the bathroom or landscaping the backyard, I discovered that many experiences—from preparing favorite meals to transporting kids to swabbing the kitchen with a five-year-old mate—had worth far beyond their market value.

My house will never be in *House Beautiful*. I'm my mother's daughter but not my mother when it comes to cooking gourmet meals or getting the stains out of tablecloths. My laundry skills were sharpened in college, where the most important thing to remember was to bring enough quarters. I still sort laundry by child rather than by color, partly because puzzling over whose foot fits in which sock can send me over the edge.

What needs to get done gets done. And as I said at the beginning of this chapter, housework is not why I came home.

The Kids, After All—Unanticipated Pleasures

In her book *Fruitful*, Anne Roiphe writes of the passion so often overlooked in early feminist literature:

> Early feminists like Germaine Greer did not give sufficient weight to the falling in love with the baby that was part of most women's experience. They overlooked the ferocity of the mother's passion for the child. They wrote about the exhaustion, demand, demeaning routine, loss of self accurately enough, but they forgot about pride, about contentment, about the expansion of self as it is poured into the child.[5]

The concept of loss of self with simultaneous expansion of self is one to which perhaps only a mother can relate. OK, so making dinner, doing the laundry, and cleaning the bathrooms were not part of my contemplated job description. Neither was sitting on the third step curled around a tiny person sounding out words from letters for the first time ever. Neither was picking out guitar chords in the soft glow of a nightlight, playing songs about spiders and picnics and trips to the zoo.

I found myself a tour guide to the wonders of the world, showing people around who'd never before smelled daffodils in the springtime or blown dandelion puffs into the wind, never watched the raindrops dance or listened to the crickets sing. The world was suddenly full of everyday marvels and beauty, there for those of us who would experience them.

Life at home seemed more immediate, more real, and ultimately more important than anything I'd done at my high-priced lawyer rates.

What's more, I was learning more than I was teaching, learning to look at the world in a different way. Children introduce parents to a range of new experiences, whether you're home twenty-four minutes or twenty-four hours each day. The at-home parents, though, get more intensive doses of heretofore unanticipated pleasures.

My two companions and I enter the restaurant shortly after noon. It has been too long, they say, since we've splurged like this. Inside, the room is bathed in fluorescent white light. Other diners are sitting down, but it is still early. Clusters of tables for groups of two and three beckon. The service is quick; we grab a cozy banquet near the window with a view.

"Oh, look," I coo happily. "We can see the cars in the drive-through line."

I am sitting in McDonald's with my six-year-old and his five-year-old cousin, the lunch a bribe so that he'll agree to go to a school orientation for two hours—two hours I need desperately to write. My preparent standards ("*I'll* never feed my child fast food loaded with fat and sodium; *I'll* never bribe my child with cheap plastic toys") are gone—vanished, poof!—faster than you can order a Cheeseburger Happy Meal.

But it gets worse.

Like an immigrant resisting assimilation, for three years I've tried to live my life in a universe parallel to that of the Power Rangers. Aware of their existence but unwilling to sit through an entire episode (or, worse, one of their feature films), I have acquired information only on a need-to-know basis, as, for example, interpreting Christmas and birthday lists. What's more, I figured that the Power Rangers would quickly go the way of the Ninja Turtles and the Ghostbusters, migrating in natural evolutionary patterns to the bottom of a box in a corner of the basement.

But as time has worn on, I've come to realize that soon I will no longer be able to communicate with my youngest son in any meaningful way. I have no choice. I want a relationship with my son; I must learn the language of the Power Rangers.

"OK, there's Jason, right?" I say, pen poised over a small spiral notebook.

My son's large brown eyes study me suspiciously. He knows I have never cared about Jason before.

"Right?" I repeat.

"Jason's a Zeo," he says, head cocked, a long slender french fry hesitating at his lips.

"OK. Great. Jason. Zeo." Images of the Toys "R" Us aisle of action figures flash in my brain.

"And he's the red Morphin, too," he says, almost as an afterthought.

I stop and look up. "He's a Morphin and a Zeo?"

He takes a swig of root beer. "He's a red Morphin and a gold Zeo. Billy, Kimberly, Trini, and Zack are the Mighty Morphins."

"Wait. Wait." I scribble.

"Aren't they all Mighty Morphins? Mighty Morphin Power Rangers?"

"Mom, I'll tell you how they morph. The mountain blaster is Justin, who uses the blue."

"Uses the blue what?"

"He's the blue Turbo ranger."

"Turbo? . . . Turbo is different from Morphin?"

He pauses. "Right, Mom."

"Right? . . . Really?" I have no idea what I'm talking about, but I feel a surge of happiness, mastery, and power.

Learning a new language is but one of the things I never associated with parenthood. Here are some of the activities women in my survey reported that they'd never imagined themselves doing before parenthood:

- clipping a pet iguana's toenails
- drying another person's wet underpants under the hand drier in a restaurant ladies' room

- having to recite, loudly and in public, the litany: "Don't eat boogies! Don't eat boogies! Don't eat boogies!"
- cheering at hockey games until my throat hurt
- asking a three- and a five-year-old what they think of my outfit and actually needing their advice
- starting to play the violin again
- sleeping with one ear open
- cleaning fish tanks
- wanting to cut short a European trip because I missed the kids too much
- looking for small translucent lice living in human hair
- climbing every piece of jungle gym equipment at the park
- using peanut butter to remove bubble gum that had spread through the dryer
- singing and dancing with a three-year-old partner and fifteen other three-year-olds and their parents
- having to think for another human being
- giving up sex for the chance to get some sleep
- having an audience when going to the bathroom or taking a shower
- cleaning up other people's vomit
- becoming a mommy monster and chasing other human beings around living room furniture
- hoarding small human teeth in a cardboard box in my dresser drawer
- reading *Goosebumps* on the Internet
- chewing up carrots so that another person can eat them
- searching for snails and actually wanting to find them
- eavesdropping on conversations in carpools
- having another person look at me and say "Mom"

CHAPTER FIVE

"So What Do You Do?"

Social Traumas, Introductions, and Identity

I n 1963, Betty Friedan wrote:

American women no longer know who they are. They are sorely in need of a new image to help them find their identity. As the motivational researchers keep telling the advertisers, American women are so unsure of who they should be that they look to this glossy public image to decide every detail of their lives. They look for the image they will no longer take from their mothers.[1]

The problem of identity that hounded women in 1963 still plagues us at the millennium, in part because many of us mistook men for our role models and job titles for our identities. Under such circumstances, when the job title departs, so goes our sense of self, and something as mundane as filling out an application, completing a college questionnaire, or running into an old colleague can cause angst and apprehension.

The Problem of Introductions

"I don't understand why new acquaintances ask, 'What do you do?' instead of 'Do you have a family?' or 'Where do you live or work?' or just 'How are you?'"
VANESSA, part-time architect with one child, age eight

It is, for some women, merely "irritating," for some "troublesome," for still others the "most dreaded question" of all. It happens most frequently during what one woman described as "the cocktail party thing," when you're stuck navigating a room full of strangers who don't know or care that:

- you've been up since 4:17 A.M., when your youngest woke up screaming that large green numbers were scaling his bed
- your nine-year-old child was sent home from school today at noon complaining that his mouth feels like there's dust in it
- you spent part of the afternoon officiating at funerals for several fish who looked just fine at the beginning of the week
- a just-begun semester-long project about "landforms of the Midwest" is due in tomorrow's seventh-grade social studies class
- your neighbor who knows about these things has detected a severe double ear infection in your dog—*the dog*—and strongly recommends an immediate visit to the vet

It is usually about then that a well-dressed adult-type person you've never seen before turns to you, flashes a gracious smile, head tilted with polite curiosity, and asks, "What do you do?"

Asking the question is, for some women who have recently left or scaled back their careers, like pulling a pin on a grenade of issues. Not asking it can be worse.

Carolyn, a publishing executive turned literary agent, recalls her anxiety during those years when she stayed home with her three small children:

"When people say, 'What do you do?' . . . if you don't have anything professional to pull out of your hat, you feel inadequate and as if you're not really worth holding a conversation with. . . . I think that 'stay-at-home mom' does feel derogatory for someone whose persona depends upon being something other than a mother. . . ."

So do we tell them about the fish eulogies or the black sludge seeping from the dog's ears? Do we discuss the existential meaning of numeral nightmares? Do we pump them for information about the topography of midwestern America, in the hope of avoiding an all-nighter when we get home?

No.

Regardless of what home activities now fill their days, many women, particularly those fresh off the fast track, feel compelled to avoid family talk and speak, instead, of their careers:

"I felt demeaned," admits Lisa. "I used to be able to say, 'Well, I teach at Penn. I'm a neurobiologist.' Now they'd ask, 'What do you do?' and I'd say, 'Well, I *used to be. . . .*' That lasted for three to five years. I had a used-to-be pattern."

"I was the ex-researcher for many years," agrees Cheryl. "That's what I talked about whenever anyone asked what I did."

Sally left New York and the *Wall Street Journal* to freelance about a year before her child was born. "For the first couple of months it was fine to explain that we'd just moved down here and that I used to be a columnist for the *Wall Street Journal*. I could rest on that, and that was fine. . . . I could say I was freelancing. But I was getting really frustrated when after a year—or even two years—I still felt I had to validate myself and say I used to be a reporter for the *Wall Street Journal* . . . as if at one point in my life I did something you might want to talk to me about."

Having a baby only made it more complex, says Sally, "because I didn't want to use that as my new answer."

Women who do come right out and say that they're home with the children also experience discomfort. "I have to admit that when asked about my occupation, I tend to answer with an edge that I am an at-home full-time mom," says Marie, the former controller and chief financial officer who now juggles her accounting work for a family business around the schedules of her four boys and her volunteer work at their school.

When introducing themselves to people as stay-at-home parents, Corrine, an elementary school teacher at home with a one-year-old, says she's "apologetic"; Donna, a compensation analyst and marketing associate, feels "embarassed." And Anne, a thirty-four-year-old public relations manager turned grad student in historic preservation who took a medical leave of absence after her second child was born, admits that she "cringes" every time she signs her tax return where her occupation is listed as "homemaker."

"Saying that I am a stay-at-home mom . . . that title is perhaps the biggest adjustment about being at home," says Allison, a thirty-four-year-old lawyer who left her job at a law firm to spend more time with her three-year-old son. "It says nothing about my backround or experience or education. When I was practicing law, people seemed more interested in my opinions. . . . Now I find that people without children have nothing to say to me because they assume that kids are my whole life."

What's more, Carol, an archivist, reports that the usual question she's asked is not as "benign" as "What do you do?"

"Instead people ask, 'Do you work?' to which I always respond, 'You mean do I earn any money?' This allows me to let the person know that I do consider my efforts at home with my kids to be real, honest-to-God work requiring serious effort on my part."

This uneasiness is not limited to women who've decided to stay home full-time.

Jessica is a physician who sees patients on a part-time basis around the schedules of her three daughters. "I say, 'I'm a doctor three days a week, and I do carpool, work in school, and so on.' For some reason, I always feel compelled to explain."

For some women, once their sights were set on the top, anything less becomes a source of discomfort. Researchers Deborah Swiss and Judith Walker interviewed female graduates of Harvard's medical, business, and law schools and found:

> Some of the smartest women in the country said that they're too embarassed to attend their reunions at Harvard Business School if they have dropped out of the work force, left the fast track by choosing part-time work, or decided not to follow anything other than the standard male career path.[2]

I Work; Therefore I Am

Part of the anxiety stems, no doubt, from our suspicion that strangers are thinking exactly what we once thought of stay-at-home mothers. (And they may well be.) What's more, we're not yet secure enough to truly believe otherwise. As Lucy, marketing consultant turned at-home mother turned professional artist, put it, "When you're a young mother, not only are you not a businessperson anymore, but you're not a seasoned mother."

Tracy, thirty-four, remembers a Christmas party she attended three weeks after she left her job as an investment house communications specialist to be more available to her two young daughters. The party, held by her husband's employer, churned up feelings of doubt, guilt, and resentment about her decision: "I felt I had to justify myself. . . .

I knew I had made the right decision to quit my job, logically. But self-ishly I thought, 'It's not fair! Why do I have to do this and my husband can't?' It was all up to me—finding a baby-sitter was all up to me. And then I thought, 'Maybe I just don't want to make it work,' subcon-sciously, I mean; no baby-sitter was ever good enough. I thought it would be easier to stay at home, but it's not. . . . Most of the women there—my husband's peers—worked. I knew when I would talk to stay-at-home moms how I thought about them, and I didn't want these women to think that about me."

Of course, cocktail parties aren't the only circumstances that cause anxiety in newly at-home mothers. Remembers Lucy, "Whenever I went places, if people would say, 'Where can we reach you during the day? Are you home during the day?' it would always bug me, because I felt like it wasn't good enough to be home during the day. It's like 'Oh, you don't have a job; you're not worth anything.' . . .

"When I went grocery shopping as a stay-at-home mom, I remember feeling it was very important to me to have diapers in the cart (even when the baby wasn't with me) so people would know I had a baby. Somehow babies made staying at home more legitimate, than, say, being at home with a three-and-a-half-year-old."

Many women say that after a while, as they come to appreciate the value of what they're doing, their priorities change and this need to justify themselves with professional credentials diminishes. Yet for others, even years of work in carpooling, homework counseling, house managing, and volunteer activities (ranging from baking cook-ies for the bake sale to producing fund-raising extravaganzas for char-itable organizations) can't fill the holes in their self-confidence left by those abandoned careers:

Kate, a former radio broadcaster, home with two children for over ten years, sings in a semiprofessional choir and has managed her church's principal fund-raising country fair. Yet she confesses: "I'm still not very comfortable introducing myself to people without call letters after my name. You know [she puts out her hand and flashes an eighty-megawatt smile], 'I'm Kate Harris, WGGB.' That was the rea-son I had for introducing myself to you; that was the reason you'd want to talk to me. . . . These years later, I still feel it. In a room full of high achievers, where everyone is a lawyer or a cardiologist, I some-times look around and say, 'How come I'm not doing anything?' And then a voice inside my head says, 'If you're not doing anything, how come you don't have a spare minute?'"

A Society of Titles
(The World's Perceptions)

Pam was a nurse coordinating a team of neurosurgeons at a major trauma center before she left to take care of her son. She remembers an exchange at a cocktail party: "I was talking to a woman, and said, 'I'm at home with my kids now,' and she said, 'Oh . . . I admire you.' She's probably with no kids, and working. If I had said I was CEO of some company, she'd say, 'Oh, I *ADMIRE* you.' But it was more 'Oh, isn't that nice.' It was just maddening. It's a constant reminder. You always have to remind yourself of why you're here."

There is no question that titles are significant tickets to certain circles in our society. In a world of snippets and sound bites, buzzwords and passwords, call letters and acronyms, a title acts as passport into worlds outside the home. Studs Terkel, in his book *Working*, found that title was important to men and women alike:

> A title, like clothes, may not make the man or woman, but it helps in the world of peers—and certainly impresses strangers. "We're all vice presidents," laughs the copy chief. "Clients like to deal with vice presidents."[3]

For those of us caught up in the corporate climb, a title was also a powerful symbol of an identity within the professional world. The significance of title in certain circles is illustrated by a December 1997 story run by the *New York Times* that was critical of what the author considered outdated official guest list practices in East Coast power circles. In particular, the White House was criticized for its practice at state dinners, where only official guests—not spouses—were identified by title.

> As president of the international division of Dow Jones, [Karen Elliott] House oversees 600 employees and $100 million in annual revenues. But [attending a White House State Dinner with her husband Peter A. Kann, publisher of the *Wall Street Journal*] Ms. House was merely 'and Ms. Karen Elliott House.' . . .

Letitia Baldrige, who was the White House social secretary to Jacqueline Kennedy, feels that a spouse's position should be on 1997 White House guest lists, within reason. She suggests as an example including the information that a woman is president of a garden club but not that she is just a member.[4]

Now wait. Presumably any spouse with a business card, no matter how low on the corporate ladder of a multibillion-dollar company would have a title and be identified by it on such a guest list. What is the point of distinguishing between members and president of a garden club, particularly since their attendance is dictated not by their occupation but by their relationship with the invited guest? And what of the titleless wife and mother who's managing a busy household? If the purpose of these guest lists is to identify something with which your dinner companion can relate, why get into judgments about the relative merit of the way one spends his or her days? The White House's practice of identifying only the invited guest—male or female—was certainly more even-handed than a judgment-laden process of identifying only those with heavyweight titles.

And how many domestic or school-related titles make it onto the guest lists, alumni bulletins, and questionnaires? Debbie, thirty-nine, a freelance social worker and a part-time medical office worker, comments:

"I get these college alumni bulletins where they profile people who've done interesting things—usually people who've graduated in '92 or '93. One person's working in the White House; another person lived in Africa for a year and is writing a book. . . . I guess they'd never put in a big glossy photo of the president of the Home and School Association, even though it's an incredibly demanding job."

Whose Identity Is It, Anyway?
Identity versus Title

Although what I thought of as "my identity" once seemed inextricably linked with my career, neither my career nor my title ever, in fact, defined me in any meaningful sense, to either people who knew me well or to myself.

In those years I toted the briefcase, wore the suits, analyzed the corporate documents, and wrote the briefs; people knew me as a lawyer. As the adult Peter Pan discovers in the movie *Hook*—"Don't mess with me, I'm a lawyer," he shouts to the unruly gang of lost boys—there are times when it's nice to throw a title around, particularly in unfamiliar territory. But as Peter also discovers, there's more to life than work.

The people who knew me *only* as a lawyer were not the people who really knew me—knew that I liked to wear jeans and sweaters and ride my bike in the park; knew I liked to sing, play tennis, listen to James Taylor, dance, and eat Mexican food. To these people the fact that I was a lawyer was merely incidental, if not irrelevant.

Similarly, titles on business cards are incredibly useful at work or when filling out credit applications or alumni questionnaires but extraordinarily useless when reading bedtime stories or trying to catch a fast ball from a child learning to pitch. Corporate titles carry impressive authority when you're trying to rent an apartment or break the ice at a spouse's work function but count for less than nothing when you're trying to set dessert limits for small children visiting their grandmother. "I don't care if you are the president of the United States," Rose Kennedy is rumored to have said to her son Jack during a visit to Hyannisport. "Pick up your socks."

Job titles, impressive as they may be at power dinners, are not synonymous with identity. The *Random House Dictionary of the English Language* defines *identity* as "the state or fact of remaining the same one, as under various aspects or conditions." Like a good part in a play, a career or a title may come and go. Identity—who I am—remains the same.

It is December 1997, and one of my best friends from high school, whom I haven't seen in years, is in the area. We arrange to meet for coffee at a local mall.

This woman is a doctor in internal medicine. She teaches, writes, and sees patients. She is also married, with two teenage girls. But when I think of Missy, I think of sixth grade and climbing the tree in her backyard, carving initials all over it in the dead of winter; I think of eleventh grade, when our code phrase for a certain boy was *blue coat*, and I think of a giddy senior year afternoon, pouring over a *Newsweek* cover story titled something like "Sex and Collegiate Life."

When we meet at the mall, hands cupped around mugs of steaming coffee, we catch up on our respective professional activities. Then, suddenly without transition, we are talking about men, the kids today, how difficult, how wonderful it is to be adults, parents, children still; growing older but not always feeling the wiser, still groping our way through life. Digging deep, our identities fully exposed, we talk not so much about what we're doing but about how we feel about it—our doubts, fears, questions, joys. We haven't talked for years, but the comfort level warms us long after the coffee has cooled.

Philosophy aside, the "what do you do?" question remains. And as secure as you may feel, it can be difficult to respond when your life no longer fits into sound bites. Alice was a model, a makeup artist, an entrepreneur, and conducted tours of South Africa, among other things, before she stayed home to raise her two children. "If I'm at a dinner party, and someone says 'what do you do?' I just pick one of those things. . . . The people who work with my husband meet me, and they don't know what I've done. They know I'm a suburban matron, stay home with my kids, play tennis. I'm part of the book club, I putter in my garden. That's how they see me. . . ."

Lawyer, wife, mother, friend, writer. Any and all of these are me. I'm not particularly plagued anymore by the "What do you do?" stress. Like Alice, I pick one of those things —whichever fits the circumstance. Sometimes I talk about writing; sometimes I talk about the law. And sometimes I talk about the kids that make the sun come out for me on the rainiest of days.

Factors That Alleviate the "What Do You Do?" Stress

1. Been There, Done That

Women who've reached a certain level of professional achievement sometimes have fewer insecurities about being home; they know it's not because they "couldn't cut it" professionally.

Julia, thirty-four, was president of her own company when she decided to stay at home with her infant son and professes little anxiety over the "What do you do?" question: "I've been president of a company and previously, a successful stockbroker. I have nothing to prove."

Similarly, Maureen, forty-three, had been a partner in a law firm and general counsel of a corporation before she left the law to be able to spend more time with her four children, ages five to twelve. "I couldn't be the mother I wanted and needed to be and continue working at such a level of responsibility. I felt I had done all I could do careerwise, given my family constraints: I felt ready to retire and enjoy the life I had with my family. . . . My identity—who I was and what I had achieved—was set, and I was more cognizant of the bigger picture, [i.e.,] spending more time with my family. I was ready for fun and developing my children into people I could be proud of."

Patricia, once a cellist in the Philadelphia Orchestra, also puts her work identity in perspective: "I used to answer the question, 'I'm a musician, and I have a family.' Now I say, 'I have a family.' If they press, it'll come out that I'm a musician. It doesn't bother me that somebody else sees me as a mom."

On the other hand, significant achievement professionally can sharpen the contrast between professional life and life at home. Cathy was executive director of a nonprofit arts alliance in a major metropolitan area. She had not only a big job but high visibility—something she found she missed when she left to be able to spend more time with her three children. She's now investigating opportunities in commercial real estate, where she will have more flexibility, but acknowledges that it's not quite the same: "Having achieved a lot in a visible way is a double-edged thing, because once you realize what you've done, and when you've been a sort of crowd pleaser, you realize how nice it is to please the crowd. . . . I mean, I'm secure, but I'm not totally secure. I want people to think what I do is interesting. I like it when the response from people is 'Oh, that's really interesting.' I mean, no one has said 'Are you kidding? That's disgusting.' . . ."

2. Time at Home

The longer women have been involved in home activities, the more comfortable they feel with the role. Lisa, a CPA and former finance manager, now at home with three boys, ages three, seven, and nine, admits she occasionally gets defensive at the "What do you do?" question, but thinks she's mellowed as time's gone by: "The older I get, the less I care. What matters truly is what is best for me and my family."

Lillian, who'd worked as a clinical dietician before staying at home after the birth of her second child, says that a sense of purpose in her work with her children has eased the uneasiness she once felt about being home: "I used to be bothered at parties and spouse work functions, but not any longer, because I see what I'm doing is important to my kids. I want to be able to enjoy my time with them, and they need me, which gives me a lot of satisfaction."

And Lucy, the former marketing consultant who used to carry diapers in her grocery cart to justify shopping in the middle of the day, says that her angst has eased with time: "Now that I'm a seasoned mother, I feel much different. When people ask me what I do, I generally say, 'I take care of three kids.' Then I also sometimes say, 'I paint.'"

3. Part-Time Work or Education

This is critical to some women's sanity, income, and peace of mind (and is explored more fully in Chapter Eleven). When faced with the reality of leaving her child with a sitter for thirteen hours a day, Emily, thirty-four, left her job as vice president of institutional equity sales at an investment house but continued to work part-time training junior salespeople. Although she misses "the control" and "the power" of her position, her part-time work has helped maintain her sense of identity. "Whether right or wrong, good or bad," she admits, "work is part of my identity. I lose a slight sense of self if I do not have it."

With a *Wall Street Journal* job behind her, Sally is now working toward her master's in writing, a program she started when her now-fifteen-month-old was six months old.

"It's been great for me to do, to have something I could say I was using my time for during these two years. It was and is very important to me to be able to say I'm doing something else worthwhile. . . . I hopefully don't discount other women who don't have that need, but I know that about myself."

4. A Supportive Community

Debbie was a neonatal social worker on call twenty-four hours a day working at a hospital with parents of premature—or, in some cases, dying—babies. After the first of her three children was born, she altered her responsibilities because the full-time job was too stressful and emotionally draining. She began doing home studies for an adoption agency and later took a job working part-time in a medical office. "The reason I haven't felt 'shunned' professionally is that social work is a field concerned with children and families."

Jill, in contrast, who came from engineering, a field overpopulated by men, finds her support in her family and friends: "My sister is at home with a Wharton MBA. And my friends are OK with staying home. That's all I care about. I think the older we get, the more like ourselves we become. At twenty-two, you don't know who you are, but at thirty-six, you're getting there. I'm OK with where I am now. At thirty-six, I have two beautiful children, a wonderful marriage. I love my new house; I have a dog. I have a typical family, and I'm happy with that."

I am moving in a black silk dress in a room filled with the same, a forest of satin, sequins, and lace. The men, in their starched shirts and cummerbunds, bow ties and black jackets, all look like waiters. The women, having roamed the shopping malls for the perfect dress, clustered in beauty salons for the perfect hair, labored under the bright lights of bathroom mirrors for the perfect makeup, now stand elbow to elbow, satin sleeve to silk shawl, bare arm to black jacket, all blending indistinguishably with one another in the great hall. Satin whispers, ice clinks, light glitters from the tips of earlobes and the bases of long slender necks.

My husband and I are at a charity fund-raiser. His job requires our attendance at many such events. Poised at his elbow, sipping a fluted glass of champagne, I smile appreciatively at the serious, nodding man to whom he listens, while wondering if Andrew got that ride home from soccer practice and whether the baby-sitter knows how to work the microwave.

The man gestures in the air, eyes wide, then leans in toward my husband with a conspiratorial smirk. Apparently something is funny. I grin. My husband nods, rocks on his heels, says something clever. It is a dance, the old cocktail party dance.

"Another drink?" For a fleeting moment my eyes lock with my husband's before he takes my glass and pivots away, leaving a gaping hole in our conversation group. I know it will be a while, for the short distance to the bar is encumbered by distractions. Five steps away from us, somebody stops him. He swivels, nods, and another conversation begins. Another dance.

The serious man's eyes roam the space above my head, then stop and settle on me. The corners of his mouth push up in what passes for a smile.

"So . . . how're the kids?"

CHAPTER SIX

Altered Roles, Altered Marriages

Who Empties the Dishwasher and
Other Hurdles; His Money, Your Kids

(Sometime in 1988)

The room is bathed in a soft golden glow, and the smell of fresh flowers wraps around me like a shawl. A basket of fresh pineapple, melon, and grapes beckons from the dresser, and a bottle of champagne chills on the coffee table. I walk to the sliding glass doors and look down at the pool sparkling in the afternoon sun. The bed is big and inviting; I throw myself down and pick up a room-service menu. Not now, but later, maybe, I'll get one of those drinks with an exotic name and a tiny umbrella stuck in a slice of orange on the rim. For now it is enough to lie back and contemplate the quiet.

The phone startles me awake, and I sit up. A pile of laundry is where the fruit should be, and I realize that it's 10:30 P.M., and he's away, not me.

"Hi, honey," says my husband. "Did I wake you? How are things at home?"

As I push aside some towels still warm from the dryer, my head begins to clear, and I pick up a sock the length of my thumb. "OK. It's been pouring all day."

"Really? You're kidding! You should see the weath—never mind. How are the kids?"

"Andrew threw up all night last night."

"Oh, no."

"Uh-huh. He woke up at 11:30, screaming that he'd had a nightmare, and I just held him awhile and then carried him back to bed, but an hour later he cried out again and threw up."

"Oh, no."

"Oh, yes. From then on it was every hour on the hour, until 4:30. Poor little guy. At 4:30 he slept for two hours."

"Oh, good."

"But Brian got up at 5:30."

"Oh, no."

"Yeah, he was really screaming. I think his front teeth are coming in."

"Boy, it was a good night to be gone. Sorry. I didn't mean that."

"Yes you did. So I'm a little tired. It was kind of hard to relax in those forty-five minutes between throw-ups, but you know what really kept me awake?"

"What?"

"Around 2:00 I remembered something—Andrew hadn't finished the chocolate custard he had last night for dessert. I thought I'd bought chocolate yogurt, but it was really like pudding—"

"Yes, so?"

"Well, Julia and Danny wanted to finish his pudding, and I said yes. I said, since Andrew's not sick—boy, was that dumb—they could split the rest of his dessert. And I spooned it out for them, one for Julia, one for Danny, you know, to be even. So now they'll all get it."

"Ohh . . . "

"So when are you coming home? . . . Honey? Are you there?"

Business trips. Once upon a time—during those fleeting years between being a child and becoming a parent—we both took business trips. It doesn't seem fair that stay-at-home parents (SAHPS, pronounced "saps") don't take them. They, after all, are the ones who need them the most.

But wait, objects the weary traveler. Although business trips may be exciting at first, they quickly become tiring, boring, sterile. Working during the day, coming back at night to an empty hotel room with nothing but a bed, a phone, and TV. Eating restaurant food three meals a day. Empty evening hours that stretch into quiet lonely nights.

Sounds good to me.

"Mom, what would happen if you cracked an egg like that just a little and then left it hidden someplace for a very long time?"

I am getting out eggs under the watchful eyes of my four- and eight-year-old sons. Dinner is a little unfocused tonight. Scrambled eggs, Cheerios, leftover black olives, and peanut butter and jelly sandwiches won't hurt anyone. The kids think this is great—"just like a restaurant."

My eight-year-old is staring at the egg preparation with an unusually introspective look.

I frown as raw egg slips from shell to bowl. "Why are you asking me this?"

The phone rings.

"Hello?"

From the receiver comes static then a faint "Hi, honey."

"Oh, hi. Danny, did you hide a raw egg somewhere?"

"What?"

"Oh, sorry. Hi, honey. How are you?" Crooking the phone under my chin, I grab a fork from the drawer and start stirring the eggs.

"Exhausted," he sighs. "It's one in the morning here. We went out late after work again. We were about to leave when somebody ordered another bottle of wine."

"Oh, too bad."

"Then somebody else wanted dessert—"

"Isn't that the way it always is?" I shake my head, licking peanut butter off my thumb.

"Yeah, well, we'd heard that the desserts in this place were incredible; anyway it was impossible to leave."

"Hmmm."

"So I'm just exhausted."

"Hmmm."

"And we have a 7:30 breakfast meeting, so I should get off. How are the kids?"

"Great. We're playing restaurant tonight, too."

I haven't done much business traveling in the last eight years. My own trips kind of dried up when I decided to work at home. And accompanying my husband on his trips is easier said than done. I used to think it was difficult to leave my law firm job for a week away. Arranging coverage for a variety of cases and corporate legal matters was a piece of cake compared to planning the lives of four kids for four days. You corral a couple of colleagues to cover for you, send a few memos notifying everyone of your departure, and bolt. There may be some grumbling, but right is on your side—the office manual provides for a vacation.

Not only is there no vacation in the SAHP job manual, there is no manual. Different schools, sets of friends, and after-school activities make for complicated scheduling. I have a house calendar on which everything is written in code that only I can decipher. Anticipating emergencies, organizing medicines in appropriate dosages, making sure that everything is locked away from the kids and accessible to whoever will watch the kids and administer their lives—finding the sitters is, of course, the last major hurdle—makes leaving close to impossible.

So he takes the trips and I take the calls, although meaningful discussion with kids pulling at my sweater is somewhat lacking. When my turn rolls around, a lot of expensive sighs ripple across the miles in an undeclared contest to demonstrate who is the more exhausted one. But then I like to talk about why we are both so wiped out:

Who is tired in nice clothes? Who is tired in jeans and a T-shirt with spit-up down the back? Although neither of us is getting much sleep, what do the beds that we are not using look like, and who makes them? Who is seeing different parts of the country, the world? Who is finding old eggs in heretofore undiscovered places right in our own home?

This discussion is not of great interest to one of us, who thinks that the other is keeping score (she is) and that he will somehow owe the other one something when this is all over (he will).[1]

It is an old debate. Who has the better deal in a marriage, husband or wife?

HUSBAND: She does. I go to work and she stays at home with the kids.

WIFE: He does. He goes to work, and I stay at home with the kids.

Today's "traditional family" has an added twist. In many cases, and in the cases profiled for this book, women have in fact "been there" at a career. Daily lives—his and hers—accustomed to being the same, or at least parallel, are now different and must be complementary.

In addition to the work and respect, a woman who's left her career remembers the coffee breaks, the business lunches, the ability to think through to the end of a sentence without a colleague sobbing because someone else used the red cup/took the last drop of lemonade in the red cup/whacked him with the red cup. Because she's been there, she might be less sympathetic to the husband who comes home at the end of a "long hard day." And she might not be the "wife" who was there waiting in 1950.

A Good Wife in the Ol' Days

Once upon a time, there was a job description for the position of wife. The following instructions sailed into my e-mail box one day, purportedly taken from a 1954 home economics textbook:

How to Be a Good Wife

Have Dinner Ready. Plan ahead, even the night before, to have a delicious meal—on time. This is a way of letting him know that you have been thinking about him and are concerned about his needs. Most men are hungry when they come home and the prospect of a good meal are [sic] part of the warm welcome needed.

Prepare Yourself. Take fifteen minutes to rest so that you'll be refreshed when he arrives. Touch up your makeup, put a ribbon in your hair and be fresh looking. He has been with a lot of work weary people. Be a little gay and a little more interesting. His boring day may need a lift.

Clear Away the Clutter. Make one last trip through the house just before your husband arrives, gathering up school books, toys, paper, etc. Then run a dust cloth over the tables. Your husband will feel that he has reached a haven of rest and order, and it will give you a lift, too.

Prepare the Children. Take a few minutes to wash the children's hands and faces (if they are small), comb their hair, and if necessary, change their clothes. They are little treasures and he would like to see them playing the part.

Minimize All Noise. At the time of his arrival, eliminate all noise of the dryer, dishwasher, or vacuum. Try to encourage the children to be quiet. Be happy to see him. Greet him with a warm smile and be glad he is home.

Some Don'ts. Don't greet him with problems and complaints. Don't complain if he's late for dinner. Count this as minor compared with what he might have gone through that day. Make him comfortable. Have him lean back in a comfortable chair or suggest he lie down in the bedroom. Have a cool or warm drink ready for him. Arrange his pillow and offer to take off his shoes. Speak in a low, soft, soothing and pleasant voice. Allow him to relax and unwind.

Listen to Him. You may have a dozen things to tell him, but the moment of his arrival is not the time. Let him talk first.

Make the Evening His. Never complain if he does not take you out to dinner or other places of entertainment. Instead, try to understand his world of strain and pressure, his need to be home and relax.

The Goal: Try to make your home a place of peace and order where your husband can renew himself in body and spirit.

Even without such a text, when I was growing up in the fifties and sixties, we all knew what wife work was. A wife was a married woman, but a good wife was something more. A good wife cared for and supported her husband without interference from her own agenda. Her own activities had to be of a sort that could complement, not conflict with; interface, not interfere with, the activities of her husband. A good wife was there when he needed her, without ego, without edge. To the extent she was ambitious, it was ambition for him. She was the hostess, the manager. A good wife. Everyone could use one.[2]

I never particularly wanted to be a wife. In my fuzzy fantasy of my future, I assumed that I would marry and that kids would be part of the package, but I never sought wifehood itself with any particular zeal.

Barely out of my official childhood, I fell in love when the boy that I would marry was twenty and I was twenty-one. Love as a new adult was mostly adventure, little responsibility. In our college, graduate school, and early years of working, our relationship didn't require significant attention. He had his work. I had mine. Aside from our confessed ardor for one another, the fact that we were together was convenient; dating was just one less activity we had to worry about distracting us from our respective career climbs.

Even when we married—backed into it after a surprise engagement party thrown by impatient relatives—I didn't particularly feel like a wife. Children who had grown into adulthood together, we were friends, lovers, partners. Neither of us changed our last name or our bank account. Neither of us did the other's laundry or taxes. Although we did buy—together—a car, a co-op, and some furniture, ours was essentially a symbiotic relationship. Neither of us felt dependent upon the other, but our free time—our nonworking time, limited though it was—we devoted to one another.

And then came parenthood, its turbulence disrupting the equity of our parallel lives like a hurricane erroneously anticipated as "some strong winds."

I never realized that becoming a mother could make me a wife, if I let it. In a world where our roles had been not only equal but similar, pregnancy became the great divide. For no matter how egalitarian we thought we were by referring to "our" pregnancy, I was the one who threw up in the bathroom at work, lumbered around like a whale out of water, and was no longer able to look at, let alone enter, the supermarket. Despite our joint interest in the welfare of the fetus, I was the one to limit what I ate, drank, breathed. I was the caretaker of our child in utero. When he was born, I breast fed him for ten months. Although my husband shared in the diapering, dressing, bathing, cuddling, and cooing, I seemed the undeclared master of when, where, and how.

The Good Wife Now

My husband and I file into a theater for a charitable award ceremony. A local businessman is being honored for his contribution to the city. After reciting his list of business and civic accomplishments, the introductory speaker lauds the honoree's smarts, his cleverness, his intelligence in all his endeavors, but most of all, his talent in choosing a wife.

Choosing his wife? The room titters politely as he continues: the wife is a brilliant, accomplished professional herself who has risen to high rank in one of the most powerful corporations in the country.

The honoree then steps to the podium, beaming. Ah, a gracious introduction, he says, grinning. And a knowing one: the wife of the man who made the introduction is an intelligent, beautiful lawyer who not only contributes to the life of the city but is both a mother and a judge! Low murmurs of oohs and ahhs rise up from the crowd. *Where am I?*

How ironic that after years of social progress women have advanced themselves only to end up back on the pedestal, a male proprietary interest with
a new twist; the good wife for the millennium: professional—mother—
executive—smart—talented—funny—beautiful. Superwife—the new model to
which we should all aspire and against which we all fall short.

I squirm in my auditorium seat, finger the pearls that drop from my
earlobes, look down at my black dress, which suddenly looks vaguely
geisha-like to me. My cheeks grow warm with a flush of anger—or is it
humiliation—or is it anger at feeling humiliated?

I steal a sideways glance at my husband, who stares ahead, seemingly
oblivious to my discomfort. He is the kid who was a year behind me in
college, who followed me to New York after I went to law school. Who earned
less than half my salary the first year we were working, but whose salary now
pays for the mortgage, the camp tuitions, the food, the clothes.

Who married a lawyer and wound up with a wife.

The question remains, hanging between the partners of the modern
marriage, like the pointer on a Ouija board: Who is more tired, more
driven, more hardworking than the other? And why are we so eager
to prove ourselves? Our expectations are so high for having it all—
financial prosperity, professional success, and a family of kids who
grow up happy, well adjusted, and with every Little League/
scouting/playgroup and other opportunity we can afford to give them—
that we're always struggling to keep up, with the housework, the homework, the office work. The complexities of our daily schedules rival
that of chiefs of state (all of whom seem to have time for golf). Our
daily to-do lists run longer than the congressional agenda. And at
the end of each day, if we're never caught up, neither of us wants to
feel responsible.

Certainly many of us, when we were working full-time at our careers,
underestimated the complexities of being at home with children. And
since we are a new generation of women, we are married to a new generation of men, many of whom no doubt felt much the same way about
domestic duties as we did: that they weren't much of a job. Not until I
experienced parenthood—especially stay-at-home parenthood—did
much of my thinking change about the value of child care and domestic services.

But what of the spouses who continue working uninterrupted, whose perspectives on life at home are still blurred by the velocity of their careers? And what happens to the dynamics in a relationship (founded on similar attitudes based on similar life experiences) when one person's experience, thinking, and daily life change dramatically and the other's continue much the same?

"My husband was supportive, but when there was a wife at home to do things, the whole relationship changed," said Carolyn, publishing executive turned at-home mother turned literary agent.

His Expectations/Her Reality

Ways in which some women report that husbands expect life to change after their wife leaves or scales back her career to be at home:

- more sex
- cleaner house
- better meals
- twenty-four-hour child care
- twenty-four-hour laundry service
- personal secretary
- Martha Stewart–style corporate entertaining
- more sex

Ways in which some wives report life changing after they leave or scale back their careers to be at home:

- house seems dirtier
- cooking becomes a drag
- too tired for sex

OK, so it's not exactly what we thought it would be. When it comes right down to it, most of us hadn't a clue about what staying home would be like or how it would affect our marriages.

The quality of life is better, say many women, but it takes work, flexibility, and understanding on the part of both partners. Plugging away full-time at two careers while trying to raise a family was exhausting and stressful; being at home (even part-time) has its own set of marital tensions. There are surface tensions about squeezing a contemporary relationship into traditional family roles. "I think he has expectations that I will be the maid," says Julia, thirty-four, who is trying to sell her business to spend more time with her infant son. Bobbi, forty-three, an in-house banker for seventeen years before going out on her own four years ago as a consultant and personal business manager, says, "The perception of my husband is that since I'm 'home' . . . (even though I'm still doing banking) everything that goes with running the house—whether it's our investments, our insurance, finding a house, improving it, all the food shopping, the cleaning, the laundry—is my responsibility. All he does is go to work. He comes home, and everything's done. He doesn't think about any of that stuff."

There are tensions about money, issues of ego and recognition. Having one spouse at home requires adjustments in the daily ways in which we relate to one another, as well as in the ways in which we think about ourselves and our family.

Surface Tensions:
Domesticity, the Kids, and Traditional Roles

My husband's regular and consistent household participation before I worked at home:

- cooked half the time
- did his own laundry all the time
- cleaned the bathroom occasionally
- shared at least minimally in cleaning the house
- dressed our eldest son (only one child at the time)

My husband's regular and consistent household participation since I began working from home:

- eats
- helps tie youngest son's shoelaces (now four children)

- cooks blueberry pancakes in the shape of the Power
  Rangers every Saturday morning

It is 6:31 when I hear the voice: the jarring, screeching voice blabbering
on about the weather, the traffic, the latest political scandal. Out from the
lump of covers beside me reaches a hand, groping for the clock, fingers
fumbling for the buttons, slamming down, and then—quiet.

So begins the morning rush hour: there are kids to be roused, breakfasts to be managed, lunches to be packed, a dishwasher to be emptied, a
dog to be taken out, homework to be checked, permission slips to be
signed, and on and on. Tumbling out of bed, I am off and running.

An hour later, I burst into the kitchen after dropping my eldest son at
early-morning band practice and picking up milk. The pajama-covered
backside of my youngest sticks out from the bottom cabinet where the
cereal is stored. My nine-year-old sits slumped on the stairs, mumbling
something about sweatpants. There is no sign of my eleven-year-old, who
must be out of the house for choir practice in ten minutes.

In the midst of it all, my husband, transformed from a lump of
bedcovers to a showered, shaved, dressed-in-a-suit man, sits reading
the paper and eating yogurt.

I am on a roll and begin barking out directions: "Brian, you need to get
dressed. Andrew, I don't know where your sweatpants are. Check your
laundry. Does anyone know where Julia is? JOE, DO YOU THINK YOU MIGHT BE
ABLE TO HELP A LITTLE HERE?"

"What?" The eyes of the boy I met in college look up from his
newspaper, startled.

I take a breath, a long, slow breath.

"Honey, I just have to tell you this. We get up; you shower, you shave,
you get dressed. You come down, get out your peach yogurt, pour yourself
a glass of orange juice, read the newspaper, and go."

He looks straight at me, forehead widening. He seems genuinely
baffled. "As opposed to what?"

Similar scenes are played out at other breakfast tables. Christine, the
former legislative analyst, says: "What happens at our house. . . . By
twenty after eight, the bus is coming in ten minutes, nobody can
find their shoes, they still haven't eaten the food I put on the table, I'm
screaming at everybody . . . and he comes down looking great, in his

suit and his tie, saying [Christine waves her arms and bellows], '*Good morning everyone!*' He is like . . . an oasis of calm for the kids! And I'm ready to slit his throat!

I say, '*Do something! Grab somebody! Find a sneaker!*'

And he says, 'I have to get ready for work.' "

∽

Many women say that the relationship changes dramatically when one spouse stays at home, because husband and wife slip into a de facto division of labor without ever having discussed its parameters. In my family, when he assumed responsibility for supporting the family financially, I assumed responsibility for everything related to home and children, a relationship that seemed vaguely unfair to me, maybe because my "share" seemed to run twenty-four hours a day.

It is a slippery slope to a state that may not be marital bliss: Start cooking his dinner, and he'll begin expecting a Martha Stewart meal every night. Get all the kids dressed in the morning, and he'll lose track of where their clothes are, what sizes they wear, and which striped sweatshirt matches the green sweatpants. Make all the lunches each day, and he'll never again be able to find the peanut butter or remember that the youngest hates jelly. In other words, as you are fighting transformation into June Cleaver (see Chapter Four), he is turning into Ward, or worse.

"At first, he even stopped hanging up his coat, expecting me to do everything because I was home anyway," says Edith, formerly a supervisor of utilization review at a health care company and now at home with a seven-year old daughter. "That didn't last long."

We are riding bikes at the seashore. My youngest is four and still light enough to sit in the plastic child's seat attached over my rear wheel. Pedaling against the cool salt air breeze, our bicycle sails alongside the long grasses of the sandy dunes. Small bony knees press against my hip, and I know this will be the last summer we can ride together like this.

"Mom!" comes a small voice, carried backward by the wind. "When I get big, I'm going to have four kids!"

I smile. How sweet. He wants to replicate our family.

"And I'm going to name them Jason, Kimberly, Zack, Trini, and Billy. Oops, I mean, five kids."

I sigh. He wants to father the Power Rangers.

"But, Mom!" he shouts.

"What?" I shout back.

"I'm going to need a mom!"

"Honey," I protest, turning my head partially, "I'll still be your mom. I'll always be your mom."

Silence. We push on, under the studied stares of an endless row of seagulls perched on the telephone lines.

"No! I'm going to need a grown-up mom. Like how Dad has you!"

I am not my husband's mother.

"I hate being in the position of acting like his mother, asking him to clean up his room," says Katherine, formerly an administrative associate in a nonprofit management company, now working part-time as retail sales associate and home with her two children, ages four and eight. "But we have a great relationship, so we handle the little stresses pretty well."

This tendency that some husbands have to lapse into Ward is not a malicious, or even intentional, transformation. It's as if some contemporary male memory switch has been pulled, and they're as confused by it as you are.

"It's on the Y chromosome or something," says Jessica, laughing. "It's universal. It's the opening of the refrigerator and not seeing the milk that's right there in front of them."

It's the kind of conversation I've had in my house:

HIM (rummaging through dresser drawer): Honey, I can't find my jeans.

ME: I don't know where your jeans are.

HIM (looking up with a puzzled frown): I put them in the laundry last weekend, and they're not back yet.

Back yet?

Cathy comments, "When we first got married, for the first couple of years, he did probably half the cooking. . . . He never cooks anymore unless I'm not here, and then he usually orders pizza. He gets into a supermarket now, and he's like—in a panic.

"He won't load the dishwasher right. He always loads it so the glasses break. . . . It's almost as if he deliberately loads it wrong.

"He can't do any of that stuff."

"Even more than the chores themselves, it's the sense of responsibility that is sometimes overwhelming," says Jessica. "My husband and the husbands of my friends will pitch in a tremendous amount and are very involved in the kids' lives, but the total responsibility of knowing what the kids do and where they have to go and how their schedules are arranged is really up to us."

So he'll drive Janie to and from ballet lessons if he's told how to get there, when to drop her off, and when to pick her up. He'll help with the schedule. But he won't help make the schedule.

In this respect women are not complaining so much about taking over what needs to be done when they are home and their husbands are not (i.e., facing up to the idea of domestic management; see Chapter Four). Instead they talk about the responsibilities husband and wife assume *when they're both right there.*

As Rachel, a former corporate counsel, describes, "I felt that . . . *he was tuning out* with what was happening to the kids. . . . I'd say, 'If there are two fighting over here, and you're home, you should get involved.'"

It is Sunday night. We have had a week of basketball practices, play rehearsals, school projects. Of these, my husband is only peripherally aware, for in his own crisis mode at work, he has been out very late four out of seven nights, merely late for dinner the remaining three. Friday and Saturday nights were business dinners, at which I played the wife. When Sunday evening rolls around, we at last have a night at home together to pick up the pieces of the week. There are dishes to do, laundry to fold, mail to sort, homework to do, instruments to practice.

And after dinner, the kids flip on the TV.

"Wait a minute," I say. "Nobody's practiced their instruments all week." Unhearing, the nine-year-old settles back in the flip chair next to the dog. The eleven-year-old focuses on the screen.

"You all have lessons on Tuesday," I say, my words hanging momentarily in the air, then dissipating like hot breath on a cold winter's day. "And there's homework left, isn't there?"

I turn to my husband, who is sagging in his chair. It's been a long week and a longer weekend, and tired brown eyes swim above half-moon circles of gray.

But I am tired, too. I am tired of husband demands for which I stay up too late and children demands for which I wake up too early. I am tired of being the one to make rules about homework and cleanup; tired of laying down ultimatums to sullen teenagers ("No going to the movie unless your room is clean.") and bargaining with quick-witted nine-year-olds ("Half hour of computer game for two paragraphs of a book report").

I look at my husband, pleading now. "Why don't we just tape the show?" I say quietly. "They really need to do homework and practice, and it shouldn't always be me to say so."

He considers this a moment, then slaps the table with his hand. "You're right," he says. Then, louder. "Kids? Did you hear your mother?"

The Undercurrents: Money, Recognition, and Competition

Money

Money is, of course, a threshold issue in many couples' decision as to whether one parent can cut back his or her career to be the primary caretaker of the children. Beyond mere necessities of food, shelter, and clothing, a couple's chosen lifestyle, whether it involves private or public schools, vacations, or fancy neighborhoods, obviously dictates their financial needs. Certainly money is a factor in all our lives, and the absence of it creates stress, particularly when one salary must stretch to meet expenses.

Cathy, who resigned her position as executive director of a non-profit corporation and is now looking into more flexible work arrangements, admits that money has been more of a practical issue than she'd anticipated:

"Our income has been dramatically reduced. That's been far more stressful than either of us realized. . . . Before, we'd had this formula for dividing up our incomes. I would contribute a certain amount, and we would divide it up. It turned out I would pay for all clothes, food. . . . Now the reality is that he's had to pay for everything."

And it is true that whereas women of our mothers' generation married husbands who expected them to stay at home, many of us married men who fully expected us to be equal financial partners. Kate, a former radio broadcaster, confesses, "Occasionally, I feel guilty because poor Ed never signed on to be the only breadwinner. . . ."

On a practical level, though, not all professional callings can ease financial burdens sufficiently to make money the justification for continuing to pursue careers. Kate says, "If I were working at a career in broadcasting, we'd need a housekeeper, and I'd have to make a whole lot more money."

Even if not necessary to pay the bills, an income of one's own is tangible—and quantifiable—proof of value of some sort and a significant factor in the self-esteem of many people. Financial dependency is sometimes blamed for unhappy marriages—marriages, no doubt, in which equality is defined in terms of financial contribution.

Uneasiness eats at some of us when *Working Mother* magazine cites research showing "that earning a paycheck often helps women have better marriages. Research shows that women who are satisfied in their work lives, *who earn a salary that is roughly equal to their husband's* [italics added], and who feel that their career is as important as his tend to be happier and have happier family lives."[3]

Many of us cringe when we read in *Business Week* that "[t]he spouses of working mothers are apparently happier, too."[4]

And there is no question that losing that paycheck, taken for granted for so many years, can exact a psychic toll. Says Cathy, "Without any income, I've had to start asking [my husband] for money. That's been the biggest inspiration to earn money. For me to have to ask somebody for money has been really traumatic."

Jill says that part of the reason she automatically went back to her engineering job after the birth of her daughter was that she was earning a salary comparable to her husband's. It was not that they needed the income to live, she says, but rather, "I was having a problem thinking, 'How would we be equal partners if I gave this up?'"

Other women express anxiety about the practical danger that lurks in the wings of financial dependency when a woman decides to stay at home. Worries one, "I live every day in fear of the fact that if our relationship for whatever reason went sour, I'd have no pension to fall back on and a child who's dependent upon me."

But this woman and many others say that they're willing to take that risk.

Recognition and Competition

The shifting of roles along gender lines—initiated during pregnancy and clearly apparent once our first child was born—only intensified once I left my lawyer job to be at home. Suddenly wifehood enveloped me like a blanket, which, after all those years of independence, felt as confining as comforting, as suffocating as secure. As with the other women, there were the money issues and the domestic sorting out of roles.

But there was something else revealed: an undercurrent of competition I'd never realized existed. Both of us had been ambitious; both sought professional success and recognition. Now, as his career shot ahead, my career as a lawyer sputtered, stalled, and stopped dead. In terms of the business and professional community, he was the person people in the outside world knew, at parties, at functions, at business conferences; I became the wife; worse, the corporate wife.

Cheryl, former research director, agrees, remembering her first days at home: "There was this whole power struggle. It was, I'm home, but I'm not a different person, and I was an executive, and I had a secretary, and if you think I'm going to sit here and darn your socks, you're crazy. I never said this, but this was where my head was, certainly."

Sally, twenty-eight, a former journalist and graduate of Yale, who says that staying home with her one-year-old has worked out well within her marriage, nevertheless concedes that there was an adjustment: "All my life I had been in school, working at the same level as my husband. We both went to Ivy League schools; we both were accomplished; we were always right at the same level. We'd always seen each other in the same roles and thought, 'Wow, we're so fortunate. This is the nineties and everybody's sharing roles. Isn't this great?' And then we moved, and I wasn't working, and neither of us realized [the adjustment we'd have to make]."

Pat, who was a city planner, says that she looked to her husband to compensate for the lack of feedback and recognition she felt once she was home with their baby: "Prior to meeting Loren, I was a project manager, where the salary and title acknowledged my efforts. . . . I married him because I felt he was a true equal. He was a great date, a great lover, boyfriend, the whole nine yards. [Once I was home] after the child came, all my needs for acknowledgment of this incredibly new, stressful, frightening, wonderful experience were put on him. And it completely changed our relationship. . . . I'm not saying it's not good, but it put the most incredible pressure for what I needed and had gotten through a title, through a discernible beginning and ending of a project development, the salary, promotions, all that stuff—it all shifted to Loren. . . . I would have spent the entire morning trying to get this kid to eat solids for the first time, or trying to get him to calm down, trying to get the dishwasher loaded or unloaded, whatever. My husband would come in the door and say, 'I'm very tired, I have to lie down' . . . instead of 'You look great, the house looks great, the baby looks terrific. Is there anything I can do to give you a moment of rest?' "

One of the consequences—a danger or a benefit, depending upon one's perspective—of having "a wife" at home is that, free of domestic concerns, a husband can devote himself almost entirely to his career. On the positive side, this allows him to excel in ways he would not otherwise be able, in some cases more than compensating financially for his wife's lost earnings. At the same time, it can widen the gap between his life and hers.

Pam, the former RN coordinator of a surgical trauma unit, says that marital stress has increased with her husband's level of responsibility. "I'm somewhere way down at the bottom of his list of things to do and see. . . . If a problem comes up, it doesn't affect him, because I'm just supposed to handle it, and I do, so he just leaves me alone. . . . For the first baby, he's more in tune. . . . With every work move, his job responsibility increases. [I've told him,] I see you rearrange your life to play golf and call it business; I see you knock yourself out at work. . . . I don't see you knock yourself out to do anything with me. . . . I don't see it as a priority . . . you don't see it as a priority . . . you see it as something you'll get to eventually . . . and if there's a problem you see it as something 'she'll' take care of . . . she'll also take care of her own emotions . . . she'll take care of whatever she needs to. . . . I become like staff. . . ."

It involved, for me as well, a continuing adjustment as his career moved forward earning for him increasing recognition within his professional community. Home life, by comparison, could seem terribly isolating.

Other women felt such comparisons within their own marriages.

Alice, who'd traveled the world before becoming a mother, remembers how it felt to contrast his life with hers when she was first at home: "I hated him for a lot for a long time. Not hated, but I resented the fact that he'd go off to Europe and say, 'Keep the home fires burning, dear,' and leave all the stuff—even though he was killing himself working."

Even without exotic travel, a husband's daily commute to work could seem like something close to abandonment. After her life as a journalist at AP and *Business Week*, Cynthia found the first months at home in the suburbs with a newborn very isolating: "My whole life had been centered in the city. [Now] I felt trapped in this town where I didn't know anybody. Eliot'd go off to work every day, and I'd think, 'You bastard. What have you done to me, and why aren't you helping me more?' For him life went on as it always had. For me, it was a cataclysmic event."

Now that her two children are older and she has begun a new career in social work, she says she still feels "left behind" at times, such as "When five o'clock comes and the phone rings, and Eliot calls and says, 'Oh, so-and-so called and invited me out for a drink. I'm going to stay in, and I'll be home late.' I don't ever have that luxury. Even now, when I've been working and going to school, I've never had the luxury of calling and saying, 'Oh, I'm not going to be there.'

". . . They [husbands] think that if it doesn't get done by them, somebody else will do it. And I know that if it doesn't get done by me, it doesn't get done. And that's been really difficult—it seems like there's a basic inequity there."

But set against such feelings is a recognition that her husband has his own inequities with which to deal: "I have always had a lot of sympathy for two parts of the male role in families like ours, where we've taken on quasi-traditional roles. First, the primary responsibility of being the sole financial caretaker is tremendous pressure. It means that if you don't like what's going on at work, you can't mouth off about it, you can't quit [without] putting the well-being of your family in jeopardy. And you can't bond with your kids the same way if you're not there all the time. I've always felt that Eliot's missed something really wonderful. And even to this day, as the kids have gotten older, his relationship with them is not the same kind of relationship that I have. . . . He'll never be as close to them as I am because I'm with them so much. And I kind of feel sad about that for him.

"I don't even know that he knows that he's missed it. . . . But I know what I've gotten out of it, and I would have hated to have missed that. So it kind of gives me a sympathy for him that I wouldn't otherwise have. Not that I always remember it."

The Glitter Gluey Silvery Lining

Ok, so there are tensions—as there are in any marriage, particularly those with children. Every marriage with children—involving two wage earners or one—is a unique complexity of tensions and adjustments to ever-changing needs and schedules. Like any adjustment, having one spouse stay at home—particularly when children are involved—requires work, flexibility, understanding, and communication.

Not every marriage has the same adjustments. Not every husband turns into Ward Cleaver. I know for a fact that there exist husbands who regularly pack their children's lunches, clean the bathrooms, and throw in laundry on a Sunday afternoon.

What's more, even the husbands who have Wardlike tendencies are not like him all the time. My husband, when he's home, often cooks Saturday or Sunday dinners, will play the piano for any child who wants to sing, and reads a terrific bedtime story.

Just as the joyful meaning that children give our lives more than compensates for the lack of romance, the sleepless nights, the drain on finances, the loss of privacy, and the other adjustments we make as parents, many of us have concluded that the benefits of having one parent at home make it worth whatever adjustments we have to make in our marriages. Many women have found that for them the practical and emotional advantages of having one spouse assume primary care of the house and children outweigh the tensions.

Says Cynthia: "In living with that issue, day to day, in every relationship you give and you get. I feel as if I've gotten more than I've given and given up. If having to give up that freedom means that I get to have this incredibly close, great relationship with my two kids, who I think are wonderful people, then I guess I'm willing to do that."

The biggest practical advantage mentioned over and over again is time, a commodity of increasing value with each new tooth, every leap in shoe size, every gray hair that different members of the family experience.

Allison, a lawyer, contrasts her married life now with her life before children: "We've had more time for each other now. That's the irony about practicing law so intensely before you have children. I was so consumed with work. Steve and I were like roommates, ships passing in the night. We didn't make time to go out on dates or to do things together." She laughs. "Not that we go out much now, but if Steve doesn't have a work commitment, we can be together."

A former sales executive says that being home "eased schedule conflicts." An environmental scientist says that staying at home with her son makes their lives "less stressful." Other women report that being at home "made me more relaxed," "improved our relationship," "gave us more time together."

Betsy, once a head librarian now working part-time, is convinced that "[O]ur quality of life is based on my being the base and anchor at home."

The key to it all—weathering the shift in roles, the issues of money and recognition—seems to be in communication, understanding, and a fundamental appreciation of each other's role in the family.

Carolyn, mother of three teenage boys, comments: "I think in your own marriage, you create your own sense of self and your own rights in the family. You divide things up as they work best, in the practical sense—what the balance is going to be, financially, and the whole business of child care. . . . If the woman decides that she's going to be the primary caregiver, there should be an understanding that when the husband is at home, he really takes over a lot of activities with the children and develops relationships with them, as well as giving the mother opportunities to do things important to her. There really has to be a feeling of support from husband to wife in dealing with children."

Conversely, many women recognize that husbands have their own adjustments to make. Gloria, a CPA and financial analyst, now at home with her four young children, says that she recognized "occasional" mutual resentment that her staying home causes: "[His] resentment of my bond forged with the children, and a seemingly "fun and games" lifestyle; as opposed to my resentment of his bonds to work and the outside world."

Making the psychic adjustment to the loss of a paycheck involves both parties rethinking their ideas about what constitutes work and how it is valued. Many of us entered into marriage with a tacit understanding that we were equal partners, without ever analyzing what that meant. There was no need to: before children, our lives were parallel—joined as little or as much as we liked or was convenient— for our contributions were both equal and similar. Neither really needed the other in any functional way; nor did we need the other's approval of what we were doing.

After children, with my decision to stay at home for a while, our marriage became dependent on a real division of labor—our contributions to the whole of our family were now much less similar, their equality much more a matter of perception. Where his contribution was quantifiable in terms of dollars, mine was not.

The divorce case of *Wendt vs. Wendt* made headlines in late 1997 and struck many at-home nerves. Although his wife had reportedly been a "good corporate wife" for years, according to the *Washington Post*, Mr. Wendt resisted her claim for half the marital assets, stating that she was not interested in business and that he had earned his money without her help.[5] On December 3, 1997, a Connecticut state court judge awarded Mrs. Wendt half of what he described as marital assets, although this was valued at $20 million of a $130 million estate.[6] The case sparked heated debates in the press about the value of a wife who "doesn't work," words that grated like unclipped fingernails on a blackboard on the sensibilities of at-home mothers, a number of whom wondered aloud if Mr. Wendt could have made his millions if he'd been picking up the kids from soccer, fitting them in shoes, carting them to the doctors, and helping them out with homework.

Sally, twenty-eight, has seen what goes on in the corporate world—both as an investment banker and as a reporter for the *Wall Street Journal*—and has also had to manage a household. She thinks that Mrs. Wendt was "100 percent correct."

"My husband probably did too. There are so many things to do in managing a household. . . . And you watch the executives in the company—me in investment banking or even the companies we dealt with. These men had committed their lives to their jobs, and because of that their wives had to commit themselves to their family, and [that commitment to the family] contributed hugely to the men doing so well."

For me, to know that my husband values my work at home with the children matters greatly. As we had our children, and I fashioned my professional activities around their preschool activities, marriage became more a partnership than ever, with much more at stake in its success or failure. Like my old law firm, where some partners did banking (bringing in the dollars) and other partners did trust administration and pro bono for charitable institutions (bringing in fewer dollars but more goodwill), we differentiated our work without devaluing our contributions.

This sense of being valued for our contribution—whether monetary or not—has played a critical role in the well-being of other marriages as well. Allison says that her husband, a doctor, really wanted her to stay at home for the sake of her son.

"Steve said, 'I want you to stay at home because you will research these parenting issues. You'll talk to our son in an intelligent fashion.' Rather than being demeaning, it was quite flattering. The marriage continued to be strong because if I had said, 'I'm going back to work,' he'd be very tempted to stay at home; he felt it was that important."

Jill, the engineer who initially felt that her income helped make her an equal partner with her husband, says now, after being home for a year, both their attitudes have changed. They've found that having one parent at home is good not only for the kids but for the smooth functioning of the household: "Michael finds that he likes having me home, knowing that if his stuff has to be picked up at the dry cleaner's, he doesn't have to worry about that, because I'll do it for him. And his dad recently died, so when it came time to getting the thank you notes all done for people who had sent flowers, I took care of that. All those things I'm happy to do now—I didn't have time before."

Kate, a former radio broadcaster, found her ego problems allevi-
ated when her husband, after moving his office to the house, learned
firsthand the nature of her contribution at home: "At first, Ed thought
that because I was home I wasn't doing anything. But two years ago,
when he started to work at home, and his office was at home, he got
to watch my day, which he'd never gotten to do before. He realized
that, number one, he'd lose his mind if he had to do it—by then we
had two kids—and number two, I was doing more than he thought I
was doing. . . . We finally had a discussion about how housework and
mothering are never completed. . . ."

Once both partners feel that their contributions are valued by the
other, it may be easier to work out the nuts-and-bolts issues of money
and domestic responsibilities.

Tracy admits that while money was "a big issue" in the beginning,
she and her husband resolved it by working out a budget, based on
the needs and income of the family as a unit: "On Quicken, he has his
budget, I have mine. It's based on what we've spent, historically. I never
feel guilty about what I can buy, because I know how much we have
and how much is allotted. . . ."

Tracy and her husband applied the same cooperative spirit to handling domestic issues. Tracy hates to cook, hates to think about cooking, and hates that it's her responsibility. When she told her husband
about it, he offered to do something to make her life less stressful.

"I finally came to the realization that I don't like to think about
what I want to make. If I enjoyed cooking, it would be a piece of cake.
But I've never liked it. If I could, I'd eat grilled cheese sandwiches the
rest of my life. But I can't, so I said, 'Why don't you take on the
responsibility of planning the meals? I will cook it, as long as you tell
me what we're going to have.' . . . And it works."

It is late morning in 1991, with the heat of the summer hanging heavily
in the air. Only 9:30, it feels like noon when I've been up since 5:00. With
three kids in camp and the fourth one nodding off on my shoulder, I am
itching to get to the computer to write. Holding my breath, I lean over the
crib rail and lower his tiny frame to the cool flat sheet. His eyelids flutter,
and his head starts to turn. I take a step toward the door, dropping down
to my knees and out of his sight. Waiting, I listen for cries of protest. But his
search is for his thumb, not for me. Finding it, he closes his eyes and
snuggles into sleep just as the telephone rings.

Darting into my bedroom, I dive across the bed. "Hello?" I whisper, breathless, into the receiver.

"Honey?" It is my husband.

"Oh, hi."

"Are you all right?"

"Yes, I just got Brian down. I've got so much to do, and I was afraid the phone would wake him."

"Honey?" he repeats, his voice unusually tentative.

"Yes . . . ?" I drawl. I know that voice; it's that "You're not going to like this, but remember I love you" voice.

"You remember that meeting with those guys from Boston? You know the meeting they wanted to have at our house on Thursday, just to get out of the city and see the burbs? . . . Remember I told you it was off?"

I listen, thinking about my writing deadline, about the swimming demonstration at camp on Wednesday and the family dinner party we're throwing Saturday night. I hear squeaking from the other room and wonder if the baby's ears are bothering him and whether he needs to be checked by the doctor this afternoon.

"Well, honey . . ."

"It's on?" I say finally.

"It's on."

"Here?"

"There."

"A business meeting. In our backyard. Thursday, " I say slowly, picturing the kids mixing mud potions on the outdoor furniture and hearing Andrew's quite excellent siren imitation resonate through the trees.

"Right. And after the meeting, they want to have a cocktail party."

"They do? Did you invite them?"

"Yes, honey. We can call a caterer. I'll call them. You won't have to do anything," he blurts.

"Of course I'll have to do something," I snap. "And I'll do it. But at least acknowledge that I'll have to do something."

"Ok. Thank you. I love you."

"I know."[7]

CHAPTER SEVEN

Desperately Seeking Soul Mates

Caught Between the Lines in the Mommy Wars

> "I might as well have landed . . . from Mars. I had
> absolutely nothing to do with my neighborhood. I didn't
> know a soul here. My whole life was wrapped up
> in my office."
>
> LORRAINE, former employee benefits manager

When a woman leaves or scales back her career to be at home, one of the most difficult adjustments can be with respect to friendships. Many of us felt very isolated initially—from our friends who continued to work full-time, as well as from the community of mothers in which we found ourselves.

My sense of isolation after I left the practice of law did not surprise me. After all, I had made multiple moves—from New York to Philadelphia, from city to suburbs, as well as from office to home. I was, in a very concrete sense, moving into foreign territory.

But even women who'd been living in the same place during their career-climbing years felt, when they decided to stay at home, as if they were moving to an alien land. In fact, for some women, one of the biggest deterrents to making the transition to at-home motherhood was the fear that they would have no peers to whom they could relate.

Christine says that her decision to finally leave her job had a lot to do with her first child starting elementary school. Up until then her daughter had attended a private nursery school, where "a lot of moms were the country club set. Nobody wore sneakers or wash and wear clothes!" Sitting in the kitchen with her third child, a two-year-old, playing nearby, Christine looks down at her sweater and jeans and laughs. "I kept thinking that maybe there was something wrong with the way I was doing it. I had a perception of stay-at-home moms; staying at home meant you wore linen, attended luncheons, and played tennis. I needed to find women who wore sweatshirts! At the nursery school, I did meet some nice moms, and I was invited to work on fund-raisers. But I still wasn't finding [many] people I could relate to. I could find them at work."

Similarly, Rachel, while working as a lawyer, had an uneasy relationship with the stay-at-home mothers who were her neighbors: "My stay-at-home neighbors would sit and chat with my babysitter. . . . It was almost as if she was their neighbor and not me."

Pat, living first in the city, then in the suburbs, also felt alienated from her neighbors. She describes the void: "I never felt I fit in with anyone. I couldn't fit in with the suburban moms who hung with the kids and who'd never had a career. People'd assume if we were the same age, we'd have everything in common. . . . Many of these women went from their parents' house to their husband's house. . . . The only thing we had in common was that we lived in the same community and had a child. I desperately needed to be part of women who'd had an education and career, but I didn't fit in there anymore because I wasn't maintaining a presence."

Similarly, Barbara, a former banker who had resigned her position with the birth of her second child, lived in the city and felt simultaneously set apart from her neighbors and estranged from her peers:

"I used to go to the park . . . there would be a smattering of people like myself, and the rest would be nannies, caretakers. So it was me and all the maids sitting on the bench having conversations about the kids, and I thought I was going nuts for about two years.

". . . After you're home, there comes this exclusion from the male network and the business community. You're not part of that anymore. People don't call you to say, 'Did you see this? Did you see that?'"

Many of us were trapped between an existence no longer ours and a reality to which we could not yet belong. We were captive of our preconceived notions—cultivated by years of career climbing in an insular world—assumptions both arrogant and naive about the kind of woman who stays at home with children. The fact that we were at home with children was incidental.

Allison remembers feeling this way: "When you've thought these [pejorative] things about stay-at-home mothers, and then you find yourself one, the only way to resolve the conflict is to say, 'Well, I'm different.'"

Anne, a college teacher, also remembers thinking that women at home were simply "not like me. [I'd think] 'Don't these people read? Don't these people care about politics? Don't these people—whatever?' And it seemed that the answers to these questions were 'no.' They love their kids and they do their wash, they drive around in minivans, and that's it."

Now that Anne's been home for a year with a one-year-old, she still grapples with these images: "I still think that that's not really me." She laughs. "But it is. I'm trying to reconcile these ideas that the women I see in the grocery store with their kids in the middle of the day could very well be like me, and I just have to get to know them."

But getting to know other like-minded women can be difficult when you're at home without the built-in social mechanism a workplace provides.[1]

When I had worked outside the home, I'd been with a group of peers, colleagues, friends, who, for the most part, had essentially similar educations, backgrounds, professional goals. Because we spent so much time at work, we had similar lifestyles and a ready-made, institutionalized network for connecting with one another.

In contrast, jumping to an at-home situation, I found myself connecting with people on a random basis, in the supermarket, in a nursery school pick up line, at the corner bus stop. In my mind I was a career person, yet my body was buying eggs in the supermarket at 10:00 A.M. in the middle of the week. I was having an identity crisis, a mind/body dilemma and an early midlife crisis all wrapped in one— not something you want to get into with a new acquaintance in the dairy aisle.

It was a frustrating, lonely period. In retrospect, I was desperately seeking soul mates.

I thought I would recognize them in the park: shell-shocked, disoriented, tentatively friendly but not quite comfortable among the wood chips, the twisty slides, and the sqeaking swings of a playground on a weekday morning. Older than the au pairs. Looking back on it, my senses were primed for them. I thought I wanted to find someone who had worked in an office, a hospital, a boardroom, or a courthouse. Someone who had once invested her passions in something or someone outside the home.

Someone like me.

A turncoat in the Mommy Wars.

Caught Between the Lines
of the Mommy Wars

The homeroom mother is a Harvard MBA who teaches Chinese part-time. The phone call comes at what I understand was once euphemistically called the dinner hour.

"The teacher wants four moms to come in each of three days to help with a Halloween project," she says.

Cradling the phone on my shoulder, I stare at a freezer full of plastic-wrapped packages. I know there is food in there somewhere.

"What day? How long?" I ask, pawing gingerly through the gray and silver shapes.

"Thursday, from 1:30 to 3:00."

I sigh. Work time. I've got an ominous deadline looming, not to mention soccer practices, piano lessons, shopping runs for school supplies, and assorted other family activities. School hours—when the kids are out of the house and I can actually think to the end of a sentence—are precious writing time.

"And this is to do what?" I ask, wondering if this octagonal translucent pink block could possibly be chicken and how long it would take to defrost.

"The teacher wants parents to help glue Halloween candy pieces onto candy maps."

What? "Candy maps?" My old life continually bumping up against my new, I envision chocolate bar skyscrapers, licorice streets, M&M people taking home late-night candy corn cabs. Then snapshots of my life as a preschool mom—cutting out snowflakes, making bead necklaces for Thanksgiving celebrations—tumble through my brain.

I think I'm too old for this.

After a moment of silence, the Harvard MBA speaks again.

"Well, I understand you have . . . this book." Has the voice grown colder, or is it just my hands? I close the freezer door. The voice continues. "Shall I just make a note not to call you for *anything* before February?"

I sigh again, crouching to pull the big spaghetti pot from the bottom cabinet. (Dinner tip: When all else fails, boil water.) "Joan, it's not as if I'm not doing anything at school. I'm helping with the school newspaper. I'm going in Monday to Julia's class to talk to them about writing."

"Oh, that sounds interesting."

"Well, at least it's something that's sort of unique. I mean, I'm talking about what I do."

"Well, maybe I should call you when something more glamorous comes up."

Pause. Damn. "Look, I'll do what I can. If you can get anyone else—"

"I'm calling you last," she says evenly. "I can't find anybody. Most of the moms in this class work."

"Right," I say, snarling to myself: And every at-home mom without some outside office hideaway is presumed to be sitting around, looking for things to do. But then I glance at my eight-year-old, huddled over a math worksheet. "Fine." I sigh. "Pencil me in."

There are not a great many issues that can pit sister against sister, neighbor against neighbor, woman against woman, and whether a mother should stay home to raise her children may not be the most volatile. Women don't really like to talk about the Mommy Wars—so designated by the national news magazines back in the eighties—those spoken and unspoken hostilities between women with jobs outside the home and women staying home with their kids. No one likes to discuss them or even acknowledge that they exist—least of all, those of us who've been on both sides, sometimes at the same time.

"I don't think there's hostility between women!" one mother told me angrily as we stood on the sidelines of a Saturday morning baseball game. A full-time administrative social worker and mother of three, she protested even the suggestion that the Mommy Wars still exist. "That whole issue is a way for the rest of the world to divide women. We ought to focus on the issues we have in common."

And so we ought. Perhaps fields such as social work—traditionally populated by women—don't foster the traditionally male attitudes about success that have a way of driving women apart.

But evidence of hostility still surfaces from time to time, especially if there is an appropriate forum. Tracy Riegel runs a local chapter of FEMALE (Formerly Employed Mothers at the Leading Edge),[2] for which she attends conferences on issues relating to work and family. She has seen and heard stories of emotions running high:

"FEMALE is about respecting choice about combining work and parenting. We want to stop the Mommy Wars . . . I do think it's women who do it to each other—women on both sides: the women who say, 'I can't believe you work. What are you doing sticking your kids in day care?' And the women who work who say, 'How can you stay at home? You must be brain dead.'"

And witness any business function where "working (outside the home) mothers" mingle with "at-home (working or not) mothers." If there is conversation, it is often staccato, the subtext speaking volumes:

"I envy you."

"I could never afford to stay home."

"You must be busy."

"Who takes care of your children?"

Or ask anyone who's tried to rally volunteers for a school or community function how many times he or she hears the response "I can't. I work."

And the newspapers still run the headlines. "DISPATCHES FROM THE MOMMY WARS" screams the February 15, 1998, cover of the *Washington Post Magazine*. In the article, author Tracy Thompson, herself a newly "at-home" mother, states:

> Feminists say they value sisterhood, but behind the scenes, stay-at-home mothers often criticize office-going moms for neglecting their kids, and working mothers often disparage their at-home counterparts for getting some sort of retro free ride.[3]

The concept of the Mommy Wars, though, is predicated on the idea that there are two distinct sides; that all women fall easily into one camp or the other—women who work full-time outside the home and women who "stay at home"; that each must defend and protect its position. It is an idea built on the old stereotypes that those of us driven by our careers carried with us through professional schools and into the workplace. It is an idea that's difficult to shake, especially for someone—like me ten years ago or perhaps like the author of the *Washington Post* story today—newly at home.

Certainly there exist some women of leisure playing golf and tennis all day—as well as fast-track, ninety-hour-a-week lawyers, doctors, and business professionals who have to pencil-in time with their kids. But more and more women fall somewhere in between, and the distinctions between them are merely matters of degree.

As Thompson observes, the concepts of "working mothers" and "stay-at-home moms" have become muddied by the reality of women's lives today. Many women fit in part-time work or work from home around the schedules of their children. Women with whom I've spoken for this book are homeroom mothers who make candy maps *and* teach foreign language. They're part-time physicians *and* head of the PTA. They're home taking care of kids *and* selling toys out of catalogs on the side. They're investment bankers *and* carpool chauffeurs. Working mothers *and* stay-at-home moms, they are part of what Thompson calls a new world of "working stay-at-home moms."

> What is then, a "stay-at-home mom"? Jayne would call herself one, and so would I. So, in fact, would every woman in my eight-member new-moms support group, a group that includes technical writers, one journalist, a nutritionist, a sign language interpreter for the deaf, and a schoolteacher. All but two of us are doing some kind of work on a freelance or part-time basis at home. But, because we are working and getting paid for it, the Department of Labor counts us as being in the labor force—just as if we were punching a clock and working 50 hours a week in an office.[4]

So "stay-at-home mothers" now include those who work at home, those who freelance, and those who work part-time around their kids' schedules. (All of these are counted as "working mothers" by the Department of Labor.) Add to these the former career women who are plotting their next moves and the women who've not had careers but are thinking about them for the future, and you have a population of mothers whose collective mind-set is not at all opposed to "working."

As I will discuss in Part Three, even the women who are out of the work force entirely often plunge into their home and volunteer activities with a commitment rivaling any paid employment. Increasingly, more women are changing the way in which they work, reevaluating their choices, and moving from one side to the other—and back again.

Then, to borrow from the old sixties song, what are we fightin' for? And who is fighting whom?

To conclude that there are no clear sides is not to say that the Mommy Wars are over. "I sometimes feel as if the conflict is in myself," says Anne. "The biases about what it means to be home all the time—I have to fight against them in my own mind."

Women who are both at home and working part-time may get the best—and the worst—of both worlds. "Murder Trial About More than a Nanny" read the headline in the *New York Times* on October 24, 1997, when a British au pair stood trial for the murder of her nine-month-old charge.[5] The mother, Deborah Eappen, may have been considered by some of her professional peers a less than ambitious ophthalmologist because she worked only three days a week and came home to have lunch with her infant child. But upon the death of her child, Dr. Eappen was castigated as one of the "working mothers who consign their children to the care of others."[6]

The fundamental conflict remains, waged as much within ourselves as between us: how can we raise healthy and happy children and fulfill ourselves professionally?

Anne Roiphe writes in *Fruitful*:

> Motherhood and work life are not like glove in hand. They are more like dog and cat, in conflict, and when one is missing from their lives women yearn for the other. Most women need both.[7]

Yet most of us have more of one and less of the other. At any point in time, to the extent we have less, we envy those who seem to have it all. Not seeing their problems, we see only someone else fulfilling the less developed part of ourselves. Under these circumstances, insecurities appear like clutter in a playroom; defensive feelings sprout like weeds after a warm spring rain. The wars—the hostilities fueled by insecurity and defensiveness, envy and resentment, guilt and frustration—persist, if mostly internally, as an undercurrent among mothers, feeding a stream of anxiety that runs through our childbearing and child-rearing years.

Philosophical Versus Practical Conflicts

Many of the women with whom I've spoken were reluctant to speak out against women making choices different from theirs—at least as to the welfare of the kids.

"The Mommy Wars don't exist anymore—at least on a philosophical level," one woman told me. "We've seen a generation of kids with
working moms grow into adults, and they're fine!"

Other women take issue with this conclusion; they fear the kids
today are not all fine but are hesitant to attribute blame to one factor—
such as mothers working outside the home. On one thing we all seem to
agree: mothers have too long shouldered the blame for all the ills of their
progeny.[8]

So the philosophical and ethical debate—as to whether a parent,
usually but not necessarily the mother, *should* be at home to raise
her children—becomes an intensely personal challenge within ourselves as individuals. I work from home for a variety of reasons, *one*
of which is that I've come to believe—on a very personal level—that
having me at home works best for *our* family—considering the number of kids, their respective ages and personalities, the nature of my
husband's job, our finances, and the dynamics of our family life. What's
more, I *like* working at home—most of the time. For others the issues
may additionally encompass extended family circumstances, the neighborhood, the schools, and a host of other particulars. Whatever I feel
about my children, I would rather befriend than judge women whose
choices are different from mine, for fundamentally we are more alike
than different.

Many former career women at home with whom I've spoken echo
these thoughts, perhaps because so many of us have felt torn between
our own career ambitions and domestic realities and still juggle many
responsibilities that conflict with undivided attention to child care.

And stay-at-home mothers are an eclectic lot, bringing as many
opinions to the issue as their different experiences before motherhood. As Rachel, a former lawyer and business executive, comments,
"You have to watch what you say and to whom."

Many women who've left careers still feel greater affinity for women
who are now, or have been in the past, working outside the home.
Complained one woman with a PhD in science, "The conversational
level of women who stay home from the beginning is pretty low. They
talk about laundry bleach and Biz for sweatsocks. I found it appalling."

The diversity of lifestyles among women at home also creates
divisions. Comments Kate, "I tend to be friendlier with women who
are either working or who do a great deal of volunteer work, like I do.

Because the kids go to private school, I know a lot of women who get up in the morning, deliver the kids to school, go play tennis, go to the club for lunch, and then play golf until they pick the kids up. I have nothing in common with them; they have nothing in common with me, and in fact, we don't want to know each other."

And many women now at home feel empathy for mothers who work outside the house all day. Lisa, once a neurobiologist, is now a real estate salesperson who sets her own hours.

"How do I feel about the tight suit brigade? With the high heels you see in the grocery store at 6:00 P.M.? I feel sorry for them, because I know how they feel. That's the way I used to feel. You're tired and there's no food in the refrigerator, and there's no milk. Before you can go home and take those shoes off, you have to go to the grocery store. Me, I can go to the grocery store at 2:00 in the afternoon and make sure there's milk."

Empathy, however, can turn to resentment, when at-home mothers feel they're shouldering too much of the school and community load. Complains one at-home mom, "What really gets me is when I have to make thirty calls to get help for a school function, an hour is all I'm asking, or a batch of brownies, and a woman says, 'I can't; I work.' I want to say, 'Well, don't we all, honey, don't we all.'"

With school, community, and church or synagogue activities depending heavily on parent help, at-home mothers express resentment about having to cover the responsibilities of mothers who are not at home. The feeling is that in giving a blanket refusal to help— "I can't; I work," "working mothers" implicitly overvalue their time and undervalue the time of at-home mothers who may feel just as busy and frantic.

Nor is it simply community work that's a source of tension, but personal responsibilities as well, with respect to both home and family. Some at-home mothers complain that the older children of some "working mothers" are less supervised and often end up in the homes of the at-home moms.

Donna, a former compensation analyst and marketing associate now working part-time around the schedules of her two elementary-age children, says that she "absolutely resents the fact that a lot of my working friends ask me for favors all the time—carpooling help, baby-sitting, groceries, educational projects, etcetera—because I am at home."

Resentment about favors as well as about any disproportionate community work stems in part from feeling overwhelmed and over-burdened, in part from the feeling that such requests are presumptive and judgmental, and comes from a lack of understanding of what at-home mothers' lives are like. Donna concludes that people must think she's "lazy for the most part. My friends that work don't realize what it's like to do everything. They have nannies, housekeepers, and landscapers. They work and make schedules by phone for their kids. They come home to the chaos I'm accustomed to all day long."

Compounding these feelings, in some women, is the notion that women who've made career sacrifices are through their favors effectively subsidizing—in time and energy with the kids—the career efforts of women not choosing to make those sacrifices. For mothers not financially able to stay at home, there is more sympathy.

Pam, the mother of two boys, explains: "There's a different feeling about moms who have to work. The moms at home will take up the slack for that mom. [But as for] the moms who choose to work, those whose husbands already have a good income, who *choose* to also have a high-powered job, the moms at home are not quite so willing to take up the slack there. When they get a call from that mom saying, 'Listen, I just couldn't get to the store for that juice [or whatever]. Could you pick up an extra one?' the moms are not quite so willing to do that—they'll do it for the kid, but not simply because that mom made those choices. Picking up kids, dropping off kids—that's [what] moms at home get used for a lot. . . . I don't think people know what we do. Unless they've been a stay-at-home mom, they don't know what we do."

It is important to point out that the perceptions of being judged go both ways. There are mothers who work all day who, despite their efforts to get involved, feel frustrated by community activities that sometimes seem deliberately designed to shut them out and resent the implication that by working full-time they are making no sacrifices for their children. Melissa is an associate professor of medicine working fifty hours a week doing clinical work and teaching as well as some research and adminstrative work. She tells a different story:

"What I feel a lot is that with the stay-at-home moms, particularly in relation to involvement in the schools, it's a closed club. For the working moms to get involved is close to impossible. The PTA meetings are all at 9:30 in the morning! . . . What many of us who work perceive is an attitude of the stay-at-home moms. . . . If you're a full-time working mom, and for whatever reason you're able to volunteer in the schools, you're perceived as a threat to the stay-at-home moms because somehow then they're less than adequate because you're volunteering and working and undermining the whole reason for being home.

"... Even if I can rearrange my schedule, people will say, 'Oh, don't worry about it, you're too busy to come.'

"I'll say, 'No, but really I'd like to. I want to participate.'

"'Oh, no, you're too busy. Don't worry about it.'

"What I find, then, is that I never identify myself as a physician. . . . I almost hide what I do."

Melissa feels the efforts of working mothers are almost "deliberately sabotaged."

"Under some pressure to have meetings at night, they have one or two token evening PTA meetings, which then get boycotted by the stay-at-home moms and are then [deemed] 'a failure.' Their perception is that they've made sacrifices in their career to be at home and they should be able to do these things at their convenience."

The gulf, though seemingly a chasm, between women and what we all in fact want out of life may not be as great as we think. But problems of perception are no less divisive, no less destructive than substantive differences. If women don't judge each other, but feel judged nonetheless, there is still a big bridge to build toward understanding and cooperation.

Sources of Conflict:
Competition and Expectations

Long before I learned how to make a peanut butter and jelly sandwich while simultaneously nursing an infant and answering the telephone, I learned how to compete. Those of us who worked in traditionally male professions such as business, law, and medicine knew we'd be competing with men, knew we'd be vying hard simply to shatter old assumptions about the relationship between gender and ability.

Similarly, women rising to positions of power and visibility in other fields kept their competitive edge sharp. Cathy had a visible job in a major city as executive director of a nonprofit arts group. She says, "One of the problems is that there's this competitive thing. . . . When you're head of an organization, when you're a big guy, when you're a girl in these big jobs, you have to act so polished and straight and controlled and so proper and so good . . . all of these things. I used to get in trouble all the time for being tactless—direct and honest, really, maybe it'd sound a little rude sometimes, too. There's stress in not being real . . . that same old horseshit competitiveness we experienced as junior high girls, on a far more sophisticated level."

Once children differentiated my life from the lives of my male colleagues, another set of expectations—both cultural and private—kicked in. Now I was to be a successful professional *and* a successful mother.

Now I competed with other "career" mothers.

And I competed with myself.

I wanted to be successful at work and at home, and I measured my success against the successes of other women—or, at least, what I perceived to be their successes. For some time after I left the law, whenever I'd see a classmate profiled for some professional accomplishment, I'd look for differences between the circumstances of our lives.

I'd look to see if she had children.

If she did, I'd count them.

Other women confess to making similar comparisions between their lives and those of others. Says Jessica, "My two closest friends are much more accomplished than I. One is a physician, one is a professor. . . . They both have three children. . . . I feel unbelievably lucky to have them as friends; there is such incredible support and understanding for each other. We're like family, because none of us has family in the immediate area. On the other hand, sometimes I think when I get overwhelmed, my God, look at what they're doing. How can I feel overwhelmed with this? I feel as if I'm not doing anywhere near as much as these other women. It's not so much a competition as it is looking at myself and saying, 'Am I doing enough? Is this adequate?'"

Sherry, a freelance editor and mother of two boys, ages eight and twelve, remembers that when she was working at a publishing company with a baby in day care, "There was this other woman. Her husband was a lawyer. She was nice. She was perfect. She had four children. Her husband was handsome. She was successful. She worked out every day. We'd talk about her, and then we'd say, 'We hate her.' . . . Had she been doing this without kids, without the husband, without being perfect in every area, we'd think, 'Go!' "

Pat, now a home-based marketing consultant, was a project manager in urban redevelopment until she left to raise her son and still feels a keen sense of competition with her women friends. "Every time I'm at lunch with one of my friends who's president of a company or executive director of a theater, I come away with a real ache in the middle of my being. But then I come home, and . . . here's my son."

Whether our expectations breed desires or our desires create expectations, many of us yearn to "have it all." And we resent being judged by those whose choices are different from ours no matter which side of the office door we find ourselves. Allison left her job as an associate at a big-city law firm to be home with her son: "I'm the same kind of person, with the same kind of intensity. That's what people don't realize," she says. "The person I want to be is the person with a successful career and happy, well-adjusted kids. . . . Those feelings, goals, ambitions don't go away."

Perhaps it is because we are both female and human, our ambitions both private and public, our standards for success both cultural and what we individually feel in our hearts to be true. The mother who by choice or necessity works all day outside the home is still a mother, with the attendant concerns, anxieties, and pleasures about her kids. The mother at home still has interests, goals, and hopes for the fulfillment of her own dreams.

At the very time we need our women friends, we push them away.

Moving Beyond the Stereotypes: Getting to Know One Another

Fortunately, with experience comes understanding and, with any luck, growth. But it can take some time.

Cheryl remembers a rocky start to a friendship with one woman: "When I was first at home, I met this woman (an accountant whose job took her all over the world), and we both had an attitude problem. She was working, and I wasn't, and I was very defensive, because what was wrong with me? Later, she became disenchanted with her job. She invited me over for lunch one day, and she was a wreck. I started throwing out these ideas about how we'd thought women who were home were stupid, and she looked at me, flabbergasted. . . . That's why it's so hard to be in this position, because you *know* what they are thinking."

Eventually, the stereotypes erode and decay, decimated by the details of daily life: a long conversation on the sidelines of a soccer field, a cup of coffee with the mother of a kindergarten child's playmate, an afternoon side by side lifeguarding the kids at the neighborhood pool. Day by day, my preconceived notions about at-home mothers gave way as I began getting to know each of them.

I discovered several things.

There were many women who had not planned to be at home; who had succeeded in their professional lives and had moved on to child raising for a variety of reasons. What's more, there were bright, intelligent, interesting women who had always intended to be at home, who had always believed that it was important, who had by virtue of personality, upbringing, or circumstance never dreamed of working full time while their kids were young.

But being at home is like being anywhere. There are people with whom you relate and people with whom you have little in common, and the work/family dilemma is but one of a multiplicity of issues that frame our friendships.

Anne, the college teacher with a PhD in English, in reconciling her own self-image with what she used to believe about women at home, reflects, "What's surprising to me is that there's no such thing as typical. When you talk about the stereotypes of the stay-at-home moms or the working moms, you think that there's some norm. . . . There are commonalities, but it just seems to me that there are so many different cases, so many different reasons that people stay at home. That's a freeing idea."

It is sometimes difficult to keep up with old friendships, particularly if paths don't cross anymore. Jean was head of the juvenile division of a county public defender's office when the chance to adopt a baby landed in her lap one day. After ten years of trying to have a child, she leaped at the opportunity. Soon afterward, she discovered she was pregnant. Now at home with a two- and a three-year-old, she says, "My friendships with other women have completely changed. I've completely lost touch with all of my other professional women friends. The only women I have contact with have children under the age of five! I can't knock it, though. They are women who were in the work force and have decided to stay home with their growing children. They are a wonderful source of information, companionship, and shoulders to cry on—and vice versa."

On one thing all the women surveyed agree: our friendships with women become more and more important as we get older. Says Jessica, "There's a support now I feel I can get only from my female friends. There's an understanding of what it's like to juggle all these issues."

CHAPTER EIGHT

Relating to the Kids

Hovering Neurotic or Positive Role Model?

"I'd never had total care of them. Anytime I had a rehearsal in
the morning and a concert at night, we'd have somebody there
all day, so the kids had some consistency. So being at home did
take some adjustment.They had learned to manipulate me,
and now I had to learn not to let them. Before I'd been the
mother figure that everyone wanted to be with, but I was
much less in control than the baby-sitters. So we had to
learn to work together."
PATRICIA, former cellist in the Philadelphia Orchestra

Your children are your children, no matter what. But when you're
around more, the dynamics of the relationship shift somewhat.
It's ironic.

In 1984, as a new mother returning to work, I found myself often
defending my choice to remain at my lawyer job. I argued that my
absence would not in any way harm my baby or impair his development.
But there were always those, shouting loudly, who said it would.

Now, as an older mother of four children, ages six to thirteen, I find
myself often defending my choice to subordinate my professional life
to the schedules of my children. I argue that my presence will not in
any way harm them or impair their development.

But there are others, shouting loudly, who say it will.

Women who left or scaled back their careers are sensitive to this
latter charge, often because it is what they themselves were prepared
to believe: that if you are home all day or for much of the day, you
do an injustice not only to yourself but to your children as well. *Business
Week*, in reviewing Joan Peters's book *When Mothers Work*, states:

[W]omen who find it impossible to balance career and family are not always benefitting their children by staying home, she says. Rather, "kids profit intellectually from exposure to many people," she argues, and "maternal employment creates an opportunity for [them] to form other close connections" at day care and with other relatives.[1]

At least three interrelated dangers reportedly lurk in the world of mothers at home with children:

1. You'll go nuts. Brain cells will dissipate from boredom and stress faster than bubbles bursting in a rose garden on a warm summer's day.
2. You'll hover and dote, turning into a caricature of a mother, in the process robbing your children of initiative and the power of independent thought.
3. You'll be a terrible role model.

Any or all of these things can and do happen to some degree from time to time. But these are perils of parenthood, not motherhood or at-home motherhood. Perhaps the argument is that the more engaged I am in mothering, the higher the risk. Maybe so.

My children are the unwitting eye of the storm of this conflict in my professional life, the source of confusion and clarity, distraction and focus, complication and simplicity, compromise and unwavering commitment. If I'd never had them, I would be a lawyer caged in a glass cubicle somewhere high above the earthworms and the crocuses, the soccer fields and the jungle gyms. I would know little of Zeo Turbo Megazords or backyard garden snakes; I'd have no clue how to play Pooh sticks at the edge of a stream.

Maybe, being home, it is more of a challenge to create a life for myself that is interesting to me and inspiring for them and that maintains a healthy balance between comfort and control in the relationship. Not every at-home mother loves babies, has the patience of Mr. Rogers, or is certain that she's doing the right thing at any given moment. But on the whole, mothers are at home because of the children: because they want to be there for them and because mothers believe and fervently hope that their presence will both nurture and inspire their children.

And so they can respond to the objections, one by one.

Objection 1: You'll Go Nuts

The daily mother-baby relationship is dramatically oversimplified and considerably underrated in the dominant discourse of the day, often reduced to "[p]laying peek-a-boo and singing 'Twinkle, Twinkle, Little Star' all day long."[2] When I stopped practicing law, my relationship with my one-year-old changed from an evening, night, and weekend thing—condensed quality moments of time—to an all-day-long affair. Yes, there was tedium. Yes, there was frustration and loneliness, particularly when children were very young—too young to be much interested in the significance of the pope's visit to Cuba; not old enough to discuss appropriate jurisdictional authority of the Independent Counsel (or on some nights, watch the evening news).

But I had been a lawyer and knew that professions with greater recognition than mothering have their share of tedium, frustration, and loneliness. Recalls Allison, another lawyer at home with an infant and a three-year-old: "People would say [if you leave the law to stay home with a baby], 'You'll miss the intellectual stimulation.' And then I would contrast being at home with doing something like a document production where you're spending hours looking through documents that might be remotely relevant to your case. You're looking at a great mass of boring, irrelevant documents, hoping to find that needle in a haystack.

"How incredibly mind-deadening that is! Much more mind-deadening than anything I've done at home.

"Plus, I've also taken those same analytical and negotiating skills and applied them to parenting, because I found that there were whole new subjects I had to learn about. With every problem that cropped up, we tended to do research. (She laughs.) We'd go out and get a book, do research, apply it. Just the same way you'd make an argument to a court."

Pat was a city person. She lived in the city; she worked in the city; her work as a city planner was about the city. Having a child taught her other things about herself; made her believe in a whole other dimension of herself: "Having a child put me in touch with the natural cycles of life. . . . You know how when they're little, every day is a new experience . . . because it was so physically demanding, during that time in my life I felt as if I could have been one of those women who won the West."

Other women confirm that having had a career gave them perspective and the confidence that they were capable people staying at home by choice, not by default.

Kelly, thirty-four, was a senior VP of communications before she first cut back to part-time, then resigned her position when her twins were fifteen months old. "I realized that my twins were 'little people,' and it was a small window of time that I'd be able to be with them before they went to school. I'm awfully glad I tried working because I have no regrets."

Similarly, Pam, who loved her job as a nurse coordinator of a team of neurosurgeons, says, "I could never have done this the other way around. I could never have been one of those women who got married and had kids the first year. I would have been a complete banana. . . . I don't feel as if I have to go out and experience what it's like to have a career. It is definitely a choice. I choose to raise my children and not have somebody else do it, because I thought this was important."

Not all women find babies intellectually interesting. Lisa, the neurobiologist, found caring for babies tedious. "They're not intellectually stimulating when they're two and four. They're work. They're physical labor. We used to nickname them 'the digestive systems.' That's all they were—you put food in one end and clean up the other end. I hated it, absolutely hated it."

But not all people like science or banking or teaching or the law; we don't dismiss entire fields because some people find them boring.

Allison found life with young children to be much more interesting than she'd ever given it credit for: "To me it's been fascinating from almost an anthropological point of view, the development of a human being. . . . They start out so unformed. . . . Then he starts walking, talking, speaking. When language develops, you really start getting . . . blown away, because you see what it means to be human. To me [raising a child] is watching the human condition."

For me, it was also a love affair and in open seas: exhausting and exhilarating, serene and fraught with turbulence, and subject to continual change as he grew, change compounded with each birth of a sibling. Every time I began to think I knew what I was doing, the current shifted.

The constant change, the daily discoveries, the very aspects that kept me off balance, also helped keep me interested.

And I learned never to think I knew too much.

On a Friday morning in 1990, the crying starts early. We are clustered around the kitchen island. The older two of the three children are slipping down off their stools in a race to catch a few minutes of the animated chatterbox before school. Left at the island are abandoned Cheerios float- ing in milk in an unbreakable ABC bowl, raisin toast rinds hanging off the yellow plate, three swallows of orange juice in a *Tyrannosaurus rex* jelly glass, and two-year-old Andrew.

"OK," I call, whirling from sink to counter to sink to trash with soggy cereal and cold coffee. "Turn off that TV. Get your jackets on!"

Amid the sounds of running feet and jumping to reach backpack straps dangling from the closet shelf, the littlest child sits staring over a bowl of sliced bananas.

"Andrew, sweetie, time to get ready for school," I gently prodded, reaching for his glass of untouched apple juice.

"No," he says to the bowl of bananas, tightening his grip on the juice glass.

"Come on, sweetie, it's time to go to school."

He lifts his head and locks his round blue eyes on me. "No."

"Gregory will be there."

"NO." His eyes begin to swim, his voice to waver, and his lower lip to quake.

We stare at one another in a silent standoff. "You like school," I say help- lessly, the words ringing hollow.

"NO."

I break the stare and walk past him for his blue windbreaker, but his sobs stop me halfway there. Giant tears slide down his cheeks. "No go school. Stay home. No go school. No." Reaching a crescendo, he blurts what he knows from his brother to be final words: "NO WAY!"

This is the end of the second of two rotten weeks of his new pre- preschool. I anticipated some tears when I left him at first, but the teachers said he perked up as soon as I left, and although this is the kind of thing mothers have to take on faith, I believed them. If it had been crying only on my departure from the school, I probably could have dealt with it. But the second day he wailed with painful recognition as we pulled into the parking lot. The third day it was earlier in the car, after we dropped off his sister, when we turned left instead of right out of her school's driveway.

"Go baaghk home," he commanded in his guttural way. As I began my cheerful blabber about toys and kids and fun things to do at school, his protests became louder, and he squirmed against the straps of the car seat. "Go baaghkk home. Go baaghkk home. Go baaaaghhhhhkkkk hooooooommmmme," he sobbed. On the fourth day it begins at breakfast, and on the fourth day I listen.[3]

They say that raising children after your first is a breeze; you are more relaxed; you've been through it before; you know the ropes. I discovered that this is true and it is not true. I'd been through the routine things, the diaper changes, the ear infections, even the nightmares. And with my second, third, and fourth children I did not make lists of concerns for the pediatrician like the one I found stuck in a notebook from my first: "Cries at night—causes?" "Flashbulb hurt eyes?" "Red spot on left thigh?" "Bathwater dangerous to drink?"

But if my first child taught me about knowing a child, the second, third, and fourth taught me how different children can be from one another. Four children, four personalities. They all go to bed under one roof, but two sleep motionless, one under, one over, the covers, and the other two thrash about their beds from side to side and head to toe. Once when checking on the kids before we went to sleep, we found our daughter sleeping soundly on the floor on the other side of the room—she had just fallen and rolled. And the older they get, the more they make themselves known to me. When they were little, they all wanted the red cup at breakfast, but chances were good they'd want four different drinks in them. In groups, one is shy, one gregarious, one deliberate, one impulsive.

When our third child was born, we vowed to keep as many records, take as many pictures, and give him as many opportunities as we had given to the first two. This is what the pre-preschool thing was all about. It was not for child care. It was for him. It was to give him the chance to have his own group of friends, his own schoolbag, his own artwork to tack on the kitchen wall. His brother had gone to this school and had loved it. Well, my then youngest told me with his tears, "School at two may have worked for Danny, but it's not for me."

Perhaps we wanted to be the same parents for each of our children, forgetting that we were dealing with different individuals, each growing up with his own spot in the family, each of whom at two necessarily had a different family from the others at that age. Perhaps we were trying to be even-handed and conscientious; we'd been through

this and we knew what two-year-olds needed. Perhaps we were just trying to do the best we could. In the midst of our struggle to impart the
wisdom of experience, we realized that we had yet a lot more to learn.
And the learning continues as they grow.

Eventually their babble turns to conversation and, as opinions take
shape, finding expression in words—sentences, paragraphs—crying
jags evolve into skillful negotiations. Nap times give way to soccer
schedules, competing with piano lessons, baseball games, and birthday parties, as the children, who were once reflections of what parents
wanted to see, develop their own interests, talents, and friends. Faster
than the red winter sun slips from the horizon into night, babies trans-
form into toddlers into preschoolers into genuine little kids.

A year or two—or maybe three—was all I thought my working
from home would be. When I first began writing for a local parenting newspaper, my bio informed readers that I was "taking a break
from the practice of law."

But as my children grew, my relationships with them grew as well—
more interesting, more challenging, more frustrating. Rather than feeling "brain dead," I felt myself continually challenged by increasingly
complicated beings. Rather than feeling less needed at home, I felt more
so. And there were still times when I thought I'd lose my mind.

There was the morning I poured orange juice on Andrew's head.

He was eight at the time.

At the time, I felt I had no choice.

It is in the midst of the morning rush to get my three younger kids out of
the house—the dressing, the picking out of clothes, the hunting through the
laundry for the sweatpants that match the shirt with the number 4 on it. I
have shepherded them through breakfast, made their sandwiches for
lunch, corraled at least one of them to practice the piano, and watched—as
the minutes ticked by—the youngest tie his shoes, his laces emerging at last
from a tangle of fingers and loops in a limp but victorious bow. Now it is
late. Very late. My five-year-old will miss his bus. The others will be late
to class.

It is now 8:50. We have to leave.

Swiping at the blueberry-stained upper lip of my five-year-old child with
a wet paper towel, I pull on my coat and round the bend of the kitchen,
ready to bolt out the door, when I see it.

A sea-green plastic bowl, milk and soggy bits coating its bottom, sits defiantly on the table. Day after day I have asked Andrew to carry his empty cereal bowl from the kitchen table to the sink. "Do it without being asked," I said. "I am not your servant," I said, again and again. Yesterday I'd asked him. The day before. The day before the day before. Today I have asked him. One too many times.

Yet there it is, sitting there, silently screaming at me.

"Andrew!" I shout.

Thump, thump, thump, he comes bounding down the stairs, his snow jacket whispering all the way.

"What?" He stands there staring at me the way he does, not a foot from me, freckles floating on his pale cheeks.

I open my mouth to say it. One more time. But I can't find the words.

I look at the bowl, then back at him. "Please take it," I think, I wish, I pray. "Please take it over."

He stares at me, blue eyes, freckles, insolence and innocence combined.

In one swift motion I pick up the glass, half full of juice, and turn it over on his straw-colored hair.

"MOOOMMMMMMM!" he screams. His eyes widen, pulp matting his long pale eyelashes together. "What did you do?" he shrieks.

"I poured orange juice on your head," I say in surprise.

And so it goes. Some days I do feel as if I'm losing it, and I'm tempted to take an outside job, a real job, any job. Some days I feel jaded by this parenting thing, my senses dulled to the miracle that is mine.

And then at an odd moment, I see them, really see them—flying on bicycles down the street or laughing and tumbling in the grass or throwing a ball in an arch across the sky or curling around a book in a patch of sunlight on the sofa or studying their reflections in the oven door or doing a thousand other things . . . I hear their laughter and their shouts, their singing and their cries. I feel the velvet arms of my youngest hug my neck. And I think, "Oh, my God." I can't believe these kids are mine.

Merry, a video producer turned writer and at-home mother of two girls, ages eight and eleven, expressed it this way: "Every time my kids say 'Mom' and look at *me*, I'm amazed, blessed, incredulous. I can't believe, even now, that I'm lucky enough to be their mother. I'm amazed that I go to teacher conferences, drive to swim team, tennis, piano.

That they look at me, thinking that I'm their mom, just like it's normal, just like automatic. It's anything but normal, and I feel like I've lived more than one life. Who I was before kids is long gone."

Objection 2: You'll Hover and Dote

hover (huv'er)—2. To keep lingering about; to wait near at hand[4]

The at-home mother is often painted as a hovering neurotic (who else would accept such a job?) "whose sole charge in life is to follow [her children] around and cater to their every nose drip, diaper change, and puncture wound."[5]

(Actually, small children in diapers with runny noses and puncture wounds probably do need someone to hover.)

Once they are out of diapers; once they are taking standardized tests, the consequences of hovering and doting are dire. *Working Mother* magazine reports researchers have "revealed" that:

> . . . children of working mothers have an edge in several areas: They have higher math and reading achievement levels than the children of non-employed mothers, enjoy higher self esteem, and report a greater emphasis on independence in their homes.[6]

OK. Fine. So we all know mothers who obsess a little, who won't let go, who still monitor their grown sons' diets and let them bring their laundry home.

So maybe I shouldn't have quizzed my three-year-old firstborn on the parts of a steam engine the morning of his first show and tell at nursery school as if he were about to make a presentation to a board of directors ("Cow-catcher? Sweetie, can you say, cow-catcher?"). Maybe I shouldn't have freaked out that Sunday night when I discovered that the same child, at eleven years old, had written exactly four sentences for his entire research project due the next day on "Landforms of the Midwest" and at 7:30 was now poking around in my office, casually asking, "Do we have any poster paper in this house?"

Conscientious student-lawyer-woman that I had been, I threw myself into this job of mothering. Other women confess to doing the same. Allison says that she felt the pressure upon becoming a mother and doesn't know if it's exacerbated by being at home: "I'm a perfectionist. . . . Mothers have such a lion's share of the responsibility for how kids turn out, I think especially if you decide to stay home. If your kids don't turn out OK or don't become successful, you feel responsible, whereas if I were working . . ." Her voice trails off. "I think you get the blame either way."

You may get the blame either way, but there's that feeling that if you're working outside the home, at least you would have accomplished something else during that time you were screwing up the kids!

It can be argued that how obsessed we are with our children is a function of personality, not whether I spend my days at home or in an office. We give our children different combinations of our time, our money, our energies. Anyone who's tried to get a parking space at Toys "R" Us during the holiday season or weave his way through the parent paparazzi at a nursery school play knows that we parents can make quite a fuss about our children. The daily experience—and exhaustion—of mothering has taught me when to pull back, when to get in there, when to let consequences happen. I don't do homework anymore, except as an occasional consultant; at those few concerts and class plays when I remember to bring the camera, I inevitably forget the film.

What is it about being at home—in and of itself—that causes critics to yell "hovering neurotic"?

Back in 1963, it was attributed to mothers' lack of interests beyond their children. Betty Friedan wrote of a "new and frightening passivity, softness, boredom in American children," which she connected to "mothers who . . . were fulfilling their roles as women in the accepted, normal way. Some had more than normal ability, and some had more than normal education, but they were alike in the intensity of their preoccupation with *their children, who seemed to be their main and only interest.*"[7] [Italics added.]

Of course, if mothers *do* have other interests, as most today do, if they have many, many interests, and if they in fact have had full-blown non-child-related careers, they may fall prey to the modern reason at-home mothers are presumed to be overly attentive to their children:

[F]ull-time mothers, *denied the attention and respect they feel to be their due* [italics added], may be inclined to manipulate rather than monitor their children to ensure an outcome that will bring them, vicariously, that attention and respect. Ironically, it is these mothers' refusal to abdicate responsibility, to allow their children to live their own lives free of a chronic sense of guilt or expectation, that makes them guilty of the insensitivity characteristic of 'negligent' parents.[8]

Yet few of us deliberately overload our kids, be it with time, money, or material things. Women at home may have more time than money to give their kids. But the women with whom I spoke were well aware of the dangers of doting. Pat has one teenage son and runs her own consulting business out of her house.

"One of my greatest fears—whether I have one child or four—I work every day to avoid being overfocused on my child so that I don't create dependency, so that I do not become an enabler. . . . I truly believe that if you don't maintain your focus, you start looking to your child for affirmation that you don't get from the spouse, from society. In my case, I have a child with a learning disability. I have to be careful that I don't let that disability create dependency. . . . I'm terrified of overfocusing because I'm at home. But I would be terrified, if I were working full-time, of not being there enough."

The line between monitoring and manipulating is a fine one every parent must draw. It's always a balancing test, from either side of the office door. How much of a presence is needed? How much is too much?

In some ways, working from home has made it easier for me to give up control over my children's lives. Whenever I've had child care, I've been sure to find someone who would play with the kids, stay in the same room with them, watch them like a hawk. I wanted her there, "in their faces," supervising all the time. Yet as they get older, I realize that growing up, breaking away, becoming adults doesn't happen in one magic moment, but in fits and starts. They pull against the reins, and I make a calculated guess as to how much to let go.

I'm uncomfortable letting a baby-sitter supervise while the kids cook on a gas stove, ride their bikes into the next town, or make transportation arrangements on their own.

On the other hand, when I'm in the house writing, my thirteen-year-old son bakes cookies for a project at school, my eleven-year-old daughter walks into the town center to pick up groceries with her friend, my nine-year-old rides his bike through the park. The fact that

I'm accessible, available to put out a fire, round up a kid who's not home on time, and tend to scrapes from a nasty fall off a bike, makes me more—not less—likely to encourage independence.

Even with a child as young as three, Allison agrees. "Since I'm at home, there's not the pressure to have every moment be 'quality time.' I can say to my son, 'Go off and play by yourself for a while.'"

Most women I know, and those with whom I've spoken for this book, are busy. Between working at home, part-time jobs, volunteer gigs, and all the wife and mother stuff—supervising homework, riding them to practice their musical instruments, driving them to lessons, to soccer or basketball practice, keeping birthday party invitations straight—they want and need their kids to develop independence. I need my kids to keep calendars, keep track of dates, and watch out for each other when I'm not around.

Objection 3: You'll Be a Terrible Role Model

(1991)

I am standing in the nursery school hallway, reading answers my three-year-old has given to questions about his home, his family, and the activities of his parents. Every year the school displays these questionnaires at the spring program, and every year I brace for the results. I look up at the paper and see, in bold red letters on the wall, what my son has chosen to tell the world about me: "My mommy sits around all day and night."

I realize that this is a three-year-old talking, not a judgment to be taken solemnly. On the other hand, these pronouncements are feedback of sorts, in a job without annual evaluations or reports. And they always seem to unsettle me.

You might think that I would have been convinced the year my daughter stated that what I liked best was to work at my desk. At least that sounded as if I do something more than sit around in a housecoat and curlers watching "I Love Lucy" reruns after everyone's off at school. The problem was that year my daughter also said that what her daddy liked best was to play with her.

What? I felt like saying to them. I am the one who gave up the career, the income, the respect I had at business cocktail parties, and the ability to have an uninterrupted telephone conversation. I am the one who changes your diapers, makes peanut butter and banana boats, hunts down neon sunglasses in January for sunglasses day at school, and spends the better part of an hour looking for the part of the toy that changes your new doll's hair color in the bath. I AM HOME. I AM SPENDING MY RAPIDLY DISAPPEARING YEARS BEFORE OLD AGE WITH YOU. I work a few hours at the computer. A few lousy hours. And your father, in his cameo appearances each week, is the one who best *likes to play with you*?

But the "all I do for you" speech sounded like words from a caricature of a mom, not what I'd want to come from me.[9]

Another reason given for maintaining one's career is that children have better role models in their "working" parents, parents who are "out there" in the "real" world. This role model issue is of real concern to many women at home.

There are two aspects, particularly for women who have struggled over the career/family dilemma:

1. what our kids think about our career status
2. what lessons we want to pass on to our kids

What the Kids Think of Our Career Status

Many of us gave up career identities measured in terms of position, money, or power—aspects seemingly irrelevant in our relationships with our kids. Still, sometimes we wonder what they think of us, especially when the subject of "other parents" comes up.

Lisa, years after giving up her career in neurobiology, had a conversation with her daughter about science: "Abby came home one day and started talking about something in science. I said, 'Well, I used to be a scientist.'

"She said, 'You were?'

"I thought my kids knew who I was. I'm in *Who's Who in American Women*, *Who's Who in the United States*, *Who's Who in Science and Technology*. So I pulled them out and said, 'Find your mother.'

"She did, and she was mightily impressed. But I was shocked that she had not a clue. That I was just a mom to her."

After resigning her position as chief executive of a nonprofit arts organization, Cathy had a lot of anxiety about what her kids would think of her: "There was this thing on the bulletin board at my daughter's preschool. . . . It said, 'It's ten o'clock in the morning; where are your parents?' [The kids had to supply the answer.] I was looking anxiously for my daughter's name, and I didn't see it. I wondered what on earth she would say about me? What was I doing at ten o'clock in the morning? . . . For me to be home all day doesn't mean a thing to them because they're not home. Maybe if I painted the house. . . . "

Rachel, a lawyer now at home for two years after working for twenty, still grapples with the issue of financial self-sufficiency: "With five kids, we don't have a ton of money, and we can't afford this or that. And they say, 'Mom, when are you going back to work so that we can afford things? Why are you . . . at home?'

"And I don't want to argue with them on this. I want their mindset to be that women work. I want my daughters to think that they should be out there working and not be dependent on men, and I want my sons to marry women who have careers. So I will not glorify to them what I do at home. . . . "

We fight not only our own notions of money and its importance, but those of our culture, which plays its own part in shaping our children's expectations.

Pam was putting her eight-year-old son to bed one night when "he began spouting off these things . . . one of them was that guys are more important because they go to work and make money, and I thought 'Where, *where* does this come from??!?' And he said, 'All girls do is talk on the phone and go to the mall.' [Pam shakes her head.]

"I just said, 'Where do you get that?'

"'It's true, Mommy!' he insisted.

"And I said, '*Who* do you see around here doing that? I don't go to the mall.' And then I said, 'Gee I've been doing entirely too much around here! And by the way, find your way to soccer.'

"It's that same kind of thing that you get from adults. Everybody will say, 'Oh, you're doing something really worthwhile,' but it's sort of like one of those niceties of the world; it doesn't make the world go 'round. If it doesn't earn the bucks, it doesn't carry real weight."

Despite such exchanges, our kids may not be judging us as harshly as we judge ourselves, and sometimes they give us glimpses of true

Table 8.1

Successful Career Characteristics

	Adult Definition	Child Definition
1. Prestigious position	Doctor, lawyer, CEO, politician	Four-term homeroom mother on first-name basis with school principal.
2. Visible	Recognized in field	Recognized on soccer field
3. Informed	Reads major newspapers	Knows Little League schedule, date of school play
4. Talented	Is creative with professional accomplishments	Able to find missing homework and to cook cheeseburgers that taste as if they're from McDonalds

understanding. Betsy, forty-three, formerly a head librarian who now works part-time around the schedules of her three children, says: "A few years ago, Phoebe made me a gift out of toilet paper tubes. A family was decorated and glued together. She told me I was 'the glue.'"

Children in those in-between years, too old to express the unconditional infant love for their parents and too young to harbor unconditional adolescent suspicion, may indeed want their parents to be important, visible, informed, and talented. Child and adult definitions of such characteristics, however, may vary, as shown in Table 8.1.

And certain careers may have a kind of glamour attached to them. The following are careers that kids have asked mothers in my survey to pursue:

- candy counter clerk at Rite Aid, near my house ("so we could have some extra money and they could come visit me")
- pizza delivery person ("so I could have a job while they're in school and I could bring home pizza every night")

- baseball player
- alternative music equipment supplier
- gypsy

What We Want Our Children to Learn from Us

Some years ago, my daughter used to wear her bathing suit backward. In January. The front scooped a little too low, and the back rode up a little too high over her cute little bottom, but overall the consequences were not terrible on the figure of a four-year-old. Nevertheless, I felt as her mother a duty to steer her, guide her in the proper way to dress herself.

"Sweetie," I'd say gently, "don't you want to wear it with the bow in the back? . . . You know, you're wearing it backward."

Thumb in mouth, blanket draped over her shoulder like an Armani silk scarf, she'd sometimes give me the courtesy of a pause, a stare, a consideration of the words I'd spoken. But her response was always the same. Not petulant or defiant, simply matter-of-fact:

"I like it that way."

By age seven, my daughter's supreme confidence in her own judgment had not abated. One afternoon after school, we were sitting at the dining room table. Julia was there to write a story for her homework assignment. I was there, I thought, for moral support and encouragement.

It was not going to be a smooth session, I could tell. Brow furrowed, elbows on the table, she glared at the blank page on her open notebook. Suddenly she picked up the pencil and in bold dark letters wrote a third of the way down the page:

THE END

"Julia," I protested. "You can't do that. Come on, now, erase that and write your story."

"That's how long it's going to be," she snarled.

I sighed. "Please start again."

"I don't have to."

"Julia."

"I'm going to write a knock-knock joke. We're allowed to do it."

"I want you to write a story," I insisted, taking a step down that ill-fated path to a mother/daughter power struggle.

"I don't want to, and I don't have to."

Taking a deep breath, I said with deliberate calm, "You're probably tired and hungry. Why don't you get some juice and a pretzel first? Then you'll feel more like writing your story."

Without brightening, she slid off the chair and disappeared into the kitchen.

Ten minutes later, I went back to the dining room to find Julia already at work, bent over her paper, her legs swinging busily under the table. It looked as if she'd already written almost two lines. I breathed a sigh of relief and smiled with satisfaction; my patience and motherly insight had worked; now that she had had a chance to rest and get a bite to eat, she'd get this done in no time.

I looked over her shoulder and read the first sentence: "One day a little girl was walking down the street with her mom."

"Oh, wow, great," I cooed encouragingly as I sat down beside her. "Are you writing about something that happened to you, or are you going to make something up?"

She looked up and smiled. "I'm writing a story about a little girl who kills her mother."

It's dangerous to cross my daughter.

"Mommy," Julia said one day while I was rocking her baby brother. She stood next to me, watching her brother's eyelids close. "When I grow up, I don't want to have children."

"What?" I asked, startled. "Oh, sweetie, I hope you have children."

"Why?"

"Well," I said, feeling more and more foolish saying this to a seven-year-old, "your children will be my grandchildren?"

She thought for a moment. "OK, I'll have one, so you'll have a grandchild."

I grinned. "You don't have to decide these things right now, sweetie."

"But only one," she warned. "Because then I'll have time to take care of it."

I feared that even at age seven my daughter was judging me, evaluating the job I was doing, the role I was playing. Now as she enters adolescence, I worry sometimes about her opinion of me. She may want to be like me; she

may want to be as different as possible; she may want both at the same
time. As a daughter, I know how daughters can judge; now I know how difficult the role can be.

I do know what it's like to be a girl growing up in the sixties and a
woman growing older at the millennium. I don't know what it's like to
be Julia.

I want her to follow her dreams and fulfill her potential—intellectual,
creative, and emotional.

I want to give her as much space to be her own person as I instinctively
give my sons; I want to guide her without manipulating her dreams; I want
to learn from her without regarding her choices as an attack on mine.[10]

So I take this role model issue seriously. Because simply by being their
parent I am a role model—good or bad, like it or not, whether I'm
president of a company or the PTA, piloting a plane or a minivan, drafting contracts, writing books, or simply scribbling notes to the teacher.

The fact that I have left the law to spend more time with my children does not mean that I want my children, sons or daughter, necessarily to do the same.

But this is a concern, particularly with my daughter, who, unless
the culture becomes more family friendly, will likely have similar conflicts to resolve, similar passions to juggle. When she looks back at my
life, what guidance will it be? At the very least, she will see someone coping with conflict and compromise. I hope she will be afraid of neither.

Jessica, working three days a week as a physician, also wants her
daughters to be prepared for conflict: "With three daughters especially,
I'm very open with them. I'll tell them, oh, here's another conflict. I'm
going to do this, but I can't do that, or I can't sit down and read
because I have to go there. Letting them know that I want them to
do whatever they want to do, but whatever it is you choose to do,
you may have to make some compromises. . . . You may want to work
full-time, you may want to spend more time with kids. . . . I have no
idea how they're going to work them out; it'll be up to them, but they're
going to have to make choices somewhere along the line."

We don't really have the answers to give them; perhaps we can only
prompt them to ask the right questions.

Elise, now divorced, struggles with finding balance among competing needs: her work as a dance therapist (which doesn't pay the

bills), her need to support her family, and her desire to be around as much as possible for her teenage daughters. "I hear myself giving them mixed messages. You need to study and work hard and play the corporate game or decide that you don't need that. I see more and more women who finally made the million-dollar mark and are more stressed. What is the bottom line? I'd like to tell them to find passion and really hold on to it. Don't let anyone tell you it isn't worth what you think it is."

A mother is a role model in the way in which she lives, the choices she makes, the values she holds dear. Maybe at-home mothers with multiple identities, professional and personal—what we were, what we are, what we hope to become—need to work harder to define for their children what success is all about.

For some women at home, being a role model is not about money or job title but about making a contribution in whatever community we find ourselves.

Cheryl, former research director at a large regional brokerage firm, has a girl twelve and a boy fourteen. ". . . I can be a role model when my children are young by being around their school, doing something that they think is cool and gets them noticed. When they're older, I hope to be involved in moving toward a career or more involved in civic and community activities than I am now. And how could they not think that that's laudable? As long as you're doing something that's productive for society at large, that's all it takes. If you tell me that being a buyer for a department store or—there are a lot of people who are making a lot of money at their jobs, but, my God, who cares?"

Alice is heavily involved in volunteer activities and has these arguments with her ten-year-old daughter: "Sarah will say to me, 'I know you do this, but why can't you get a real job?' Her notion of a real job is one that provides an income. I try to explain that everyone has roles, that there have to be people who don't 'work' who have time to do these volunteer jobs.

". . . I would like the kids to realize that there is more to life than a nine-to-five career. I don't want them to value stuff in terms of the letters after their names."

Kate, the former broadcaster who, as a child, could never understand why her mother left a career in the theater, says, "One of the reasons that, even when I'm tired, I drag myself out to rehearsals, and even though I might not want to get involved in the pumpkin sale at school, I do it, is because I want the girls to understand that being a mom does not preclude other interesting work. My mother felt that being my father's wife and our mother took all her day. When people ask Elizabeth what her mother does, she says that her mother sings. [I want her to know] that being a mom doesn't mean that you give yourself a mental lobotomy, [or that you can't do] anything else."

We're role models, teaching by example, not only in what we do for a living but in how we live our lives. Marie, a CPA and former company comptroller, talks about lessons having nothing do to with finance that have rubbed off on her eleven-year-old son: "I have never been more proud of anything than when my eldest son, completely on his own, recognized the need to include a special needs basketball teammate in a particular play and therefore passed him the ball rather than taking an easy layup. I only knew of this because the teammate's mom called me in tears to relay what my son had done and how it had absolutely made her son's day! There is just no way to express how satisfying that experience was to both of us as parents. Finally, we realized that some part of our moral teachings and examples had sunk in!"

Tracy, former communications specialist, now at-home mother of three little girls and founder of a local chapter of FEMALE, an advocacy group for at-home mothers, explains it this way: "It's hard to be a woman, because you do it all. I've done both working and being at home. It's important to have the self-esteem to say, 'I don't care what anybody else thinks, I'm going to do what I want to do.' That to me is the foundation of what to tell our daughters. We will put them through college, and . . . after that if they want to get married and have children, that's fine. It's never a waste—you can always use your education. Knowledge to me is power. I went to school for four years and worked for eight years, and I'm still using all the stuff I've learned in FEMALE."

In the end, I want my sons and daughter to know that I have worked—as a lawyer, a teacher, a writer—and that those jobs are part, but not all, of who I am. They are but paths I have taken, choices I have made, in no way indicative or prescriptive of the choices they themselves will make.

Parenting, like life, is going with your gut. Embracing each challenge as it comes. Even though it's never quite what I expected.

The sun has slipped from the red winter sky by the time I open up. Flipping the switch for the high-hats in the ceiling, I sigh with satisfaction. The room looks pretty good: oak bar stools lined up, glasses clean and ready on the shelves against the wall. You'd never guess there was a brawl here last night—drinks thrown, bodies tangled, chairs upturned.

Now, as the afternoon shadows disappear in the darkness of the night, the stillness is broken only by the quiet blare of the corner TV announcing the five o'clock news. I move around to the back of the bar, check the mixers, and pull down some dinosaur jelly glasses from the shelves.

At 5:17, the first customer—er, child—appears from the shadows of the back hallway. His shoulders sag, his footsteps lumber, and a frown has settled on his young brow.

I take a deep breath, ready to do what bartenders—er, moms—do best.

"Hey, buddy. What can I get you?" I say with my gentlest smile.

"I'm hungry. Got anything to eat?" he says gruffly, climbing onto the last stool along the line.

"You know we don't serve dinner 'til 6:30," I say, wiping the counter in front of his place. "What about a drink?"

He glances up at the clock on the wall. "I'll take a sandwich or something."

I pause, looking from the clock to the cabinet behind the counter back to his scowling mug. "Look, you can have dinner at 6:00. Have a pretzel. What would you like to drink?"

"I hate pretzels. What about peanuts?"

"Sorry. We're all out."

He moans. With elbow bent, hand cupping his chin, he slides his body across the damp surface of the bar. "Fine. I'll have a lime."

"Lime. No drink. Just a lime?"

"Cut up."

I raise my eyebrows. "Yes, sir."

"So how was your day?" I ask after giving him half a lime sliced into quarters.

"Terrible," he says, ripping at the pale green flesh with his teeth.

"Terrible. That's too bad." I watch him sucking the wet fruit into his mouth, the juice dripping down his chin.

I wait. Years of serving the regulars have taught me not to push. The clock ticks. The oven beeps. Finally, he continues.

He tosses the first piece of peel down. "Ya see, Aaron wasn't there again. And Dylan is not my friend anymore. He spent the whole afternoon with Jamie."

His eyes fill, his narrow shoulders lift, his small body swells with a sigh of sadness. I come around and wrap my arms around him.

"Mom," he says, voice breaking.

"Yes?"

"Do we have any blueberries?"

Another figure appears from the shadows. Taller, more intent, he stands quietly, collar up, eyes darting, drumming his fingers on the side of the bar. I know the type: he wants something, or someone.

"Hi, sweetie," I say, putting a cocktail napkin in front of him. (I call all my customers sweetie.) "What can I get you?"

"Just water." His eyes scan the room. "Have you seen . . . a dictionary around here?" he says casually. His steel-blue eyes quietly comb the room.

I stare. My customers are always waltzing in here, acting as if I'm supposed to know everything. Who do they think I am, their mother?

I shrug. "Haven't seen it. You hungry?"

"There was that big one around here a couple days ago."

I sigh. "Which one? Can you describe it?"

His jaw tightens. "You know what I'm talking about. A big one. Heavy. Doesn't fit most places."

I roll my eyes to the ceiling, exhaling a long, thoughtful sigh. "Sorry."

He pauses, then pulls up a stool. "Maybe I'll just hang out here for a while. Have a soda."

"Can I get a glass down here?" comes a strident outburst from the end of the bar. The little guy's face is red, his knuckles white. "No one's listening to me!" he wails.

"Take it easy, buddy. Have another half," I say, setting down the other half of lime and an empty dinosaur tumbler in front of him. "Your favorite. . . . You want anything in the glass?" He shakes his head. Strange guy, but I'm used to him.

A blond beauty with fear in her eyes looks back at a brooding dark-eyed man lurking in the shadows on a snowy mountainside. *Murder on Ice* proclaims the cover of the worn paperback framed by waves of dark brown hair. I can't see the face behind the book, but I don't need to. This bookworm babe comes in every night, head buried in a different trashy tale. Sightless for anything but the words on the page, she feels around for the stool, slithers onto it, and plants herself without a word to anybody.

Every so often, a hand meanders out from behind the book groping for pretzels, or popcorn, or whatever might happen to be out. Resting on my elbows, I study the back of the book and wait. When it sinks slowly to the surface of the bar, I am staring into troubled eyes.

"How's it goin', babe?" I ask.

She frowns. "My head hurts, and I'm thirsty. Can I get a ginger ale?"

"Sure thing."

The dictionary guy groans.

"You OK?" I ask.

"Yeah . . . I guess."

"Wanna talk about it?"

"Naw, it's just that . . . well, I lost my umbrella, and my girlfriend likes someone else."

"That's tough. I hate losing umbrellas."

"She told this girl that she really likes the girl's boyfriend."

"Instead of you?"

He nods, staring into his drink.

"Geez. Girls can be cruel."

"And not only that, now she wants me to do something."

"Who?"

He curls his lip, annoyed. "The girl whose boyfriend my girlfriend likes."

I wipe the bar in big circular sweeps, looking from the lime guy to the bookworm babe to the dictionary man, hoping something inspirational will pop into my head.

On the other hand, maybe they just want someone to listen.

Suddenly the door swings open, and the room is filled with a blast of warm, gusty singing. Silhouetted against the beam of the outside light, a figure croons as if he's already partied the night away. "I'VE BEEN WORKING ON THE RAILROAD ALL THE LI-IV LO-ONG DAAAAAAAAAAY," he roars in a deep grovel.

"He should be an opera singer," comments someone.

The door slams shut and the singer writhes, squeezing his fist around an imaginary microphone. "AH HIVE BEEN WORKING ON THE RAH—HAIL RO-HOWED JUST TO PASS THE TAM AH HA-AH WA AYYYY."

"Now he sounds like Elvis," says the babe.

"In his dreams," mumbles the lime guy.

"Well, I wish he'd be quiet," snaps the voice behind the book. "I can't concentrate."

"OK, you—" I say, raising my voice. "Pavarotti or Elvis, whoever you are, keep it down. There're other people here—"

"YOU AIN'T NOTHING BUT A HOUND DOG, CRYIN' ALL THE TIME—Why doesn't she *read* somewhere else?" he asks, eyes wild. Taking a running start, with arms raised, he slides the length of the floor behind the bar on his knees, passing behind the tall man, the bookworm babe, and the lime guy.

"OOOOWWWW, HE HIT ME!" shrieks the bookworm babe.

"Hey, it was an accident. My arms were out," Elvis says innocently, standing up, eyes wide.

"You poked me right in my back." She glares.

"Can I have this banana?" asks the lime man. "It was just lying here."

"Wait—no—oh, fine. But that's it," I say to the lime man, who is already looking a little bloated. "Listen guys, settle down. I'm not having another night like last night."

"Whaddya goin' to do, call the cops?" sneers Elvis.

"Yeah, put 'em all in jail," slobbers the lime guy.

"Enough," I say, thinking I ought to have a drink, just to keep up with these guys. "You can take a seat and engage in polite conversation, or you can leave."

"Anyone want to hear a joke?" asks the dictionary man suddenly. "Why did the monkey fall out of the tree?"

The bookworm babe groans. The lime guy's eyes roll to the ceiling. Elvis climbs onto a stool and cups his chin in his hand.

"Because he was dead."

I stifle a groan and clear away a banana peel and assorted lime peels. This job doesn't pay enough.

"Why did the second monkey fall out of the tree?"

We stare.

"Because he was stapled to the first monkey," he says, grinning, searching the faces of the other customers for a reaction. "Get it?"

"That is really stupid," says the babe.

"Yeah," he says, smiling.

"Ohhhhh, I don't feel so good," moans the lime guy.

"Maybe you've had enough," I say. "Maybe you've all had enough. How 'bout some dinner?"

"Not me, I'm full," says lime guy. "I don't feel so good."

The clock on the wall reads 7:24: closing time. The bar crowd has long gone, scattered into the night. I put away the glasses, sweep the floor, line up the oak bar stools, and wipe the bar surface till it gleams. My hand poised on the light switch, I survey the room. Another night gone by. Things look . . . not bad. Not bad at all.

CHAPTER NINE

Invisible Accessibility

Parenting Teenagers:
Contradictions and Confusion

O K, so here is the plan (plan K? L? P? whatever): take a break from the practice of law until the youngest child is in school all day, at which point I can reenter the legal profession, and get back on the track of sixty-plus-hour weeks.

I discover that there are many problems with this plan, not the least of which is that when my youngest enters full-day kindergarten I have two adolescents and a third nearly there.

They are good kids. They baby-sit, they acolyte in church, they do well in school. But they are adolescents in a changing world—their moods, their days as variable as island weather.

> I catch a glimpse of my oldest son when he comes in the door from school. His step is heavy but quick on the wood floor. Hands in pockets, he tilts slightly forward, his once narrow shoulders muscling the weight of his overstuffed backpack.
>
> "Hi, Dan." I smile.
>
> He looks past me, perhaps out the window at my back. "Hi." He rounds the bottom of the stairs leading up to the bedrooms. "How're you doing?"
>
> "Fine," he says, the word disappearing with him up the stairs.
>
> Sometime later he appears, and I am glad because he is company for me for a dinner on the run. His father is working late; his brother is at soccer practice. His sister and youngest brother have already scarfed down leftovers.
>
> "Sit with me?" I ask, pulling down two plates.
>
> "Huh?" Standing at the open refrigerator, he looks out from behind a shock of brown hair that hangs over his pale blue eyes, and then, in a mumble, he says, "OK."

We sit at the table, my firstborn child and I, eating pasta.

"You should drink milk," I say, glancing at the glass of water he has poured for himself.

He picks up his glass, takes a drink, and puts it down.

"Are you OK, honey?" I ask, resisting the urge to brush his hair aside.

"Yeah. Fine."

"How was school?" I lean forward, smiling.

Frowning, he moves the spiral twists around the plate with his fork. "Fine."

"Did something bad happen?"

He looks up, twisting one corner of his mouth up into his cheek; his eyes narrow. "What?"

"I just wondered. You seem . . . quiet."

"I'm *fine*," he says.

"OK, OK. So how was the field hockey game you stayed to watch?"

"Fine."

"You know girls on the team, besides Sharon?"

He nods.

"Who's on the team?"

He chews and looks at me, considering. "You wouldn't know them."

I take a breath. "Heather?"

"No. Mom, you wouldn't know them."

"OK." We eat in silence. "Were there other people watching?"

"What?"

"Well, you weren't the only person watching the girls' field hockey game. There was an audience, right?"

He winces. Maybe *audience* isn't the right word. "Yeah."

"OK, well, who?"

"Who what?"

"Who was watching?"

He sighs. "You wouldn't know them."

"None of them? I wouldn't know anyone?"

"Nope."

"Well, maybe if you told me their names, the next time you told me a story about school, I might recognize them, and then, even though I'd never actually met them, I'd sort of know who you were talking about."

He stares.

"And then," I continue, building up steam, "someday, I might actually see one of them, you know, in person—if I go to school to see a play or a concert or something like that, and THEN, when people are milling around afterwards, I MIGHT—I mean, it could happen—I might actually meet one of them. Someday . . . who knows?"

He is looking at me . . . that way, that incredulous, how-am-I-going-to-survive-my-teenage-years-with-this-woman? way.

I hate this. Now is a good time in life to have a job. Any job. Or a volunteer gig. Or an active interest in plants, which don't keep up a conversation any better than your teenage child, but at least they're not . . . well, mean.

"You know," I say, rising from the table. "I do have feelings."

It is a difficult, turbulent ride from childhood through adolescence, from a vulnerable child reliant on his parents for so many things to an independent adult. It is new territory for me as a mother, knowing when to let go, when to hold firm, when to just sit by silently.

As adolescence looms, other mothers feel the same tension, the same challenge. Pam is at home with two preadolescent boys, ages ten and twelve, and bracing for the teenage years: "We're all afraid of the Beaver Cleaver stereotype—those of us who have quit decent jobs and high-powered jobs to stay at home with kids. I think that when we do that, we think that Beaver Cleaver's mom is who we're becoming, and that's not the case. . . . The world is too complicated and moves too quickly. There're too many issues . . . and the pressures on our children are different. I'm sure every generation has said that. . . . But the pressures on our children can kill them . . . if they don't have some kind of grounding. You have to be so much more than Beaver Cleaver's mom."

And then suddenly, you're in the midst of it—hormones, rock bands, and telephone bills, as your child struggles to fit within his growing body.

Another irony of motherhood: career women at home who plan to go back after the early childhood years sometimes discover that it is the adolescents who need them more.

At Home for Teenagers: Why

What I've concluded so far about teenagers:

1. They need us.
2. They don't want us. (Or if they do, they don't want us to know.)

3. Therefore, parents must be invisible, but around.
4. Figuring out teenagers is more challenging than navigating office dynamics, managing a staff, or pleasing the boss.

Rachel was never at home when her first four children were babies. She left her nearly twenty-year careers as a lawyer and businesswoman when her fourth child was five years old and her eldest was thirteen.

She didn't leave because of the preschooler. And after her fifth child was born, she continued to stay at home, but not because of the baby.

"It's the teenagers I feel really need me," she explains over coffee, her five-month-old playing at our feet. "When you have a two-year-old, you can find someone to do arts and crafts and play the games. But when your teenager walks in the door and wants to discuss *things*, you can't get a duplicate. No housekeeper, no baby-sitter in the world is going to work."

Carolyn found the same to be true when she had a housekeeper at home to be there for her three middle- and high-school-aged sons after school. The situation seemed workable: the literary agency she'd cofounded was a short cab ride away from her home in the city. But by the time the boys were eleven, thirteen, and fifteen, she decided to move her office into the house in an attempt to make life easier for her as well as satisfy the varying needs of her three adolescent children.

"When the housekeeper told the boys what they could and couldn't do, they would tend to say, 'We're going to call Mom.' As soon as 3:00 or 3:30 rolled around, I'd be on the phone trying to put out the fires, trying to run the house from my office. Living in the city . . . it seemed very safe, but there was the lure of Main Street. . . . I wanted to know where they were after school and what they were up to.

"What I found was that children don't always need you when you're available. When the kid really wants to talk to you is when he comes home from school. What was so wonderful for me was to see that when I did move my office into my home, my third child all of a sudden seemed to develop a sense of security; he was a new person when I moved in. This seemed to be a child who needed a presence, and he didn't want a housekeeper."

Carolyn's presence turned out to be helpful for the child who needed her as well as for another child who didn't—or didn't appear to: "Within a year of my moving the agency back into the house, the older boy came into the house with a trail of girls, eighth-grade girls with their skirts up to their navels—unbelievable! I took one look at this . . . my husband was away, and all of a sudden I had a panicky feeling. My son was in high school, and one of those eighth grade girls was after him. When the kids had left, I asked him to come into my office. I said, 'That little girl has something else in mind. You'd better be very, very cautious. . . . Any trouble for her will be big trouble for you and for us. . . .'

"Sometime later, there was a knock on the door on a Sunday night about 8:00. This girl's much older brother stood there—he looked like a bodybuilder. He banged on the door and walked in and said, 'Your son better give my sister back her ring!' My son was quaking. My husband didn't know what was going on. After a lot of unpleasant conversation in the hall, we resolved it, but the point is, if I hadn't been here and seen the kids in their after-school wear, I wouldn't have known what was going on.

"When you're at home when your kids are teenagers, you get a very different sense of what their attitudes are, who they're spending time with, and they're a little more cautious about what they do, because they know that their family is aware of what's going on. You still lay down rules, and they still break them. I'm not saying that staying home solves all the problems with teenagers, because it doesn't. But in my case, I know there were certain situations that I was able to defuse because I was here."

At Home with Teenagers: How

I am sitting on the grass with Doug's mom, watching our eleven-year-olds play in a Little League baseball game. Doug is on third, and as the ball flies past, he runs, he races, he slides toward home. The players are shouting, the fans are screaming, all eyes are trained on the clouds of dust rising up from the tangle of bodies at home plate.

He is safe. We yell. We cheer. We clap.

Doug pulls himself to his feet and hobbles over to us on the grass behind the team bench. He grins at his mom and holds up a bloody finger.

"Oh, my gosh, Doug." She rises, pulling open her bag and searching for a Band-Aid.

"Mom, I'm fine," he says, turning his back and heading for the bench.

She runs to follow him; quiet words are exchanged; she returns to the

sidelines, Band-Aid in hand. "He says not to embarrass him." She sits
and sighs. "He wants me to know he's bleeding but doesn't want me to do
anything about it. I don't know what he wants from me."

I know what he wants: invisible accessibility. Not an easy feat. Sometimes you desperately want to be part of their world. They desperately
want to include you. But neither of you can press the issue too hard.

Cathy describes it this way: "You don't sit and hang with your
teenagers . . . you're in the middle of doing something, and the kid says
something earth-shattering, and you have to stand there looking as
if you're just cruising, *because if you actually sit down, they'll stop talking to you.* But their need to connect is so important, you almost have
to accommodate it any way you can, because if they don't connect
with you, they'll . . . just get sucked out, no matter how careful you
are. You can see that when they hit adolescence, how precarious it is,
how they can just get slurped away."

It's an intellectual challenge—not only dealing with their problems
but finding the right time and place to be part of their lives.

Says Lisa of her two teenage daughters: "They're becoming more
private, which they need to do. They need to separate, to become their
own independent selves. . . . It's none of this 'Tell me what your school
day was like.' . . . You won't get a word out of them. . . . When they're
teenagers, they have teenage problems, and they wait until the
moment is right."

When Carolyn's at work in her office at home, she doesn't hover
over her son when he comes home from school. "He walks in, and if
I'm not on the phone, I come downstairs and say, 'Hi, how was your
day?' And then I go back upstairs, and that's usually the extent of it.
But he knows that if he needs me, I'm here. That's been the pattern.
You have to use your intellect to a greater degree as your children get
older because they become far more challenging intellectually, and
they'll argue with you about almost anything, and you have to try to
understand how teenage children think and work and how you are
going to relate to these young people who are trying desperately to
break away and at the same time desperately clinging to you. It's a very
difficult time in the parent-child relationship.

"When they are teenagers, in some ways you feel a lot more useful, because if you can get through that difficult period, if you can be there for them, physically and emotionally, if you can be around most of the time when they need you, you're going to have a good dialogue, they're going to understand what your values are, and even if they seem to leave you, seem to spit in your eye and do things you don't approve of—that they *know* you don't approve of—eventually kids who feel loved and secure in their own families do come back to that, because that's what they want to re-create in themselves. If it's been a positive experience living in your family, that's what they want for themselves."

What I sometimes think my teenager thinks I'm good for:

1. driver
2. shopper/cook
3. driver
4. phone-bill subsidizer
5. driver
6. comic relief

The Payoff

Every once in a while there are flashes—of cooperation, of acknowledgment, of love—producing feelings in me more powerful, more validating than anything experienced in preparent days.

Carolyn's children are now nearly all out of the house. Two are in college, and one is a junior in high school. She is a woman who can't imagine not having a professional direction, at the same time acknowledging that being at home with her children forced her to compromise her professional drive. Her career has had its fits and starts, but she says, "I don't regret in any way having been at home with my children so much of that twenty-year period, because it's really paid off. What we all hope for is that we're going to produce offspring who are interesting, secure, self-confident people who lead productive, happy lives and who still like to be with their family—who'll come back and spend time with you!

"Our older child dyed his hair flaming turquoise in college and was always pushing the envelope with us. That same boy is the boy who, the second night I was in the hospital after I had surgery, came back a third time that night. This was the kid who didn't like the sight of blood! Nobody else was there, and I was really uncomfortable. He came back to be with me and rub my feet. . . . As long as I live, I will never forget this boy coming, like an angel from heaven. My family had been there twice that day, and this boy came back, all by himself, and said, 'Mom, I just thought you needed somebody here.'"

I am sitting writing at my computer at 9:30 at night, aware of the soft clicks against the hard drive's gentle hum, my hands cold from the night chill.

Suddenly my teenage son appears silently at the door, tall and still, his shirttails out, a lock of hair falling over one eye.

"Hi," I say, glancing toward him. In the middle of a thought, I turn back to the screen.

He disappears from my sight line, but I hear the muted bounce of the mattress of the guest bed as he settles behind me. I glance over my shoulder. He is opening a looseleaf notebook and lining up pages in a three-hole punch.

I type another thought, then turn.

"Are you here because you want to watch TV?" I wonder aloud, unaccustomed these days to his willing presence. Glancing up toward the darkened screen of the small TV on the top of the high dresser, I brace for a debate. He knows the rules: limited TV on school nights and only after homework's done.

His eyebrows lift in quiet surprise. "No." Head bent, he squeezes the puncher. He lines up the pages, punches, slides them out, then inserts them in the rings of the binder.

"Oh." I turn slowly back to the computer.

His voice, gravelly and low, speaks softly. "This is my script for the play. We have to put it in a binder, the teacher said. And then I've got to mark my part."

I turn. He looks up and smiles. "Cool," I say, then turn back to the computer.

I can see his reflection, blue-gray against the screen. Tall, quiet, bent over his work on the bed. As seconds slide into minutes, the room is filled with steady soft sounds of quiet companionship: the computer hums, my keyboard clicks, and his hole puncher snaps, scattering small circles of white paper over the bed.

PART THREE

STRIKING A BALANCE AND COMING TO TERMS

Hard-driving, ambitious workaholics who leave their jobs or scale back their careers don't automatically chill out, kick back, and begin chronicling soap opera plots. Many women throw themselves into other activities—both child and nonchild related—with the same energy they previously poured into their careers. In the process they are collectively changing the face of at-home motherhood.

Here are just some of the things that the at-home mothers who participated in this book are doing besides minding the kids:

- running school newspapers
- starting businesses
- rowing in Chinese dragon boats
- leading the Girl Scouts
- running the PTA
- investment banking
- organizing a publishing center so that elementary-school-age kids can have their own books published
- running for political office
- writing books
- playing in community orchestras
- performing stories for local libraries
- doing part-time office work, learning about new fields

- working at soup kitchens
- starting a jewelry business
- freelancing in professional music groups
- leading efforts to improve town traffic safety
- producing newsletters for civic associations
- using accounting skills to help community members at tax time
- teaching reading
- consulting—on business and just about everything else
- leading the Boy Scouts
- producing a weekend-long antique show to benefit charity
- participating in local government
- serving on boards of nonprofit organizations
- selling real estate
- selling toys
- teaching nursery school
- lawyering
- tutoring adults in computer skills
- part-time teaching
- part-time library work
- social work
- working for the county doing—and learning—statistics
- organizing support and political advocacy groups
- practicing medicine part-time
- going into schools to share their talents

CHAPTER TEN

Volunteering

Hidden Needs, Hidden Payoffs

Crossword puzzle clue: nine-letter word syn. with
frozen dinners, pin in children's underwear,
laundry in refrigerator, five-hour meetings, no pay,
no health benefits, causing head to hurt a lot.

Answer: VOLUNTEER

from ERMA BOMBECK'S
The Grass Is Always Greener over the Septic Tank[1]

W hen our lives were propelled by paychecks, it is what many of
us never had time for, what we disregarded, what we suspected
was social busywork: volunteering.

In *The Feminine Mystique*, Betty Friedan offered an indictment of
volunteer work, which, twenty and thirty years later, may still color
our perceptions:

> In some suburbs and communities, there is little work left for the non-
> professional that requires intelligence . . . there are simply not enough
> posts to go around. As a result, community work often expands in a
> kind of self-serving structure of committees and red tape, in the purest
> sense of Parkinson's law, until its real purpose seems to be just to
> keep women busy. Such busywork is not satisfying to mature women,
> nor does it help the immature to grow. This is not to say that being a
> den mother, or serving on a PTA committee, or organizing a covered
> dish supper is not useful work; for a woman of intelligence and abil-
> ity, it is simply not enough.[2]

In retrospect, many of us who felt this way were desperate to be taken
seriously in what we considered "the real world," where a salary, aside

from paying the bills, was evidence that we had reached adulthood, could support ourselves, and had something of value to offer the world. A paycheck could put a number on that value. A paycheck could give us identity, make us real. We believed what Friedan also wrote, that "even if a woman does not have to work to eat, she can find identity only in work that is of real value to society—work for which, usually, our society pays."[3]

A paycheck was proof that people took us seriously.

Volunteers, on the other hand, didn't seem to be legitimate professionals, no matter how important their work.

Barbara knew that volunteers were critical to the functioning of many organizations. Her mother, whom she considers "a wonderful role model," had run the volunteer efforts at their local hospital: "My mother was at the hospital from eight to five every single day; she volunteered for twenty years without a single drop of pay. We were comfortably off, and Dad said, 'You shouldn't take the money away from a man supporting his family.' . . ."

But Barbara also believed she'd never be taken seriously unless she proved her value in monetary terms, earning a salary. "When I came here, my dad said, 'Why don't you volunteer and work for free to learn the business?' I said, 'No, Dad, there's a perceived value there, and I can't do that.'"

And so today, for many of us, the forces collide: women accustomed to being "economically productive" are thrust into a home and family life in which volunteer work plays an integral and critical role in creating community. As any at-home mother of a school child will tell you, once word gets out that you're at home for even part of the day or week, volunteer work will hunt you down faster than a retriever can chase down a dry leaf dancing across the yard.

And sometimes the work that finds you is not the work you might choose. Christine found her initial forays into preschool benefits difficult. "Nobody was there to do things efficiently. It was truly a social thing, everybody wanting to be on the best social committee, nobody wanting to clean up. Some women would commit to things and never follow through. I would get very irritated."

The good news is that women participating in this book report that the world of volunteering is no more uniform in its challenges and frustrations than the world of working for money. Volunteer activities are as varied as the interests and available time of the workers.

The substantive range of activities that depend on volunteer efforts is far reaching. Volunteers help educate children in our schools, help care for the sick in hospitals, staff religious, library, and other civic institutions. In museums, orchestras, theaters, and other arts endeavors, volunteer efforts preserve our past and enrich our present. Volunteers support medical research, protect our environment, and contribute financially to countless other efforts that, although not economically viable, protect the future of our civilization.

Just as with paid work, volunteer work varies in its intensity and level of commitment. Many of the women with whom I spoke plunged headlong into positions of significant responsibility.

Yes, there are plenty of bake tables that need cookies and brownies baked (the skills required for which, by the way, are vastly underrated). But there is also the need for someone to run the event, be it a church fair or a community block party. Anne works part-time as a registered nurse and has also helped manage her community's Memorial Day parade and block party, which require, among other things, skills in management, negotiating, computers, finance, politics, communications, marketing, and public relations. Just a part of the to-do list includes:

- coordinating the efforts of different interest and talent groups
- soliciting participation from community groups as well as local celebrities and politicians
- negotiating and drafting contracts with a band and a group of jugglers
- meeting with members of the fire and police departments
- planning the layout for crowd control
- securing the appropriate permits and insurance
- coordinating the preparation and sale of food and the disposal of trash and garbage
- arranging for setup and cleanup
- all this while motivating people to work without pay *and* making sure that the event continues to be fun for everyone involved

As Anne remarks, "You have to be much more politically correct and savvy as a volunteer than when you're in a paid situation."

Alice produced a three-day-long antique fair to raise money for the American Cancer Society and, aside from her practical-life crash course in the antique business, found herself learning the nuts and bolts of town politics. (Among other things, a town resolution had to be rewritten to allow a banner to be hung announcing the event.)

Many volunteer organizations are run like businesses. Lorraine runs a nationwide seed distribution program for a horticultural society. "When people ask me if I work," she says, "I say, 'Yes! But not for money.'"

Former career-driven people bring to volunteer jobs their education, experience, and expectations. Jessica, a part-time physician and full-time mother of three girls, is an officer of two home and school associations, and when she can she attends school board meetings. Volunteering has given her a greater appreciation of the work and the people who do it—whether they have outside jobs or not. "It's a necessary commitment to make sure your community works."

With such an array of possibilities, it can take time to find a niche, especially for those who feel, as one woman expressed it, "between two worlds." Yet volunteer work can often bridge that gap while providing balance between family demands and the outside world. Women surveyed for this book report additional benefits from volunteer work, including:

- regaining a sense of community, often felt as a vacuous loss during those first months at home
- keeping career skills honed
- rediscovering old interests
- enjoying "a free education" in developing new skills sometimes leading to new careers
- showing their children, by example, the importance of values beyond money
- making a positive difference in the world, which is what so many of us wanted to do in the first place

Sense of Community

Once Barbara left her position at the bank, it was volunteer work that helped her regain her sense of community and feel better about her decision to be at home with her kids. "I helped out at the school a lot and thoroughly enjoyed it. Then I started chairing things at the city's children's museum and tried to get the funds going for the science museum. I enjoyed that part of it, so I did calm down."

Other women agree that volunteer work grounded them in their new lives. After Pat left her job as a city planner to be with her child, she felt as if she existed between two worlds—that of the business community and that of at-home mothers. Wanting some sort of balance, Pat sought volunteer work that would use her professional skills within the demands of her family schedule. While she was home with a preschooler, she joined with other mothers to found a before- and after-school child care center—a project that both brought Pat in contact with like-minded women and helped the community.

Rachel's circumstances were different than Pat's, but her feelings were similar. After nearly twenty years of working full-time, Rachel says that being home was truly traumatic and that volunteer work is what helped her weather the turbulence of conflicting emotions: "I got very involved with volunteer work for my synagogue. I think that's what saved me. I had never volunteered before, with four kids and a full-time job. As soon as I stopped working, my synagogue found me. They put me on five committees."

Maintaining Career Skills and Connections

Rachel's volunteer work for her synagogue not only gave her a sense of community; it placed her smack in the middle of a network of professionals and enabled her to use her business skills.

"I'm running a search for a full-time youth director. I've got résumés coming in, I'm interviewing people, checking references. I'm chair of the youth committee. I'm on the rabbi search committee. I'm probably going to run focus groups and surveys, which is good for my marketing end of things.

"I'm working with full-time professionals. I'm learning from them. The woman who cochairs the search committee works for an executive search firm. It's very nice. It's good, high-level work."

Sometimes, as in Rachel's case, the perfect volunteer job is waiting. Other times women have found it necessary to create their own opportunities.

When her son was in school, Pat began part-time consulting work in commercial space planning, but missed the involvement she'd had as a city planner with "the bigger picture." Combining her business skills with her interest in the arts, Pat volunteered to organize a fund raiser to benefit the city's symphony orchestra. The event would showcase a real estate development site, provide networking opportunities for leaders in the real estate industry, and raise money for the orchestra. The first benefit was so successful that a group of real estate corporate leaders was formed to continue such events. Eleven years later, the Corporate Round Table created to organize these events still exists, although its annual benefit event has become a golf tournament. Pat continues her involvement. "Even though I don't play golf, I get the satisfaction of seeing a project grow to where it meets my personal, professional, and philanthropic needs."

Through her efforts, Pat felt once again connected to the business community. "It's not always easy to find a place [that uses your skills and fits your schedule]," says Pat. "Sometimes you have to create your own forum."

Tracy is another woman whose initiative paid off. After a friend suggested she join FEMALE, a support and advocacy group for professional women making the transition to at-home motherhood, Tracy discovered that there was no chapter anywhere near her community. Undeterred, she decided to start one, an experience she's found to be "extremely rewarding":

"It's not a paid position, but I'm using my management skills that I learned from my many years of paid employment. . . . I also know that this little project will be a nice item for my résumé, whenever I do decide to return to work."

Thinking along similar lines, Sherry, once an editor at an academic press, says that in each of the new places she's lived, she volunteers to start a newsletter or newspaper if the need is there. Although each project can turn into a large time commitment, Sherry feels that this kind of volunteer work supplements her freelance editing jobs in keeping her writing and editing skills sharp.

Rediscovering Old Interests

From dusting off a college instrument to play in a community orchestra to acting out children's stories at the local library to putting those carpentry skills to use in an inner city renovation, volunteering can sometimes provide the forum to return to interests long buried under work and family commitments. Before Kate entered broadcasting, she studied ancient civilizations, obtaining a joint college degree in communications and comparative religion and mythology. Now, twenty some years later, she is once again reading up on the Mayans, the Aztecs, and the Olmecs, preparing for her job as a docent, or tour guide, for the University of Pennsylvania's Museum of Anthropology and Archeology. "It only took me a short time to get up to speed on Mesoamerica," she says, smiling. "Although I discovered that historians had completely changed their minds about the nature of Mayan civilization! It's been fascinating."

Volunteering has brought her back to some original academic loves while expanding her interests further. "I really want to ghost Caanan, the new exhibit," she says, grinning. (*Ghosting* is the term for following silently along a tour led by an experienced guide to learn the drill.) "It's biblical archaeology, with emphasis on the Bronze to the Iron Age."

Developing New Skills and Meeting People

Volunteer work provides opportunities to develop new skills and meet people with whom you'd never have had contact in your career.

As copresident of one Home and School Association, vice president of another, and a regular attendee at school board meetings, Jessica deals with a wide variety of significant issues and works with professionals she'd not otherwise meet in her medical practice. "I love the school involvement . . . going to school board meetings! I need to know what's going on on an overall level." The work involves social interaction and gives her a connection to the community in which her children are growing up. "Medicine can be so isolating. The training itself—college, medical school, internship, residency—your whole life is centered around it. I don't want my whole life centered around that anymore."

∾

Meghan, thirty-two, a former full-time elementary school teacher, had been fascinated with statistics since taking an introductory course in graduate studies and was seriously considering going back to school again to learn more. At home with her two-and-a-half-year-old daughter, she was already working part-time running an accelerated math program for fourth graders and doing volunteer work for FEMALE when she saw a notice in the local paper that the county was seeking volunteers to work with statistics. She called, had an interview, and soon found herself helping with a variety of interesting projects. "Most of my work has been with a database that they have of a household survey about health related issues—insurance, wellness care, care for children, those kinds of issues. . . . They use all this information to focus their educational materials, to determine how successful their child immunization programs have been, to teach women about breast cancer, and things like that. . . .

"I go into the database and work out the numbers. Now I'm putting presentations together, showing them to my boss's boss. We're trying to figure out if there are press releases or other things that should come from that. Sometimes they'll ask me to work on grant material."

While county personnel gratefully accepted her work in areas with which she had some familiarity, they were also willing to train her in areas she knew little about. Meghan raves about the experience, which has provided her a flexible way to contribute her talents, learn new skills, and meet a whole new group of professional contacts.

"I've been able to learn a lot this way without having to commit myself to carrying a load of courses. I do some work from home, and I do an afternoon a week there. This way if my daughter's sick, or if something comes up, it's OK. I can try to make that time up during the week.

"It's been so much fun for me, the greatest thing. The first afternoon I went, my daughter was still napping, so I had it set up during her nap time. I was probably there for four hours that day of uninterrupted intellectual activity. It was so exciting. I came home so invigorated. I still feel that way every time I go."

Meghan's pleasure with her work is apparently mutual. The county recently offered her a part-time job, which she declined: the time isn't right for her to make that kind of commitment. Still, the offer shone some light on future possibilities.

"I've been a teacher, and I am a teacher, and when I think, 'Where will I be working? What will I be doing in years to come?' I think it'd be nice to use this time [at home] to consider options. Maybe this work will be something I can relate to education, or maybe it'll be a separate field."

ᴄᴏ

Before Tracy became involved in FEMALE, she was suffering a rocky adjustment from her career as a communications specialist at an investment house to being an at-home mom. Adding to the stress of the transition was the tragic death of her father in a plane crash three months before she left her job.

"The first year at home was really hard. I was executor of the estate. I was freaking out. I had to deal with litigation attorneys, estate attorneys. I grew up a lot and learned a lot. But I needed to get out and meet people."

Once she was approved as leader of a local chapter of FEMALE, Tracy established the board, formed officer and committee positions, and began promotional activities. She conducts two meetings a month and administers the chapter of now more than fifty members—all around the schedules of her three little girls.

"Had my father not died, I don't think I would have had the courage to do this. . . . I did it for myself, and a big bonus is that it's helped other people. And that makes me feel really good."

Tracy has—at least for the moment—the balance she wants: "I'm not the kind of person to play with the kids. I know some women who actually sit down and play games. Sometimes we'll do a craft project, but I have things I need to do. I was up until midnight typing the agenda for FEMALE . . . But I meet my daughter at the bus, I can help out at school. . . . I drop my daughter at the preschool. . . . I take them to see the doctors. I like to know what's going on, and I'm there for them when they need me.

"My husband's on the periphery. It's my job to inform him of all this stuff. This is my little company here, and I'm the manager of it all. That's how I see myself."

Children and Values

It is not merely that volunteer work is not as boring as we once thought it would be. Many of us have come to realize its true importance—to the institutions and organizations that could not otherwise afford the services, but also to ourselves and to our children.

The March 11, 1998, issue of the *Princeton Alumni Weekly* ran a cover story titled "Careers or Kids," which asked whether "Princeton graduates who stay home to raise their children are wasting their educations."[4] That such a question was asked underscores the negative perceptions that still plague at-home parents, including active volunteers. Mary, a CPA and a member of the class of '75, worked from forty-five- to fifty-hour weeks as a financial manager before she had children. Now at home with two children, ages six and nine, she added her thoughts to the Internet discussion sparked by the article:

> In my current 'public life' as a volunteer, I do important stuff that would otherwise just not get done to the same level—not-for-profit accounting and financial management; one year, just being the story hour lady at the local library. I can be selective in using my time. I can put in 20 percent of the time and get 80 percent of the results—a force multiplier of four. . . . The questions I ask are 'If I don't do this, what else can I do?' and 'If I don't do this, who else will do it?' The answers to these questions, not how much I am paid, guide me in evaluating my use of time and talents.[5]

Rosemary ran for school board after nine years of teaching and fifteen years of being at home with four children. "My high school junior said, 'I always thought you were stupid; now it's confirmed. How can you work so hard without money?'"

That's why she ran for school board—to demonstrate to her children (now ages eleven, thirteen, fifteen, and seventeen) that not all responsible, important work is paid and, conversely, that working and making money are not the sole means to satisfaction.

"I could have gone back to teaching, and I would have enjoyed that. I'm fortunate that I can invest the time and energy in volunteer work. I guess I wanted to show my kids that if you have the means to give, you should do that. I also wanted them to know that staying at home doesn't have to mean you do nothing outside the home. You should channel your energies and make use of your time in a positive way."

"I always thought of volunteer work as a time filler," confesses Anne, a former public relations executive and grad student turned at-home mother of three who is also president of her children's school parent association. "But you start to think of how empty life would be without it. . . ."

A world without volunteers would be a stark world indeed—driven only by economic incentives. Essential services—hospitals, for example—would be stripped to the bone. Low- or nonprofit cultural activities—music, theater, and the arts—would shrivel. A world without volunteers would be a world without Little League, scouting, or library activities. There would be no receptions after school plays, no spring fairs, no drives to help feed the hungry or clothe the poor. Doing good things simply because they need to be done fosters connections between people and creates a sense of belonging, without which we have a collection of autonomous individuals, not a community, for a community needs a collective heart.

It is right after we move that the house surges ahead again in the giant scoreboard in the sky: HOME 974; ME 43.

Up until now, I have been, if not winning, at least keeping at bay the laundry, the dishes, the floors, the dustballs, the breakfast-lunch-and-dinners, the food shopping, not to mention clothes shopping, homework, birthday parties, doctor appointments, team practices.

Maybe it is the new house, which came complete with 1,001 things to do.

Maybe it is the five-foot-high pile of dirt the kids have discovered outside, which has become the site of all their games, and which, sneaker sole by sneaker sole, is moving into our house.

Maybe it is the action figures, Barbie dolls, baseball cards, tiny metal cars, plastic Lego blocks, tiny plastic pieces of toys, assorted birthday bag paraphernalia, paint, braids, crayons, stamps, and other kids' stuff spilling out of the toy boxes, over the carpets, into the hallways. They are reproducing, it seems, on every surface.

Whatever it is, I snap.

"Ok! Ok! Ok! Ok!" I scream in my habit of fours, one day soon after we move in. "If we lived on a farm, you'd be milking cows, gathering eggs, feeding the horses! Well this is like a farm, only it's a house. We all need to pitch in and take care of it."

"Can we get a horse?"

"NO. What you'll get is an allowance."

In the years since, we have been in continuous negotiations about what chores qualify for what payment, if any. We've had job charts where each child qualifies for allowance after doing seven chores of his or her choice; we've had regular daily rotating chores; we've had jobs that merit separate payment, like baby-sitting and heavy yardwork.

And we've had a great deal of volunteer work. Work that we do just because it needs doing.

Because, like so many other things, volunteerism begins at home.

CHAPTER ELEVEN

Career Moves

Old and New Careers, Working at Home

My writing and I found one another soon after I stopped practicing law. My one-year-old son had just consumed a fistful of evergreen bush alongside the sailboat reservoir in Central Park, and as I hustled his stroller home up and down the curbs and over the sidewalk cracks, block after block to our apartment on the Upper West Side of Manhattan, I watched the back of his head and worried. I worried about whether you could die from eating evergreen bushes. I worried about how to phrase the question to the new pediatrician. And I worried about my worrying.

In the hospital after my baby was born, I had asked the old pediatrician if flashbulbs could hurt a baby's eyes. When he told me we'd better get a seeing-eye dog, I decided that what we really needed was a new doctor.

The new doctor seemed nicer than his predecessor, at least to a hormonally charged new mother, but I wasn't certain how he'd take the evergreen question. Not that I had a choice. My child's life was on the line. Swallowing my dignity, I called the nurse.

Later, I sat down to write about it.

My son is now a healthy thirteen-year-old, and I am still writing about family.

For the first four or five years I was at home, I wrote because I liked to write and writing about life at home helped me sort out thoughts and feelings that had no other forum. I liked turning feelings into words with sounds and rhythms all their own. But I never thought of my writing as a job.

In those first several years, my desire to have more children kept me from jumping into another full-time job. At least I thought that was the reason. In retrospect, I was treading water in a sea of uncertainty. I took on limited and short-term work commitments, one after the other:

- I interned at a television production company and, after watching movie credits my whole life, finally learned what a grip was, not to mention best boy.
- I taught a law school course in writing and entertainment law for three years.
- I wrote a column for a local parenting publication.
- I wrote a column for a regional city magazine.
- I became a freelance writer.

Thirteen years later, I am up to my graying bangs in basketball and soccer, baseball and school plays, choir concerts and camp car lines. Still a lawyer, I participate on a committee of the local bar association and chalk up credits each year in required continuing legal education courses.

I write for three reasons: I love it, I can afford to do it, and usually my writing work can yield to my wife and mother schedule.

And it occurs to me often that—at least while I have kids living at home—I may not return to the practice of law.

Many women have said that the break that motherhood caused in their careers provided a time for reevaluating goals, assessing options, and redirecting professional paths.

Reworking Careers

A number of women have become consultants in their fields, maintaining contacts and building their own businesses.

Bobbie was a successful banker for seventeen years, moving up through the ranks of the New York banking world. With loyal clients and experience in corporate lending, corporate buyouts, and private and entrepreneurial banking, she was poised to go out on her own when, at thirty-eight, her first child was born. Now with two children, three and four, she works from home, consulting on problem loans for her former employer, handling business affairs for two wealthy clients, and brainstorming possible business opportunities for the future.

Although she once enjoyed working long days at the bank, entertaining clients at night, she wouldn't want the same kind of life now that she has children. Nor is the idea of a 'normal' full-time job, say, 8:00 to 6:00, appealing.

"Many of my friends who are mothers are working full time, most as attorneys. They're totally harried and out of their minds, working 8:00 to 6:00. They're doing it for the money. It's not like they're getting fulfillment out of their jobs. There's no real career going on there. They're tapped out. This is it. They're doing a competent job, but there's nowhere else for them to go.

"I would never want to be in that position. I'm far too ambitious, and I work too hard for that. I would cringe to do that. That's why I don't know if I could work for another bank, unless I worked in a totally different field where I wasn't expected to bring in the business and entertain clients that way."

The answer, for Bobbie, is to work for herself. "For a woman with kids, sometimes it works best to be more entrepreneurial and not work for an institution. That's why more and more women are off doing their own thing. You can structure work to meet your needs, not the other way around. You can control when and where you fit your time and your efforts."

Similarly, Judith, a former public relations manager for a symphony orchestra, finds great satisfaction running her own public relations and communications consulting business from home. She's gained not only flexibility to be available for her two children, ages five and nine, but control, without sacrificing her professional persona.

"I love making my own project choices and being my own boss.... I'm aware of being a somewhat senior member of the profession with a much broader portfolio than I had. I think I receive much more respect as a part-time consultant than I ever received in an office."

Starting New Careers

Barbara: From Banking to
Motherhood to Newspaper Publishing

Barbara jumped from managing people's money to managing a household without missing a beat: "When the kids were little, I proceeded to run them ragged, because I'm a very active person.... I transferred my energies from work to them. They saw every museum before they were four, and now that they're fifteen and seventeen, they don't remember much about those early years. . . . I think I did it more for me than for them. But I was there for them, and I was active in their school. . . ."

And all the while she was trooping through museums, dining on playground benches, and volunteering at schools, she was plotting her next career move: "In those years, I probably came up with thirty-two ideas of how to start a business. . . . My best friend and I—she was a Wharton MBA and in a similar situation—would be sitting on the bench talking about what business we were going to start and how to do something at home. There weren't really many people working out of their house at the time."

Now Barbara was fortunate; her husband owned a chain of local newspapers. But she didn't want charity; nor did she want to merely dabble in the family business. Noticing that the chain had little coverage of antiques and fine arts, she determined to fill that hole. As soon as her children all reached school age, Barbara went about assembling a separate section of the paper on arts and antiques.

"I put that together for six years, and that was perfect. I could go to work, come home, and pick up the kids, go to all their games. . . . I did miss the financial world because every day is different, and there's a bit of glamour attached to it because of the travel. . . . But the newspaper field is truly interesting; you're always aware of things happening. . . . I was talking to people around me, exchanging ideas. . . . "

Increasing her contacts in the business, Barbara continued to brainstorm about the future. In March of '95, she and the business manager of the newspaper chain decided to launch a new local weekly paper, despite the fact that there were two already-established papers that serviced the same community.

"It became a lot of work. I told them I would work 8:00 to 2:00, five days a week. But it's stretched a bit. I do work at home, I do stuff on weekends."

The paper has been a huge success, winning an award for the best suburban newspaper in North America two years in a row.

Now with two teenage boys, and working with her own newspaper, Barbara is once again juggling, running from meetings to basketball games, teacher conferences back to the office. Because she has a large degree of control over her life, it works. And she feels as if she has, for the moment, at least a piece of it all.

"The boys are gone 8:00 to 6:00 but I leave every day when they have games. If they need me to pick them up, I pick them up. If they're in a play, I do that. . . . Sometimes I feel funny leaving, because I don't want to set a bad example, and this is not a dilettante situation—I have work to do. So sometimes it's hectic. But I hope there's something left at the end of the day for the kids. I don't want to shortchange them or my husband."

Lisa: From Neurobiology to
Motherhood to Residential Real Estate

Science may still well be the professional love of Lisa's life, and in some ways she regrets not having kept her hand in during those years her children were young. But as they grew older, she knew that she wanted to do something besides mothering, something that would give her flexibility and control as well as bring in an income. Seven years ago she became a sales agent in residential real estate, a field she has mixed feelings about. It is not, in her mind, "a high-status job," nor does it give her the same kind of intellectual stimulation that science did. On the other hand, learning to sell real estate has given her—aside from critical schedule flexibility—a chance to develop skills she didn't have to use before:

"When I worked at Penn, 99 percent of my time was alone, 1 percent lecturing. I was slicing brains, reading research articles, writing. Real estate is completely different. It's all people skills. So I had to reach inside me to find those people skills. . . . I used to analyze a buyer's needs and say, "OK, here are these five houses that are perfect for you. I'd take them to see them, and they wouldn't buy them . . . and I slowly realized that this is an emotional decision. It's a connection between them and . . . sunlight, or some sort of lifestyle, or the way the house smells. It's completely unpredictable, and an analytical mind doesn't help you one bit. So I had to refocus how I dealt with other people . . . and that's a good thing. I'm a much more well-rounded human being now."

Liz: From Prosecuting to Motherhood to Lactation Consulting

Liz was first a civil litigator, then an assistant district attorney in a large city before she left the law to be at home with her first child. She enjoyed her work, which included child advocacy. But seven years later, as the youngest of her three children approaches full-day school, she is thinking about resuming her professional life, not as a prosecutor or even a lawyer but as a board-certified professional lactation consultant, commonly known as a *breastfeeding counselor*. It is a career change she says she would never have anticipated.

"I never in a million years would have said to myself seven years ago that I would be accredited in the medical profession and considering hanging out a shingle as an allied health care professional. But right now that sounds a lot more appealing to me as a mother of school-age children than clawing my way back into the legal profession: (a) struggling to find a part-time job, (b) being able to keep it a part-time job, and (c) not losing my mind trying to get back to speed without taking it out on my family."

When Liz thinks about her former life as a prosecutor, it is not simply the seventy-to-eighty hour weeks that deter her but the accompanying emotional drain: "I gotta tell you, as a mother, it's very hard to go back and work on the kind of cases I was prosecuting. It was hard doing it before. . . . When you have a three-year-old, it makes a lot of difference in the way you hear facts about a case about a three-year-old raped by a fourteen-year-old."

In contrast, her seven years of volunteer work as a lay breastfeeding counselor have given her the satisfaction of helping other women in a job with real positive feedback. Now that she has passed the board examinations, the possibility of setting up a private practice is both tempting and daunting.

"As a lay counselor, the kind of problems you're given are usually solvable. As a professional lactation consultant, you see the difficult problems: the preemies, the cleft palates, the teenage moms, the babies who aren't sucking because of neuromuscular problems, cases where the first time you figure out that a kid has a real problem is when he's not nursing well.

"Another thing that has crossed my mind is that when you're the lawyer, and you walk into the room, there's a certain panache, whereas when you're the lactation consultant, and you walk into the room and there's the doctor standing there, guess who thinks they're the king of the world? You hear lots of stories about these people, that just because they're more credentialed, they think they're smarter than you. . . .

"But the charm of it is that I can do it out of my house, on my own time. I can be my own boss. . . . The thought of doing it is exciting and a new challenge. I feel as if I'm standing on the high diving board. I'm there on the edge, looking down, trying to muster the courage to jump in. I know I'll make it; in fact I'll probably do a pretty good job at it."

Cynthia: From Journalism to Motherhood to Social Work

Cynthia left a full-time job in journalism with solid experience behind her—first at a suburban newspaper, then at the Associated Press, and finally with *Business Week* in New York. Once she was home, she continued to take on freelance editing and writing projects, fitting them around the schedules of her two growing children. But as with Liz, experiences with her children introduced her to subjects she found increasingly more interesting:

"When Sam was going through his difficult toddler phase, I was reading everything I could get my hands on on human development, personality development, behavior, and the makeup of the human psyche. . . . I found that whole body of knowledge really interesting. . . . to think about how people work, what makes them tick."

As the kids grew, Cynthia became involved in a lot of volunteer work in the schools, among which was a committee of teachers, administrators, and parents in a school-based management program, a "political snapshot" she'd never seen before. There the idea of working with children and children's issues took on new significance.

"Having a say in how my kids' education was structured was important to me. To have input, for example, into class size and see the impact the next year . . . was significant. . . . Also, I became interested in social issues, issues of class, race. How do you bring your kids up to be aware of other parts of society that are not in your immediate neighborhood? To be caring and active citizens?"

Volunteer work with parents at a school for developmentally disabled children and teenagers was another rewarding experience, and an idea began to form in Cynthia's mind:

"I thought, 'I need to have a plan, so that if I do stay home for ten years, I don't end up like those diary-of-a-mad-housewife women, suddenly on the doorstep with my husband out with a younger woman, and with no kids at home anymore.' . . ."

A future in journalism, despite its earlier allure, no longer had the same appeal: "Nothing about journalism is conducive to family life. Your family is going to be a very adjunct part of your life if you're full-time employed in journalism. You have deadlines, you've got to be there. Things happen at odd hours. You've got to have the flexibility to do that. . . . I really didn't want to go back to that kind of life, because I didn't see how it would fit into the rest of the way the family worked.

"I began thinking about being in a helping profession, working with social issues, human development issues. . . . I found it really rewarding, and I was good at it."

Cynthia made a decision and over three years, got her master's in social work. She now works twenty hours a week at a psychiatric hospital as a medical social worker, doing a lot of counseling, combining her social work education with many of the interviewing and writing skills she learned as a journalist. Her new career, she says, is, if not financially lucrative, personally rewarding and because "you can command some flexibility," easier to integrate into family life.

Cathy: From Nonprofit Administration to Motherhood to Commercial Real Estate

When Cathy left her job as executive director of a nonprofit arts group, she knew she needed a different professional direction. "I don't know whether it's just caught up with me, you know—going ninety miles an hour; I'm just too old to go ninety miles an hour—or whether the demands and needs of the kids—and this is probably it—are just so much greater."

She began searching for whatever job would have that impossible combination every parent dreams of—good money, meaningful work, flexibility, and time to be around for the kids.

It wasn't easy. "I was alternating between low-paying meaningful jobs and high-paying jobs I couldn't get excited about." She tried doing consulting work at home but discovered that there were too many distractions. "Made me realize that being a consultant at home was a bad idea for me. If I was going to earn money, I'd better go someplace and earn it."

Frustrated, but determined to find the right match, Cathy networked, talked to other women, and even went to a psychologist. "I think he didn't understand what I was doing—from his male view—not that girls think one way and boys think another, but I don't think he had a clue of what I really needed. I needed somebody to say, 'You can do it, you'll make the right decision, don't worry. Give yourself a break. Go earn some money, because you have to, and something will show up.' . . . I wanted to do something really different. I couldn't tell you what I wanted to do, but I could tell you nine things that I didn't want to do. I just had faith that something would turn up."

After months of searching, something did turn up. "This real estate thing fell in my lap, and I thought, 'Why not?' The last thing I did in my old job was to move our offices from one end of town to the other. The broker thought I'd be a good broker because I have such good contacts. He kept calling me, recruiting me. I finally met with him, and it sounded fine. So now I'm in school, taking these classes to get a license."

It was an odd fit at first—a Quaker social worker hawking commercial real estate. But Cathy realized that her requirements for a job now were very different from what she'd wanted fifteen years ago.

"To do commercial real estate was a real family-based decision. There are a couple of factors. First, starting something new that required a minimal amount of time—like I don't have to go to law school—and a minimal learning curve. The potential was for super-flexible hours and the potential for making a whole lot more money. I've never been motivated by making money before. This is a new thing. I don't feel greedy, but the idea of making money is extremely appealing."

Reigniting Old Passions

Fine arts was Lucy's passion before she ever got into marketing. Graduating from Penn with a degree in psychology and art, she started graduate study at the Pennsylvania Academy for Fine Arts, waitressing at night. After a year she grew impatient with art, tired of waitressing, and eager to find a career with which she could support herself.

A marketing professional was born. After several jobs and promotions, marketing became Lucy's professional identity. Her love of painting faded but never quite disappeared into the recesses of her mind, her day-to-day life taken up with her marketing work and then with the work of raising three young children.

It turned out, however, that staying at home with her children was the break she needed to get back to painting. But it was not an easy reentry.

"I remember thinking when I gave painting up, 'Maybe I'll get back to it when I have children,' because I'll have time! I'll be home with my kids, and I'll have time!" Lucy laughs.

"After I was home, I kept thinking that I was going to paint . . . but I felt like I couldn't get back to it." Overwhelmed by the demands of a small child, and hanging on to her professional identity, Lucy tried working on individual jobs for the marketing-communications firm she'd left. When her first child was three, she took a large job for one of its clients. Two weeks later she discovered she was pregnant again. She laughs, blushing, "I finished the project, and that was it." It took a while to break free from the sense of obligation to keep going in marketing. "Once I had come to terms with that—yes, I'm a stay-at-home mom—I needed another outlet for myself. . . . After my second child was born, I started to go one afternoon to a painting group at a local arts center. . . . I took a landscape painting course that summer, submitted a painting to a show, and got an award. I thought, 'Gee, maybe I *should* pursue this.'"

Lucy persevered, working in the family's basement and increasing her painting time to fifteen hours a week. The birth of her third child slowed her momentum somewhat, and she realized that she needed to get space out of the house.

"When Matthew was a year old, we decided I would rent a studio and see how it goes." She grins. "It was cheaper than therapy. I was, at that point, a mess. I didn't feel as if I could support it, but I wanted to give it a try. The first open house I had, I sold three paintings. That didn't cover my rent, but I felt like it was a success. Two months later I put together a portfolio and went to see one of the best galleries in the city, and they said they wanted my work!"

Despite setbacks from time to time, Lucy has doubled her income each year, as word of her work has increased along with her productivity. Soon to have her work published, she's maintaining a web page and exhibiting in three galleries.

Working Part-Time

Often the decision to leave work or scale back significantly comes only after a couple has decided that their lifestyle can be maintained, or adjusted, if necessary, on one income.

But money remains a concern for most families.

Some women work part-time in their former fields, maintaining contacts and scouting out opportunities for the future. Meghan, an elementary school teacher, works at her school part-time, teaching and administering an accelerated math class. Emily, formerly vice president of institutional equity sales, now works ten to fifteen hours a week training junior salespeople. Marie, a former chief financial officer, does accounting work part-time, especially at year end and other "crunch" periods. Kelley, former merchandising manager of an automobile company, now works two to three days a week as a consultant, with much better pay and the autonomy of being self-employed.

Other women find their former professions incompatible with their family priorities, even on a part-time basis, because the work requires too much time, too much emotional commitment, or both.

Sheryl has found it difficult to establish a part-time legal practice, in part because the business is so client-driven and in part, she says, "because other lawyers don't take you seriously. There's this attitude of who are you? Where did you come from? You're working *part-time*? Or when you're answering the phone yourself—a lot of lawyers aren't used to that. . . . When you answer the phone and they hear a child in the background, they think you don't know what you're doing. . . ."

Similarly, although Jill says her part-time engineering job on balance "worked," it was not ideal: "Did I feel like I was taken seriously 100 percent of the time? No. I would take work home with me and work on it at 2:00 in the morning. If I had been in the office at 2:00 in the morning working on it, yeah [I'd be taken more seriously], because I would have been seen."

Another consequence of part-time work, she says, was that she didn't get the same kind of work, the kind of work she felt she needed to keep current: "Obviously I didn't get jobs with hot deadlines. I felt that since I wasn't there all the time . . . I was losing my skills because I wasn't getting the difficult stuff."

But it is not merely the high pressure of an industry that makes it difficult to combine some work with child rearing. Some professions demand a full-time commitment:

Anne was just finishing her dissertation when her daughter was born. She's been home for a year now but feels that if she's going to advance in her career as a college teacher she needs to look for full-time work: "In academics, for career advancement, there's no such thing as permanent part-time. . . . To get recognition in that profession, you need that full-time job."

On the other hand, one of the reasons she chose academics was that even a full-time job will give her some flexibility in the way she'll juggle her time.

Conflict can also be created by competing passions, where family and job each extract too high an emotional toll.

When her first child was born, Debbie, with a master's in social work from Bryn Mawr, worked in the neonatal unit of a hospital, counseling parents of babies who were premature, sick, and in some cases dying. Working with a team of neonatalogists, she was on call nearly twenty-four hours a day to be available to parents when emergencies arose. She counseled those who had lost children, those who were having trouble conceiving babies, and those who spent days, weeks, and months visiting their tiny infants who were holding on to life in intensive care units. It was a draining emotional experience. After working part-time for several years after she began having children, she opted to take a break from this kind of social work while her children were young.

She first taught a college course, then plunged into a potpourri of other part-time work and volunteer activities, with her biggest time commitment made to working part-time in a medical office doing administrative work. The money's OK, the people are friendly, and most significant, the hours are flexible enough to work around her children's school and activity schedules.

"I miss the excitement and responsibility of being on call, having business cards, a professional identity. But I wouldn't want to be in a

full-time job yet. . . . I enjoy what ten years ago I would've viewed as
mundane or outside my career aspirations."

Elise, a dance therapist, understands the emotional drain of certain
careers. Before having children, Elise worked as a therapist with autistic children and families doing mother/child interaction and later as
assistant director for a state project in arts and special education.
After she married and began having children, she continued to work
in her field but focused more on her administrative and teaching skills.
"My work was still passionate to me—it just wasn't living the pain. As
a therapist, no matter how good you are, you live the pain."

When her children were young, Elise trained interns, did a session
or two a week with patients, and ran workshops here and there, all the
while doing the wife and mother thing. Now divorced, with two daughters ages thirteen and sixteen, Elise wants and needs a job but is trying to find something meaningful beyond her field.

"If someone were to say to me, here's a job with adolescents, I'd
run! I'd say, 'Are you kidding me? I'm living it!' I couldn't work with
autistic kids the way I did for eight hours a day before I had my own
babies. I knew I'd have to transfer—find something that's not so loaded.
I couldn't put my heart and soul there and come home and shift to be
there for my kids."

Working at Home

On a day in 1990, as I stand at the kitchen counter making a cup of coffee
before work, little feet step up on mine. Little arms wrap around my
knees, and fingers clutch at the back of my skirt. I look down to an uplifted
face of saucer eyes and honey hair.

"Sweetie, I have to go to work. I'll play with you later, ok?"

A small whine ascends from below, and the tugging on my skirt
becomes fierce as he tries to shimmy up my body.

I bend down and take him under his outstretched arms, lifting his
compact mass up to me. Little legs lock around my waist, arms cling
around my neck, and he burrows his head into the groove of my shoulder.
I swing my body gently side to side and lean my head to nuzzle against
his soft fine hair.

"Baby," I whisper in his ear. "You'll have fun this morning. I'll see you this afternoon."

In response, his head presses harder into my shoulder and his little legs squeeze my waist. No way, José, he says more clearly than with words, are you going into that office without a fight.

I press his small body to mine and put my lips to his hair.

"I love you, sweetie." Wrenching him gently but firmly away to the waiting arms of his baby-sitter, I say with my best actress smile, "I have to go to work. I'll see you later." I turn my back on the anguished red face, the pleading cries of "Mommy, Mommy," and the hands that clutch at the air for me. With jaw set, I walk out of the kitchen down the hall and turn left at the stairs. I pass quickly through the living room into the den and shut the office door.

At 10:45 the same morning, I am at my computer, blocked. The cursor on the screen blinks with the impatience of a tapping foot, waiting for my next thought. I swivel around in my armless blue desk chair, surveying my home within a home. A box of photographs lies waiting to be sorted according to year, event, and degree of blurriness. A pile of trade papers lies waiting to be read so that I am current on legal matters for the class I will teach next spring. A picture of a cowboy with eleven fingers on each hand stands guard on the wall above my printer.

I really have to go to the bathroom. Crossing to the door with the special lock, I ever so gently turn the knob. After a soft click, the door swings silently open. I stand still, listening to the muted sound of familiar voices. Slipping off my shoes, I creep through the living room to the bottom of the stairs. If they are in the kitchen or breakfast room, I will have to go back, because the bathroom is in the hall next to the breakfast room. If they are in the basement or upstairs, I can make a run for it. The sounds seem to be coming from the bedrooms. I quickly pass by the staircase and dart down the hall.[1]

Somehow I'd thought it'd be different, working at home. Of course it is different from my office existence in many ways, but it isn't the perfect fantasy existence I'd once imagined, the having-it-all for which so many of us strive. The good part is that the mom in me is always here, close to the front, the skinned knees, the hurt feelings, the jubilance of riding a bike for the first time. And then there's the relaxed dress code for workers at home.

Says Bobbie, the banker now managing her client's personal businesses from home: "I don't want to get dressed like a banker every day. It doesn't give me the flexibility to run to my kids and pick them up if something's happened. I don't care if I get covered with grape jelly at this point."

Yet there are drawbacks, among them isolation from colleagues. After a fast-paced professional life in investment banking and financial journalism, moving to a new community in a different state exacerbated the isolation Sally felt working as a writer from home. "It's gotten much easier to work at home once I met some friends outside. I met most of those through having a baby and taking classes like gym or music classes with the baby. He was definitely my entree into a new group of friends, which everybody said he'd be, but I didn't believe them. Now that I do have a couple of people I can call on and say, 'Hey, what're you doing?' it's easier to work at home. I don't feel that there's no chance I'm going to speak with anyone."

Computers, the Internet, e-mail, fax machines, and other technology have also eased Sally's sense of isolation. "With all the technology, these decisions about whether to work at home have been easier. I can freelance for magazines in New York. . . . If I wanted to work for the *Journal*, that would be entirely feasible now. Just sitting with my phone and computer, I have an entire office with me."

But the conflicts between work life and children don't disappear when working at home—indeed, they seem at times stronger or at least more immediate—without the distractions a busy office and co-workers can bring.

Sally had visions of continuing her writing with an infant by her side. "I was not a woman who was so utterly taken with the experience and the responsibility. I wanted it to work out and combine with a lot of other things I had interest in. So during the first six months I was having difficulty because . . . his needs were so constant. I'd thought, 'This will be perfect, the baby will sleep, and I'll put him in my office while I'm working'. . . and it was impossible."

Unquestionably a baby-sitter helps. Yet there's still the problem of saying good-bye—and once gone, staying out of sight.

"Sometimes I feel trapped in my office because if he's out there, and he sees me, it's over for the next ten or fifteen minutes," says Sally. "I have French doors on the office, and I'm going to have to get curtains up so he can't look in! When I see them leave out the front door to go to the park to play, I feel like a teenager, like my parents have left for the weekend. Wow! I have the run of the house! I can go get some chips! I have the place to myself."

Even as my children get older—when they are home—the competition for my time and energy is constant. A closed door is not a big thing for a determined child, whether he's two or four or nearly fourteen.

And then there are the telephone calls, during which anything can happen. The phone rings, their radar is activated, they materialize—inches from my face—down from their bedrooms, up from the basement playroom, in from the yard; suddenly bored with games or stuck on homework, pressing questions on their lips, urgent pleading in their eyes, demanding my attention *now*.

Carolyn was teaching writing with small children at home when a call came in from an official at the bank where the course was being offered. "We were on the phone going over the details of the coursework. I was trying to be smooth and professional when my three-year-old came running into the room screaming at the top of his lungs, 'Mommy, *I have to do a poo-poo now!*'"

"Every time you're on the phone," says Bobbie, "even if you have help in the house, they know you're on the phone. There were occasions in the apartment where I'd have to lock myself out on the balcony—*in the winter*—to get away from the kids so the clients wouldn't hear the noise of them screaming, saying, '*Mommy, I need this!*' because the nanny couldn't keep them away from me."

Smooth and professional, at least the way in which we once defined those terms, are not always possible.

Of course, there are also times when you get on the phone and the house fills with an unnatural silence. Very quiet. Too quiet.

It is an evening in 1990, about 5:00 in the afternoon. The phone rings. It's a new editor at a magazine to whom I've just sent a story. He is interested, I am thrilled, and I do my best to sound focused and articulate, despite the fact that out of the corner of my eye I see my two-, four-, and six-year-old children begin a parade in and out of the house, collectively dragging an old scratched bucket, a large bottle of dishwashing liquid, and what appears to be the entire contents of our silverware drawer.

"Yes, I moved here from New York . . ." I say, the words on automatic pilot, saying something about writing and law, my attention riveted on three small figures in shorts and T-shirts, who aren't even allowed knives at the dinner table, there with enough sharp implements to skewer a whole banquet table. With their rumpled hair and growing feet, stubby legs and skinned knees, they look like character models for a comic strip, crouching in the dirt, knees at their chins, stirring.

"Lunch? . . . Sure," I say, watching the tallest one disappear from view, the middle one squeal as the hose he is holding jerks to life and water gushes full force into the dusty dirt where the grass never grows in the shade of the big tree . . .

I am trying to stir up a career, and they are making mud soup, mixing mud and suds, water and leaves.

Suddenly I have an idea. After a few more minutes of polite conversation, I hang up the phone. I have a lunch date with the editor and the lead for a story. Even better, a commute of less than half a minute brings me hand to grubby hand, shoulder to dusty shoulder, with the most inspirational distractions of my life.

Imperfect perfection. Working at home.

CHAPTER TWELVE

On Overload

Safety Valves and
Finding Time for Yourself

"Hello, you've reached the home of Jim, Jane, Tommy, and Katie. To leave a message for Jim, press 1, for Jane, press 2. . . . "

"Hi, this is Jane. If you're calling to buy Terrific Toys, press 1; for the information about the Bake Table at St. Anthony's, press 2; for sign-up for Mrs. Ryan's third-grade open house, press 3; for information about the school board meeting, press 4; and if you need to speak to me immediately, my beeper number is 123-4567."

Ok. So we thought staying at home would ease our tensions, give us some breathing spaces, slow us down.

Not necessarily.

Some of us have never quite shaken the perception that if we're home, even part-time, we should—theoretically—have an enormous amount of time in which to accomplish many things. Perhaps it is because our schedules have become more flexible, perhaps because we do "leisure" things—like buying milk or picking up dry cleaning or taking the dog to the vet—in the middle of the day, or perhaps it's simply because we can "work" in jeans and sweatshirts. Whatever the reason, many of us make an irrational cognitive leap that because we no longer serve our professional master—boss or institution, whoever supplied the paycheck—we have no masters. And so we say yes—to part-time work, to school committees, to community associations, to charitable fund-raisers, to sports teams, and to music classes. Commitments build up like packed snow on a snowman, until instead of Frosty, we have Godzilla. All because "we're home, and we have the time."

We have, in fact, replaced the pressure and stress of a career with the pressure and stress of too many commitments—all competing for time with the kids, who were the reason we left our careers in the first place.

Jessica leaves her physician work at the office but works at home on multiple volunteer commitments—as president of one PTA and vice president of another. Although she loves the school involvement, attending school board meetings, "trying to get involved in what's going on," she admits that her life is getting beyond her. "I'm almost maxed out now," she says. "I almost can't read to my eight-year-old because there're all these phone calls coming in. I need to step back to spend more time with my kids."

Even women who consciously decide to spend more time with their kids feel pressure to do more. Gloria was a CPA and financial anaylst before she left to be at home with her children.

"I get a lot of pressure to fill up my days with activities. Nobody seems to understand my wanting to be at home (and really be at home) with my kids instead of leaving them with sitters while I 'get a life!'"

Cynthia had been an assistant attorney general for the state of Colorado. After the birth of her first child and a six-month parental leave, when she decided that she would be the best caregiver for her child, Cynthia left the attorney general's office. When her husband changed jobs and the family moved from Colorado to Pennsylvania, she took a career/interest test as part of the relocation package. The results indicated that she should be "the administrator of a recreational facility or an occupational therapist."

Coincidentally, her new home was close to a nature center, where her volunteer activities soon went from three hours a week to ten hours to a twenty-hour paid part-time position as executive director.

It seemed the perfect fit: interesting, meaningful part-time work ten minutes from home. But part-time turned into much more: "I'd bring home paperwork and work until one in the morning. Extra night meetings would pop up. I was pregnant again, and this time with a worrisome pregnancy, with lots of extra appointments at the hospital."

But this part-time job—at least the idea of this part-time job—was just too good to leave behind. Cynthia went back after three months of unpaid leave.

"Work continued to spill well over the twenty hours. . . . Because I thought of my job as part-time, I wanted to do all of the special activities with the kids [as well as things that were] time-consuming [but] rewarding [like] music class, shopping for kids' clothes. . . . I would work in the morning, be with the kids in the afternoon, make and serve dinner, often work some more at night, and then be up with the baby in the middle of the night. . . . I was trying to squeeze two full-time jobs into one twenty-four-hour life. I felt . . . successful at neither. . . . Nothing was getting done around the house. Lightbulbs burned out and stayed that way. Finally . . . we were living in the dark. It was like trying to run a race with your feet tied together. My dream job was turning into a nightmare."

Cynthia scaled back once again. She left her job but continued her volunteer commitments, including serving on a community environmental advisory council to maintain her contacts in the field. Today she is enjoying her two children, ages two-and-a-half and six-and-a-half, keeping up her legal license, and staying current on environmental issues.

Safety Valves and Finding Time for Yourself

It is just before 9:00 on a Friday morning, and I am walking my children to their elementary school. The cool September breeze cuts through the late Indian summer haze; the trees cast long shadows across the playground. When we come to the road in front of the school yard, we watch and wait as Land Rovers and minivans roar past, chassises bouncing, slowing only for the turn into the school driveway.

We cross, then pick up speed down the path to the school door. As the kids break into a run, I grab at arms, bookbag straps, trying to snatch a last kiss, before they disappear into the sea of bobbing heads filing into the side door of the two-story brick building.

They are gone. I shift my weights. Literally. I have been carrying five-pound weights in my right hand, and it is time for my stress walk. In my T-shirt, shorts, and running shoes, I swing the weights, pick up my pace, and head down the driveway.

A car passes me on the way out, with a palm raised at the window. Then another. The third slows, and the smoked glass on the driver's side slides down. A too-cheery voice comes from a perfectly made-up figure wearing silk blouse and blazer. "Going for a walk?"

No, I'm pacing a runway in a fashion show. Of course I'm going for a walk—correction, I'm walking—for exercise, to reduce stress. It's a medical thing. I flash a close-lipped smile, hoist a barbell in greeting, and pick up the pace.

Down at the end of the driveway, two women in sweaters and jeans are unloading crates of paper and notebooks from the back of a van.

Whoops. Little alarms ring in my ears about a meeting I forgot. *Book publishing committee. In the cafeteria. Friday at 9:15. Damn.* My path is set. I can't turn around without them seeing me. I can't go on without them noticing that I'm going the wrong way. "Hi!"

"Hi! You coming this morning?"

I smile weakly. "Yeah, I think so. For a little while. As soon as I put these weights away."

Taking walks. Running. Playing tennis. Drawing. Playing the guitar. Acting. Singing in a choir. Many of the things I gave up to be a young professional workaholic are theoretically still there, waiting.

Driving across country in a van. Taking a long biking or canoeing trip. Learning to play jazz piano. Many of the things I never got around to are theoretically still there, waiting.

But as with many women, there appear to be many forces working against doing the things for myself: Time. Money. And of course, guilt.

There's a great deal of guilt about being at home—often after years of education, training, work experience—guilt that prevents many of us from really ever doing anything "for us." Still haunted by our former opinions of at-home moms, we're driven to produce, to justify our existence, and to refrain from activities that smack of leisure time.

"The toughest thing was and is allowing myself personal time," said Judith, former director of public relations for a major symphony orchestra, now at home running her own public relations/communications consulting business and parenting her two children, ages nine and five. "Although it's not necessary, I usually still feel office demands are more important than my own needs. I still shop one day every six months for two hours and rarely do social things during the day. I haven't turned on the TV yet!"

Other women express the same thoughts. Caught between professional pressures (external or merely internal) and ever-expanding parenting demands, it's difficult, sometimes, to make time for ourselves. But after a while, many of us rediscover ourselves.

Despite ourselves.

But for some women, the first step is escape . . . just for a little while.

I'd never been away from my family alone, with the exception of a Friday overnight in New York in connection with a law firm reunion. But away—really away, for a week—I didn't know which would be worse, the logistical nightmare of anticipating everyone's schedules for a week or the emotional searing of not being part of their daily lives and their not being part of mine. I've found all the sappy stuff to be true. From pregnancy on, every pulling away has been wrenching. After my child was born, I kept thinking he or she was still inside me. After I stopped nursing, my arms sometimes ached to cradle my oh-so-soft child. I can still feel the warmth of a toddler's velvet embrace, though even my youngest is now nearly seven. These children—young people, soon to be adults—once briefly housed in my body, have moved permanently into my consciousness.

And so it's not easy to leave them.

"Carving time away for yourself is difficult," agrees Cathy, mother of three and former executive director of an arts group, "but it's so important." Cathy had been away from her children for work reasons, sometimes with dire results. "The first time I'd ever been away for a night for work, my daughter was taken to the hospital because she swallowed a penny. She's fine, but it made it difficult to go away again."

But after she left her job, she needed to pull her thoughts together and find new direction. Taking advantage of an offer from her brothers, she went skiing for a week. "I missed everyone so much it made my bones ache. When you go away, you look back at your life and your family and think, 'My God, I'm so lucky!'" Cathy plans to try to get a week away every year.

"And a Little Child Shall Lead Them . . . "[1]

Sometimes it takes the kids to bring you back to yourself. Women who participated in this book spoke of rediscovering aspects of themselves they'd pushed aside years ago. In the company of children, it often seems possible to do things we once gave up as "unrealistic" or taking too much time or not sufficiently adult for our serious professional lives—from playing musical instruments to singing to painting; from sitting down and writing to getting up and running around, playing soccer, hockey, or baseball.

Pam had given up playing French horn when she switched from music to nursing. As the team coordinator of a surgical trauma unit, she didn't find much time to nurture her old passion for music. Nor did the time appear during the early years of staying at home. But when her children began playing instruments, she decided to try to pick up where she left off:

"I think the thing that never occurred to me was finding that spot to be replenished. We're at work twenty-four hours a day, seven days a week. . . . It's not a mean thing; it's just that there's always somebody who wants something from us . . . *including* your husband when he walks in the door. As [my friend] put it, '*I can't even go to bed without somebody wanting something from me!*'" She laughs. "The answer? I don't know, for me it's playing the horn . . . or"—She giggles— "Ted asked me what I wanted for my . . . birthday. I said a week away in Florida. Alone."

If you run into Sherry in the hall at the elementary school her son attends, she will probably be on the run—to the library for a meeting with students, to a classroom to take photographs for the school newspaper, or to a committee meeting for the PTA, of which she is vice president this year. When you see her with her bobbed blond hair and sea-green eyes, her ready smile and her easy manner, you think perhaps that this is a woman who has this wife and mom thing down cold. You don't think of a classics major from Princeton who thought of going to law school as a means of becoming attorney general; an editor of an academic publishing house who is fluent in Latin and conversant in Greek. And it never occurs to you that this 5'6" perky blond plays right wing on an all-male—except for her—ice hockey team.

As I was saying, looks can be deceiving.

Sherry began thinking about ice hockey as she watched her seven-year-old race around the ice. When he was four, she'd started taking figure-skating lessons with him, "simply so I could go to family skate with him," she remembers. "So he wouldn't be falling all over the ice with no one to pick him up."

So began the life of a hockey mom, complete with before-dark awakenings (practices at 6 A.M.) and hours of her life spent sitting on cold bleachers, watching.

"I started to notice that I was spending an awful lot of time at the ice rink and also that he seemed to be having so much fun. . . . I knew what he was doing out there. He'd close his eyes and put his arms out—and just pretend to fly. And I thought, 'Cool! That looks really fun!' And then when they start chasing the puck, I thought 'Wow, that looks really neat.'"

A germ of an idea, a kind of wild and crazy idea, began forming in Sherry's head. Nearly three years later Sherry is in her third year as right wing on her hockey team. The experience has taught her about herself—that she can do things she'd never before thought possible.

"The first practice, I was petrified. I was more scared than I have ever been in my entire life. I couldn't believe I was doing this. . . . They all knew I was Sherry." She giggles. "Who else am I going to be? . . . Names are not great with me, and I've got all these Mikes and Joes and Sams—I didn't know who was who. So I just did the practice, managed to live through it, got off the ice at the end."

If Sherry thought scrambling around an ice rink fighting over a puck with guys the size of linebackers was difficult, she had yet another challenge to face: the team locker room. The men's locker room. The locker room where the plays are analyzed, strategy is planned, team business is conducted.

"The first time, I went into the women's room to put my stuff on because I didn't know what else to do. . . . The guys were all in their locker room, but I wasn't going to go in there. Afterward, the captain came out and said, 'It's ridiculous that you're not in the locker room. The guys don't have any problem with it, so if you don't mind, why don't you come in there—it's no big deal.'

"Well, from the second practice on, I was in the locker room with them, and that made all the difference, because if you're changing in the women's room and then waiting outside, you miss everything."

Although she says she's "not that good," she holds her own and is having a ball. Last year her team won local championships and went to Toronto for a long weekend. But the best part of all? When her husband brings her sons to watch. "It thrills me when my family comes. I think, 'Oh, this is so cool!'"

∽

It is the summer of 1997, and, with the exception of the overnight law firm reunion in Manhattan in 1991, I have never been away from home alone, away from my husband and kids. Away from the place where I do the wife and mother thing. They leave me—my husband travels for business, the kids go to friends' houses overnight. I don't leave them.

Until now.

I have signed up for a writing conference to study fiction. I am going to pack a small bag with jeans, sweaters, and a laptop computer. I am going to drive five hours on a highway that becomes a street that becomes a winding road through wooded hillsides and small New England one-street towns. I will live in a dorm for a week, going to classes all day, writing at night. I will try my hand, lay out my thoughts, bare my soul before an audience of people I've never met before.

I am terrified.

So is my husband.

I've prepared a few notes for him to help him through the week:

Schedule for Week of June 30

General:
Water plants, esp. hanging basket outside front door.
Feed dog.
Make sure kids take care of fish, hermit crabs, chameleons.
Make sure kids read and practice instruments every day!!!

Monday:
> 8:45–9:00—Drop off Andrew and Brian at day camp (see map)
> (put yellow card in windshield; have ID, credit cards)
> DON'T FORGET for each: lunch and drink
> (see Handbook)   bathing suit (with name)
>   towel (with name)
>   must wear sneakers and socks

> 9:00—Julia to park.
> Dan to park (he has tennis 11–12).

> 2:45–3:00—Pick up Andrew and Brian from camp.

> 3:00—Julia and Dan home from park.

Tuesday, July 1:

Don't forget to give Lacey her Program flea pill today.

> 8:10—Take Andrew to his 8:20 lesson.
> Pick him up at 8:40 or stay there the whole time.

> 9:00—Drop off Andrew and Brian at camp.

> 9:00—Julia (maybe Dan?) to park.

> 1:00—Julia (and Dan?) come home.

> 1:15—Take Dan and Julia to middle school for band (1:30–2:30) and jazz band (2:30–3:30).

> 3:00 (2:45–3:15) Pick up Andrew and Brian.

> 3:30—Pick up Dan and Julia.

> 4:00—Julia's piano lesson (Dan and Julia can change order if they both want; but you adjust time because Dan's lesson is 45 and Julia's is 30).

> 4:30—Pick up Julia; drop off Dan.

> 5:15—Pick up Dan (Andrew has no lesson this week).

Wednesday

> 9:00—Drop off Andrew and Brian at camp.

> 9:00—Dan and Julia to park.

> 1:00—Dan and Julia home.

> 1:15—Dan and Julia to middle school for band and jazz band.

> 3:00—Pick up Andrew and Brian.

> 3:30—Pick up Dan and Julia.

Thursday

(Remember, trash has to go out a day early.)

> 8:10—Take Dan and Julia to their lessons at middle school (take all four and wait? eat breakfast in car?).

> 8:40—Pick up Dan and Julia.

> 8:45–9:00—Drop off Andrew and Brian at camp.

> 9:00—Dan and Julia to park.

> 1:00—Dan and Julia home from park.

> 1:15—Dan and Julia to band and jazz band.

3:00—Pick up Andrew and Brian at camp.

3:30—Pick up Dan and Julia.

Friday, July 4:
NO CAMP??? CHECK.

Saturday, July 5:
10:15—All four kids have dentist appointments.
Julia will have a tooth pulled.

P.S. I love you all.

CHAPTER THIRTEEN

Great Expectations Revisited

So, Are We Happy Now?

I am in midthought for a story I'm working on when the phone rings. Forgetting that this is telemarketing prime time and I have promised myself to work undistracted, I answer it.

"Is this Ms. Suzanne Lewis?" comes the voice, slightly nasal, mispronouncing my first name. I knew it.

"Yes? I'm sorry, I can't talk right now, I'm in the middle of something." I say. Truthful but abrupt.

"Ms. Lewis, the president would like to speak with you."

I sigh with exasperation. This is a novel approach. "What president?"

"The president of the United States. He has named you as the next secretary of state and wanted to let you know."

I stare at the phone.

"Ma'am? He's submitted your name, and confirmation hearings are scheduled for next—beep—month."

"Uh . . . could you hold on for a second? That's my call waiting . . . Hello?"

"Is this Suzanne Lewis?"

"Susan. Susan Lewis."

"Ms. Lewis, I'm working on a story for the *New York Times*. Could you tell me what your qualifications are to be secretary of state?"

"Could you hold on? . . ." Pressing the hold button, I look wildly around the room for a newspaper. What happened to Madeleine Albright? And who is this Suzanne Lewis they think I am? I never heard of her. I run to flip on the TV.

"This is CNN news. This just in. We've just received word that the president has named Susan Lewis, a one-time Wall Street lawyer from Pennsylvania, to replace departing secretary of state Madeleine Albright."

I gasp, as my law school graduation picture flashes on the screen.

"During her days on Wall Street, Lewis worked side by side with former cabinet members before all but disappearing to have not one, not two, not three, but four children." Another picture appears, this one of me in a sweatshirt and shorts at the bus stop balancing a baby on my hip while crouching to wipe another child's mouth with my sleeve.

Where did *they* get that picture? "More on the Lewis nomination. Critics are calling it an outrage. A bipartisan effort is being organized in Congress, with an unusual alliance between the Republican majority and the National Organization for Women, calling for a full accounting of her activities between 1985 and 1998."

Whoops.

Does Ambition Still Burn?

After all the adjustments, the social, the domestic, the working it out with husband and kids; after getting to know the neighborhood, getting involved in community, working part-time or volunteering; after doing everything you can think of doing and dropping dead tired into bed each night, the conflict doesn't go away—not entirely.

Professional ambition, the forbidden fruit of the prefeminist era, still burns. Yes I did, in fact, have that weird dream about becoming appointed secretary of state. And I still cringe—part envy, part incredulity—when I read about people like Bonnie Fuller, editor of *Cosmopolitan*, on the phone cutting deals while nursing her newborn.[1]

Other women have twinges of discomfort as well—ranging from a vague sense of guilt for not "using my degree" to anxiety about failure to "be some great career woman." Katherine, who was in nonprofit management before she left to be at home with her children, now eight and four, still feels internal pressure "to do more with her education," saying that the decision to be at home "is much more complicated than I thought it would be." She laments that "child rearing is still not truly valued in our society."

Ever present, also, are the practical worries—those that pounce in the middle of the night—about the risks of financial dependency and our abilities to fit into a commercial world where youth or experience count more than commitment to family and home.

Despite these concerns, many women are optimistic. Tracy, the founder of a FEMALE chapter, reasons, "If I ever go back, and they say, 'What did you do all these years?' I figure I can say, 'Well, I did this and this, in addition to raising my children.' I think the key is to get involved."

Laurie is similarly booked with multiple activities and philosophical about the future: "Right now I'm a sort of jack-of-all-trades. Between teaching preschool, starting a small business, repping a jewelry line, coleading a Girl Scout troop, teaching Sunday school, and being involved in all aspects of our children's school and sports, I have no specific plans for the future. I keep busy, and life has a way of turning out."

And some women say that the break of being at home with children has given them perspective:

Anne, a former public relations executive was a graduate student in historic preservation when she left to be home with her children. She finds that time off has given her "more confidence" and that "moving in an entirely different direction now seems possible. Before I had children, I so closely identified with what I was professionally, and now I feel better able to take risks. I also am much more compassionate and patient."

So back at the bar stool, er, kitchen stool, I am busy working—listening to problems, learning how to take off training wheels, signing permission slips, assisting in the research of rare breeds of dolphins, learning how to put training wheels back on, catching occasional snippets about girlfriends and love notes and who said what to whom in the cafeteria.

Anna Quindlen wrote some years ago of her decision to work part-time, a decision that she says would have been "unthinkable" to her younger self, who burned with ambition.

> I am not sure when or why it all changed. It is tempting to say it is because having children has reordered my priorities. . . . But the children are not the only factor. My work is a big part of my life, but experience has taught me that the other things—friends, family, time alone—fill some of my deepest needs. . . . I want to do good work. I want to play with my children. I want to enjoy myself. I want to be happy. I once wanted to be a personage. Now I am comfortable being a person.[2]

But being a person—a full person—requires attention and commitment and, most of all, time.

I am squeezing in time to write, and there is never enough time.

I am trying to get to know each of my kids as they careen through childhood—as they learn how to pitch a baseball, play the piano, figure out new math problems, muster the nerve to get up on stage. I am trying to be there when I'm needed, to listen to their problems, to share their joys, and there is never enough time.

I am trying to have a little romance—candlelight in the kitchen—with the baritone I've loved since college. And there is never enough time.

So conflict remains, but of a positive sort. I am content not with my accomplishments but with my priorities. Despite my ambitions, I feel a hammerlock on my heart and a certainty that at this time in my life, my children are where my first energies belong. As I tried unsuccessfully to explain to a male friend of mine, I am confused but not unhappy; I am tired but not weary.

The experience of having children and growing older has not eradicated those great expectations of twenty years ago but modified them. I have not abandoned my ambition but refocused it. I want to be a success, but not by some corporate culture's definition. I want to contribute to a community, but not necessarily a community of suits and briefcases. And I want to do something for me, ideally something fulfilling, perhaps worthwhile financially—that doesn't detract from my responsibilities to my family.

All of which is easier said than done.

Old Values (Letting Go)

It's tough to let go of old values, old routines, old identities—particularly when you've worked hard to prove yourself capable within the system. "When you've invested a fair amount of your adult life in one thing, it's hard to say, 'I'm going to scrap that and start from scratch,'" says Cynthia, a journalist who, after being at home with her kids, went back to school for her degree in social work.

Starting from scratch—whether in another career or as an at-home parent—means learning not only new activities, but new attitudes. Once upon a time, success could be measured in terms of how much money you made, what title was on your office door, and whether your picture made it into the college alumni bulletin. Success could bring status, respect, and recognition from people you hardly knew.

In contrast, parenthood tosses us a new set of challenges that has little or no connection to professional life, and our success impresses no one but ourselves and our kids—who become the people who matter most.

The idea of a philosophical awakening—taking a hard look at what we value, wondering if the paths we've taken and the sacrifices we've made have led us to where we want to be—isn't new to the culture, to our generation, or to women.

It's just that many of us didn't expect motherhood to trigger a midlife crisis.

Women at home vary in their circumstances, their interests, and their aspirations. But nearly every participant in this project has agreed that we never realized how much family—and our participation in family matters—would come to mean to us.

New Insights (That Help)

No matter how many books you read, people you talk to, research you do, parenthood is full of surprises, full of learning, full of revelations about the world. I knew, when I had a party of seven-year-old boys at my house, that I'd have to make rules: Don't go near the street, no playing with sticks, no using tools from the garage as weapons, etc. I never thought of saying, "Don't dig up the cable wire from under the grass in the backyard."

So I learned. I learned little things about children that helped me get through the afternoon. And I made larger discoveries about myself that helped me deal with the larger issues of my own life.

For many of us, the search for balance in our lives today is predicated on these discoveries—epiphanies that dawned on us at various times over the course of early mornings and late nights, in carpool lines and on soccer sidelines, in darkened auditoriums at elementary school plays and brightly lit high school gymnasiums. Similar thoughts were expressed again and again in my discussions with women for this book.

1. "I Never Realized How Much I'd Love My Kids."

Of course I knew I'd love my kids. I knew it when I was a child playing neighborhood softball, when I was a gangly teenager scouting out boys at the mall. I knew it as a college student studying Aristotle and Plato, knew it when I was a young lawyer, planning to take on the world. Everybody loves their kids. That's what parents do.

I knew I'd love my kids, but I never really understood the power of such love:

- Never understood how it would feel to lie on the floor next to a sick child in bed, heat radiating from his tiny body, listening for soft steady breathing, lying there staring at the ceiling all night so that if he cried out I'd be there to smooth his brow and whisper, "It's all right, I'm here."
- Never understood how I—who before I had kids could count on one hand the number of baseball games I'd watched as an adult from beginning to end—could willingly spend hours and hours of my life sitting on hard metal bleachers baking in the hot sun, my eyes glued to a small figure in right field, hoping and dreading that a ball would come his way.
- Never understood how another human being's growth and development, happiness and sorrow, discoveries and frustrations could so engage my time, energy, and consciousness.

Like me, Jessica, a physician, never truly realized the joy children would bring: "What surprised me most about having children was how much I loved them! How much I truly enjoyed being with these kids and watching them grow and participating in their fun. It's like seeing everything through three completely different sets of eyes. . . . I'm growing at the same time they're growing, and things are changing a lot. I never realized how I would really want to be there."

Cynthia had had the excitement of being an assistant state attorney general and directing operations of a nature center. Yet it was those quiet moments with her two small children she increasingly cherished: "In the winter when the baby was about five months old, I took her to the pediatrician to have her ears checked for infection. It was such a sweet moment in that little examining room, playing with her, alone, without interruption by first child, phone, work. . . . Then about a month later, the same thing happened again. I enjoyed taking her to the doctor's office. This is a sign, I thought. . . ."

2. "I Never Understood the Influence I'd Have."

Nor did I understand the power of parental love over a child. Anna Quindlen wrote in *Living Out Loud*:

> I am aghast to find myself in such a position of power over two other people. Their father and I have them in thrall simply by having produced them. We have the power to make them feel good or bad about themselves, which is the greatest power in the world. Ours will not be the only influence, but it is the earliest, the most ubiquitous, and potentially the most pernicious. Lovers and friends will make them blossom and bleed, but they may move on to other lovers and friends. *We* are the only parents they will ever have.[3]

After our first child was born, I remember thinking, there we were, two people who had never had a pet and couldn't keep a spider plant alive—entrusted with the well-being of a real live person, an eight-pound stranger with tiny fingers and toes and intense blue eyes that could see deep into the core of my being.

"Are you sure you know what you're doing?" those eyes seemed to ask, searching my face for reassurance.

"No, not at all," I thought. This is the most incredible experience of my life. More breathtaking than scuba diving; more exhilarating than the first loop of a roller coaster; more challenging than a million-dollar deal; and more terrifying than everything combined.

We were young professionals who'd been engaged in high-level work involving millions of dollars.

But it was only money.

Raising kids—especially toddlers and teenagers—can be life and death.

Although she'd loved her work as a communications analyst, Christine couldn't shake the feeling that her work as a mother mattered so much more: "When I used to think of motherhood, I thought of children and not the adults they'd become, which is why it didn't occur to me till my oldest got bigger how much of an impact I'm having on her values and her life.

"One of the things that was profound for me was, it became clear to me that as a mother one of my greatest accomplishments in life was going to be raising good people and not my career or my mark on the world. I expect to make a mark on the world, but right up there equal to it is going to be these good people I am working very hard to raise."

Cynthia, once writing regularly for a national audience, now working part-time in social work, finds irony in the way her priorities have shifted: "In journalism . . . writing stories that people would read and throw away, I didn't feel as if I was having the kind of lasting impact I want to have. There's an argument that you have a lot of impact that way, that you reach a lot of people, that you educate, you entertain. That's true.

"But for me, I felt much more fulfilled by having a big impact on one or two people, like my kids, than I did trying to reach this big audience out there—where you never know if you made an impact, because they're just this anonymous body of people."

Allison, once a big firm lawyer, echoes this concern for making a contribution to the future: "What could be more important than people dedicating themselves to trying to foster the development of the best human beings possible for the next generation?"

3. "I Never Really Understood How Fast Time Moves."

The continually evolving nature of life with children gives new meaning to time-worn clichés: Time flies. They're the best years of your life. Childhood is gone in the blink of an eye.

Jessica reflects that time has sped by faster than she'd ever anticipated: "I have this habit of not printing photographs we take for several years! And then I take something like fifty rolls of film and get them done all at once. We have rolls of film of when the kids were two, three. They're now thirteen, ten, and seven. I look at these pictures and want to physically go back and grab that child at that moment. It was precious, and now it's gone. . . . Even though they're older now . . . I feel really special about this time also, and I don't want to lose it.

"You start realizing that life is real fast, and you don't know what's going to happen next year or next month. Which is not to say that I'm going to go climb a mountain in Nepal, but I don't want to put off doing things that are important to me, and being with the kids is one of those things."

4. "I Don't Need to March Lockstep with Every Friend."

For a great long stretch of my life, from childhood through the years in which those great expectations took hold, I had many soul mates along the way—contemporary role models, women whose lives tracked mine and provided a kind of implicit approval of and support for the personal and professional paths I followed. But then life began to diverge like bifurcating limbs of a large tree. Some women had one child, some two, three, four, or even five. Some went through divorces. Some stayed single. Some stayed at work; some left. Some started their own businesses. Some thrived in volunteer work.

Life is varied and heterogeneous. The people with whom I relate are men and women, young and old, of varying education, dreams, desires. Each of my friendships taps into a slightly different part of myself. My close friends are no longer exactly like me, if they ever were.

Regrets

Around midlife many women as well as men take stock of their lives, their career and family decisions. Mothers who scaled back or left their careers offer some regrets, not as bitter grapes but as constructive criticism for younger women—and men—approaching similar conflicts and choices.

1. The *philosophical regret* that many women express is not that they chose to pursue careers but that, in our current culture, excelling in so many careers was—and is—incompatible with the time, energy, and emotional commitment they want to devote to parenting. Some reasons are intrinsic to the nature of the career, but others are imposed by a culture that still devalues child-related activities.

The cover of the April 1998 issue of *Working Mother* trumpets the "10 Hottest Careers for Working Mothers." I eagerly flip open the magazine, wondering where the thirty-five years since *The Feminine Mystique* was published have brought us. And the 'hottest careers' are:

In health care
- private and group practice social worker
- occupational therapist

- registered nurse
- physician assistant

In computer science
- network architect
- systems analyst

In education
- schoolteacher
- employee trainer

In finance
- financial planner

In marketing and communications
- public relations specialist[4]

Conspicuously absent: lawyer, physician, corporate executive, scientist, etc. In fact, many of the "hot" careers in 1998 look like traditionally female vocations women have always pursued. These jobs are attractive because of their flexibility and good pay—reasons no less relevant in 1998 than in 1963.

What are we to make of this—that we are back to where we started? Hardly. Women have proved themselves capable and significant players in every field of endeavor, competing with men in traditionally male fields according to traditional rules.

Some careers, by the very nature of the activity involved, are difficult to combine with family. Women—or men—who want to be transplant surgeons or airline pilots may not be able to coach their children's Little League teams.

But other careers are inconsistent with family not because of their inherent nature but because of the ways in which they are conducted— weekend business meetings, golfing retreats, command dinner performances on the night of the school play—with rules and customs created largely by men—single men or men with wives, who have not had to consider family issues in the way they structure their professional lives. In law firms, partnership decisions are made after an associate has been with the firm for roughly seven years or, for a woman going straight from college to law school to practice, not before she's thirty-two years old. In academic medicine, tenure decisions are made at roughly the same time. "The timing of career development is abysmal for family life," says Dr. Melissa McNeil, an associate professor of medicine.

"I'm in an academic setting where moving up the ladder from assistant to associate to professor is how professional success is measured, and that ability to move up the ladder is strictly dependent on hours committed. For many women, tenure is considered at the same time as when women are starting their families."

Still others argue that the global economy has forced us into an ultra-competitive, workaholic culture where work must take priority over family. The truth probably lies somewhere in between.

The hope expressed by many is that as our society moves forward, professions and institutions will be structured so that raising a family can become more valued and be better integrated into professional lifestyles.

"I wish I could give Margaret a different view of the world," says Anne, a college teacher home for the time being with her one-year-old daughter. "A view where it wasn't a split between home and work, with some women working, some women at home, a view of the world where work and family were more integrated. . . . Friends of ours are home-schooling their children. I think of that mother as a feminist. She works very hard giving her kids a diverse sense of the world out there, and it works. They perceive her teaching and her mothering as significant as their father's career as a reporter. I'd like it if it were true for more people."

2. Given a culture in which some careers are more family friendly than others, a *practical regret* expressed by many is that, when we were college and grad students planning our grand life designs, no one warned us of the giant conflict looming just beyond the horizon of our professional aspirations. "A constant lament of the women I work with is that we didn't get the right mentoring," observes Dr. McNeil.

Jill, with a degree in engineering from Princeton, echoes these thoughts: "They have to do a better job—not only for women but for men, too—of telling students what's really involved in their fields [and how compatible they are with family life]."

I admit that when I was in college or law school, if someone had said to me, "When you're deciding what kind of career to pursue, you should think about how you're going to juggle that career and the raising of your children," I would have been insulted. Dr. McNeil agrees. "It was the same for my generation of med students."

Part of the reason we felt this way is that there was—and is—a cultural, indeed in many fields, an institutional bias against anything other than a 100 percent commitment to career. Acknowledging a concern with anything else showed less than a serious commitment to the job. Acknowledging an interest in family in particular was to leave ourselves open to the chauvinistic charge that women, because they thought the home was important, somehow "belonged" there. The consequence: we grossly underestimated the time and undervalued the effort that family would take in our lives.

Some good news is that students today may be giving more consideration to family than we felt able to twenty years ago. In her role as a fourth year adviser for medical students, Dr. McNeil talks with them about combining family and careers.

"It's much easier to pick a residency when they're coming out of medical school if they have a significant other and they know what they're doing. They say, 'If I don't get married and have a family, I want to be a transplant surgeon. If I do get married and have a family, I want to work part-time in an ER.' But it's being in that black box that's so very hard—deciding how to plan your own career if you don't know what your family situation is going to be; whether you're having kids and whether you're going to marry a transplant surgeon."

But at least they're thinking about the issues. And at least they have someone in authority who thinks it's important they consider them.

"The point that I try to make when I counsel young people is— they always have this vision that they can put their careers on hold for a few years while they pop out babies, and then they can gear right back up again, full swing. The message I try to give is that in many respects it almost gets harder, not easier. Because when you think of what you can and cannot manage, I want them to be aware of the demands. . . . "

3. Even mothers who chose traditionally "female" fields have sometimes found themselves in conflict between competing passions for their work and child, particularly because traditionally female careers often don't make enough to pay the bills. Elise is a dance therapist who worries that the attention given to the work/family dilemma in the corporate, medical, and legal professions overlooks the dilemma of women

in fields less recognized: "What happens to women who are in the not-for-profit place in the world, in the helping/healing professions, who don't have the notoriety and never will? Our dream was that by the time we were grandmothers in our profession it would be understood. What is dance therapy? I've been doing this for thirty years, and every new person I meet says, 'What is that?'"

Now divorced and the single parent of two teenage girls, Elise laments the lack of recognition in terms of money and power given to so many female professions. "I will never regret having put my career on hold for my kids. I will only regret the inertia that I feel at the moment because of my circumstances. . . . I can train teachers. There are creative ways to use my skills, but it's contract work. Not anything I can pay my bills on. My conflict is that I will never work sixty hours a week until the last one walks out the door."

Are We Feminists or Betrayers of the Cause?

Most of the women interviewed for this book are women who did not originally intend to compromise their careers by staying at home with children. Regardless of the circumstances, most women assert that their decisions to scale back or leave their careers were personal, not political.

But personal decisions can have political implications, particularly when people start writing about them. What these implications are, however, is subject to debate. It is important, therefore, to be clear about several facts:

- Not one of the women interviewed for this book advocated turning back the clock to the fifties, or anytime when women were foreclosed from pursuing whatever careers to which they aspire. Most women here, particularly those who had acheived a certain level of professional success, are grateful for the opportunities made available to them by virtue of the feminist movement over the last thirty years.
- Nor did any suggest that all women who can afford to do so should stay at home with children. Most recognize this as

an intensely personal decision, dependent on many practical and emotional issues.

- Nearly every woman considered herself to be fortunate to be able to make the choice to spend more time with her children. Many look forward to making the choice to continue their former careers or start new ones.

I consider myself a feminist, and because I am writing a book about women who leave careers to take care of their chidren, it seems necessary to say so. But what exactly does it mean to proclaim myself a feminist? *Webster's* defines feminism to mean "the principle that women should have political, economic, and social rights equal to those of men."

This is classic equity feminism, a humanistic social movement begun more than 150 years ago when women demanded the same legal rights that men enjoyed. Since then feminism has fought battles that needed to be fought over inequitable laws relating to marriage, property, divorce, and child custody, among other things.[5]

When Betty Friedan wrote *The Feminine Mystique*, there was an urgent need to get women out of the home, because at that time the home was, for many women, a trap likened to "a comfortable concentration camp."[6]

But the darkest prison, once its walls come down, floods with sunlight. Women at home today are largely there by choice, a critical difference in defining the nature of home life.

What's more, the home itself has changed, becoming for many today a computerized workplace, connected to the world by fax, phone, and e-mail on the Internet.

And feminism has changed.

Many women I've interviewed feel strongly about it. Pat says, "I'm a product of the sixties; I'm a feminist! I went to Woodstock—the first one! I come from that whole generation of women who wanted independence and careers and to be able to do it all." Nor did staying at home change that feminist identification. "I felt that I was doing exactly what I wanted to do. I was being more of a feminist because I don't choose to live by other people's standards when it comes to the safety and care of my child.

"Once when Chris was three years old, I was told that it was OK for him to go play in the yard at a friend's house. When I went out to find him, and the gate to the pool area was unhinged, I made a decision right at that moment that from that point on, no one could tell me what was right for the safety and security of my child. From that point on, I promised myself that no pressure from anywhere would change my innermost feelings about what my kid needs."

In contrast, a number of women are hesitant, if not averse, to identify themselves as feminists. "I don't consider myself a feminist," says Barbara, an MBA who runs her own newspaper. "There's such a thing as equal pay for equal work, but I don't think there's a major feminist drive today."

This reluctance may stem from two related factors.

Some believe that feminism as a social movement has fulfilled its purpose since so many inequities of the laws (if not all the social ramifications) have been addressed.

What's more, feminism in recent years has acquired ideological connotations beyond its classic equitable roots. With the momentum from a clear, undeniable agenda gone, feminist philosophers have gone in different directions, with perhaps the loudest and angriest voices reaching the most ears. In her book *Who Stole Feminism?*, philosophy professor Christina Hoff Sommers describes at least one split:

> Most American women subscribe philosophically to that older "First Wave" kind of feminism whose main goal is equity, especially in politics and education. A First Wave, "mainstream" or "equity" feminist wants for women what she wants for everyone: fair treatment, without discrimination. . . .
>
> [O]ther current feminist notables . . . adhere to a new, more radical, "Second Wave" doctrine: that women, even modern American women, are in thrall to "a system of male dominance" variously referred to as "heteropatriarchy" or the sex/gender system.[7]

This latter strain of feminism, expressed as a vocal social movement, may be expressed as anti-men, anti-family, and even anti-women (at least to those women who, by virtue of their choices, seem to be in collusion with or duped by men). Under this theory, a woman who stays at home with her children—despite her education and opportunities—is considered an anti-feminist.

Further, even women who don't ascribe to radical gender feminist theory find themselves judging women who leave their careers for family reasons. As many of us portrayed in this book acknowledge, our own prepident attitudes about such women were none too forgiving.

The irony of this "feminist" position is that women who would condemn other women for staying home with children are implicitly buying into the whole value system that subordinated women in the first place; the same system that said that what women traditionally did—whether it was taking care of children and a home or working in "female" careers—wasn't as important or worthwhile as what men did.

Feminism true to its equitable roots will benefit everyone. The lives of men, women, and children are too connected to pretend that the problems facing any one group of us are irrelevant to the others. Among the issues that frame our lives, family has been taken for granted for too long, and it is not only women who are reevaluating their priorities.

"The trickle of top business and political figures who say they are resigning to spend more time with family has widened to a stream," writes Sue Shellenbarger in her "Work and Family" column in the *Wall Street Journal*. In addition to women examples, the article cites John Site, Jr., who left Bear Stearns in 1995 for an 8:30-to-5:30 job that allows him to sometimes go home for lunch and pick up his kids from school, and Reed Hundt, who left the chairmanship of the Federal Communications Commission in November 1997 to write a book and spend more time with his wife and kids, ages nine, twelve, and fifteen.[8]

Early feminists fought to prove that women could compete with men in traditionally male jobs in business, politics, and the professions. The fact that women now have more opportunities and choices should not dictate what those choices should be. And if the underlying philosophy is one of equal opportunities, those opportunities should go both ways, for men and women.

The doors from the home to the professional workplace have been opened. True equality demands movement the other way, for the other sex, as well—and the encouragement of men to participate more fully in parenting responsibilities and traditionally "female" concerns, without professional stigmas. Perhaps it is time for feminism to be true to its humanistic roots and take on its next challenges: to recognize the importance of families and to support the choices we make for our children.

Notes

Chapter One

1. See *Reader's Digest's Our Glorious Century* (1994; Reader's Digest Association 1996), 348, citing Equal Pay Act of 1963.

2. Ibid., 348–49, citing Civil Rights Act of 1964.

3. Executive Order 11375, 32 Fed. Reg. 201 at 14303 (October 17, 1967).

4. Madeleine L'Engle, *A Wrinkle in Time* (New York: Farrar, Straus & Giroux, 1962).

5. Christina Hoff Sommers, *Who Stole Feminism?* (New York: Touchstone, Simon & Schuster, 1995), 18, citing "Sex, Society and the Female Dilemma," a dialogue between Betty Friedan and Simone de Beauvoir, *Saturday Review*, June 14, 1975.

6. Sommers, op. cit., 257.

7. Reed Abelson, "When Waaa Turns to Why," *New York Times*, November 11, 1997, D1.

8. Nikhil Deogun, "Top Pepsico Executive Picks Family over Job," *Wall Street Journal*, September 24, 1997, B1.

9. *Wall Street Journal*, October 8, 1997, B1.

10. *Wall Street Journal*, November 11, 1997, B1.

11. Betty Friedan, *The Feminine Mystique* (New York: W.W. Norton & Co., Inc., 1963), 30.

Chapter Two

1. Sigmund Freud, *Civilization and Its Discontents*, ed. and trans. James Strachey (New York: W. W. Norton & Co., 1961).

2. Juliet B. Schor, *The Overworked American* (New York: Basic Books, 1991), 85.

3. Ibid., 85.

4. Ibid., 84.

5. Friedan, op. cit., Chapter 10 and note 2 therein.

6. Studs Terkel, *Working* (New York: W. W. Norton & Co., 1962), xvi.

7. Reed Abelson, op. cit.

8. Deborah J. Swiss and Judith P. Walker, *Women and the Work/Family Dilemma* (New York: John Wiley & Sons, 1993), 52.

Chapter Three

1. Arlie Russell Hochschild, *The Time Bind* (New York: Metropolitan Books, Henry Holt and Co., 1997), 44

2. Elizabeth Perle McKenna, *When Work Doesn't Work Anymore* (New York: Delacorte Press, 1997), 132, 133.

Chapter Four

1. Schor, op. cit., 96, citing Daniel T. Rodgers, *The Work Ethic in Industrial America 1850–1920* (Chicago: University of Chicago Press, 1978) 202–8.

2. *Random House Dictionary of the English Language* (Unabridged Ed.), 689.

3. Susan Lewis, "From Wall Street to Sesame Street," *Philadelphia Magazine*, January 1992.

4. Schor, op. cit., 98.

5. Anne Roiphe, *Fruitful* (New York: Houghton Mifflin, 1996), 237.

Chapter Five

1. Friedan, op. cit., 72.

2. Swiss and Walker, op. cit., 65.

3. Terkel, op. cit., xvii.

4. Elisabeth Bumiller, "2d-Class Guests on 'A' lists," *New York Times*, November 12 1997, B1.

Chapter Six

1. Susan Lewis, "Daddy's on the Phone," *Philadelphia Magazine*, April 1993.

2. Susan Lewis, "The Wife and Mother Thing," *Philadelphia Magazine*, November 1992.

3. Susan Seliger, "Special Report: The New Achievers," *Working Mother*, December/January 1998, 22, 23.

4. See "The Second Income: Is It Worth It?," *Business Week*, August 25, 1997, citing *He Works/She Works: How Two Income Families Are Happier, Healthier, and Better Off*, in which author Rosalind Barnett argues that the security and flexibility provided by two careers put less stress on the marriage.

5. Sharon Walsh and Devon Spurgeon, "Divorce Means an Equal Split, Judge Rules in Big Money Case," *Washington Post*, December 4, 1997, E1.

6. "Word For Word/The Wendt Divorce; What's a Corporate Wife Worth in Court? Go Figure," *New York Times*, December 23, 1997.

7. Susan Lewis, "The Wife and Mother Thing," op. cit.

Chapter Seven

1. Contrast the situation today, when an increasing number of groups are forming to support women at home. These support groups vary, however, in their focus and their degrees of connection to the professional lives their members may have had. Some focus on developing connections within the at-home community; others help in maintaining professional connections, an example of which is Lawyers at Home, a subcommittee of the Women in the Profession division of the Philadelphia Bar Association. Lawyers at Home meets monthly and assists members in finding part-time or temporary work and low-cost continuing education programs and discusses issues related to juggling family and professional concerns.

2. FEMALE, Formerly Employed Mothers at the Leading Edge, is a national nonprofit support and advocacy group with local chapters. For more information, contact FEMALE national headquarters at P.O. Box 31, Elmhurst, Illinois 60126, telephone (630) 941-3553.

3. Tracy Thompson, "Dispatches from the Mommy Wars," *Washington Post Magazine*, February 15, 1998.

4. Ibid., 29.

5. Carey Goldberg, "Murder Trial About More than a Nanny," *New York Times*, October 24, 1997.

6. Ibid.

7. Roiphe, *Fruitful*, op. cit., 235–36.

8. See, for example, "Mothers Can't Win," the cover story of the *New York Times Magazine*, April 5, 1995.

Chapter Eight

1. "Maybe Working Women Can't Have It All," *Business Week*, September 15, 1997, reviewing Joan Peters, *When Women Work.* (Reading, Mass.: Addison Wesley, 1997).
2. "The Second Income: Is It Worth It?," op. cit., 194.
3. Susan Lewis, "Not Yet, Andrew, Not Yet," *Parents Express*, January/February 1991.
4. *Random House Dictionary of the English Language*, op. cit.
5. Ellen Wyse Goldman, *My Mother Worked and I Turned Out Okay* (New York: Villard Books, 1992), 102.
6. Harriet Webster, "What Your Kids Learn From Your Career, *Working Mother* (January 1997).
7. Friedan, op. cit., 282, 287.
8. Melinda Marshall, *Good Enough Mothers* (Princeton, N.J.: Peterson's, 1993), 77, citing David Elkind, *The Hurried Child: Growing Up Too Fast Too Soon* (Reading, Mass.: Addison-Wesley Publishing Co., 1981).
9. Susan Lewis, "The Wife and Mother Thing," op. cit.
10. Susan Lewis, "Mother's Nature," *Philadelphia Magazine*, November 1994.

Chapter Ten

1. Erma Bombeck, *The Grass Is Always Greener over the Septic Tank*, republished in Erma Bombeck, *Four of a Kind*, (New York: McGraw-Hill, 1985), 125
2. Friedan, op. cit., 345.
3. Ibid., 346.
4. "Careers or Kids? How Five Princetonians Have Dealt with the Conflict Between Parenting and Jobs," *Princeton Alumni Weekly*, March 11, 1998.
5. From Parent-Net, an on-line discussion group from the Princeton University Alumni Council. Reprinted by permission of Mary Hurley Begley.

Chapter Eleven

1. Susan Lewis, "Working at Home Doesn't Always Work," *Parents Express*, October 1990.

Chapter Twelve

1. Isaiah 11:6.

Chapter Thirteen

1. Janny Scott, "Cosmo vs. Reality: It's Power Juggling," *New York Times*, May 22, 1997, C1.
2. Anna Quindlen, "Blind Ambition," in *Living Out Loud* (New York: Random House, 1988), 59.
3. Anna Quindlen, "Power," in *Living Out Loud* (New York: Random House, 1988), 138–39.
4. Karen Cheney, "10 Hottest Careers for Working Moms," *Working Mother*, April 1998.
5. Sommers, op. cit., 22.
6. Friedan, op. cit., 307.
7. Sommers, op. cit., 22.
8. *Wall Street Journal*, March 11, 1998.

Index